THE CONSTITUTION AND THE PRIDE OF REASON

THE *Constitution*
& THE *Pride*
OF *Reason*

STEVEN D. SMITH

New York   Oxford
Oxford University Press
1998

Oxford University Press

Oxford   New York

Athens   Auckland   Bangkok   Bogota   Bombay   Buenos Aires
Calcutta   Cape Town   Dar es Salaam   Delhi   Florence   Hong Kong
Istanbul   Karachi   Kuala Lumpur   Madras   Madrid   Melbourne
Mexico City   Nairobi   Paris   Singapore   Taipei   Tokyo   Toronto   Warsaw

and associated companies in
Berlin   Ibadan

Copyright © 1998 by Oxford University Press

Published by Oxford University Press, Inc.
198 Madison Avenue, New York, New York 10016

Oxford is a registered trademark of Oxford University Press

Library of Congress Cataloging-in-Publication Data

Smith, Steven D. (Steven Douglas), 1952–
The Constitution and the Pride of Reason / by Steven D. Smith.
p.   cm.
Includes index.
ISBN 0-19-511747-6
1. Constitutional law—United States—Interpretation and
construction.   2. Law and politics.   3. Reason.   I. Title.
KF4552.S63   1998
342.73'02—dc21   97-3692

1 3 5 7 9 8 6 4 2

Printed in the United States of America
on acid-free paper

The Revolution of America . . . [s]eems to have broken off all those devious Tramels of Ignorance, prejudice and Superstition which have long depressed the Human Mind. Every door is now Open to the Sons of Genius and Science to enquire after Truth. Hence we may expect the darkening clouds of error will vanish fast before the light of reason; and that the period is fast arriving when Truth will enlighten the whole world.

Letter from THOMAS RODNEY
to THOMAS JEFFERSON,
September 1790

And then a Plank in Reason, broke . . . .

EMILY DICKINSON

And the sea rolled on as it rolled five thousand years ago.

HERMAN MELVILLE

◼ Preface

*U*p until just a few years ago, constitutional law enjoyed a widely acknowledged preeminence—albeit one often resented by, say, commercial law or civil procedure professors—among law school subjects. This preeminence was hardly inevitable or foreordained; indeed, it was of fairly recent origins. Think back to the first half of this century: The celebrated legal scholars—Wigmore, Pound, Corbin, Llewellyn, Prosser—were mostly associated with subjects other than constitutional law. (Outside the ivied walls of the legal academy these names will not be familiar, of course; trust me that they are for the legal academic what names like Ruth, Gehrig, Mays, Mantle, and Aaron are for the baseball fan.) The most famous judges—Cardozo, Traynor, Hand—did not owe their reputations entirely or even mostly to constitutional decisions, although some of them such as Hand and of course Holmes achieved eminence in that field as well.

But in the last few decades—roughly, and not coincidentally, in the period since *Brown v. Board of Education*—constitutional decisions and scholarship have won pride of place. With some exceptions, such as Richard Posner, it seems that the best known scholars (Wechsler, Bickel, Tribe, Ely, Dworkin) and the most famous or infamous judges (Warren, Marshall, Douglas, Brennan, Scalia) are primarily renowned for what they have done with, or to, the Constitution. Most law schools have had a glut of faculty members who teach, or want to teach, constitutional law. And many of those whose place in the queue means that they cannot *teach* the subject nonetheless *write* about the Constitution, so that constitutional law scholarship inundates the pages of the leading law reviews.

Nor is the dominance of constitutional law scholarship purely quantitative. I would not presume to say (in part because I do not believe) that constitutional law scholarship is qualitatively superior to other kinds of legal scholarship. But I think it *can* be reported that the most elaborate, exotic, or noticeable theoretical work, often condescendingly contrasted with more unpretentious "nuts-and-bolts" or "black letter" scholarship, has occurred in the area of constitutional law and theory.

Indeed, the attractions and prominence of constitutional law have caused the subject to become so overcrowded that in recent years, entry level candidates for scarce law teaching positions have often been coached by their mentors to insist that they do *not*, under any circumstances, want to teach constitutional law. And wary appointments committees sometimes interrogate a candidate suspiciously looking for hints that, vehement protestations to the contrary notwithstanding, the candidate is secretly planning to demand to teach constitutional law as soon as his or her position is secure, thereby aggravating the bloated condition of that side of the curriculum.

I began this description by saying that constitutional law enjoyed preeminence within the legal academy "up until just a few years ago." It's hard to say; perhaps the situation is still the same. But my own sense is that things have changed—or at least that they are in the process of changing. Constitutional law seems to be experiencing a kind of malaise. Events such as the Bork hearings and the Clarence Thomas–Anita Hill fiasco have probably left the public with a more cynical view of the Supreme Court and its constitutional pronouncements. And there are signs that a similarly demoralized attitude has infected the legal academy.

Thus, a prominent constitutional scholar, Sanford Levinson, wonders whether the "death of constitutionalism" may be the central event of our time. A beginning teacher who was recently favored by the assignment to teach the Constitutional Law course at a leading law school expressed to me the discomfort he felt throughout the course; he was more at ease with less glamorous subjects like Local Government because at least there was some "real law." Another friend who has achieved a national reputation while teaching and writing about constitutional law for a couple of decades at another school recently confided that he plans to get out of the course. There just isn't any integrity to the subject, he explains, and it becomes almost a degrading experience to have to teach, say, the equal protection clause and pretend that the Supreme Court's decisions manifest any coherent thinking at all, "originalist" or otherwise.

Students in constitutional law courses increasingly echo the Critical Legal Studies slogan from the last decade: It's all "just politics." One student wrote on an exam in one of my courses: "The principal skill needed to understand why the Supreme Court rules the way it does on any particular constitutional issue is the ability to count to five." Unlike the Crits, though, these students are not reporting conclusions earned through years of careful study, and they don't think of themselves as especially radical. To many students, it seems, the purely "political" character of constitutional law is unmistakably manifest on the face of decisions of the last decade or so. Just read, say, the Court's abortion and affirmative action decisions, and unless you are truly obtuse you should be able to see what's going on. In this climate, the mandarin discussions of hermeneutical theory or political-moral philosophy bequeathed to us by our elders may come to seem not merely beside the point but indeed laughable—like something Jonathan Swift, or perhaps Kurt Vonnegut, might have dreamed up.

People experience things differently, of course, and not everyone will agree with this description. And indeed, my own reaction to the malaise I have been describing is mixed. Although I share the growing frustration (and partly as a consequence, rarely teach the basic constitutional law course), I also can't think the peremptory diagnosis which says "It's all just politics" is very helpful. The problem with that assessment is not so much that the assessment is out-and-out wrong, perhaps, as that it is far too crude, and thus unilluminating. Or if constitutional law is "politics," then it certainly is a bizarre, labyrinthine sort of politics. Indeed, one might wish that constitutional law *were* "just politics"; at least "politics" is something that we know and understand. One cannot say as much, sometimes, about constitutional law.

At the very least it would be nice to have a more searching account that would explain how we find ourselves in the position of practicing *this kind* of very peculiar politics, if politics is what it is. So in the midst of some frustrating sessions in constitutional law courses, I began to wonder: Would it be possible to give an account that would "make sense" of it all—or perhaps make sense of how and why it *doesn't* make sense—in a way that would be illuminating not only for people in my position (that is, law professors) but also for students, for scholars in other disciplines, and even for members of the general public who are concerned about the Constitution and about what courts and others do in its name?

My purpose in undertaking this book was to see if such an account could be supplied. But my method of inquiry will perhaps seem a bit backward: I have tried to focus on a claim—one that was common at the founding and is common today—that is the exact opposite of the "It's all just politics" diagnosis. The claim I have tried to investigate insists that the Constitution, or constitutional discourse, is the expression or embodiment not of politics but rather of *reason*. In trying to figure out just what *this* claim means and whether it is valid, I believe we can achieve some understanding of how we came to be blessed, or afflicted, with the peculiar discourse that pervades our political life and that we call "constitutional law."

That at least is the basic objective of this book. But it is common, I suppose, for an original purpose to expand, or perhaps to encounter an occasional detour, as a project proceeds. And such alterations in course or scope are almost inevitable when the subject matter is constitutional law, which, as commentators sometimes note, is in a sense a vast and ever-moving mirror of the human experience of millions of people over many generations, and hence is not easily confinable to a preselected theme. So if the persistent purpose of this book is to give an account that "makes sense" of the seeming chaos that we call "constitutional law," other purposes may sometimes be evident as well. I can only hope their influence will enhance the discussion without deflecting it from its principal focus.

▨ Acknowledgments

*I*n the summer of 1979 I moved to San Francisco with my then-small family to begin a one-year job as a law clerk to Judge Joseph Sneed, a federal appeals court judge. As law clerks often do, I expected among other things to use this time and experience to sort out various career plans and options. Even before starting law school I had thought about going into university teaching. So that was one of the options I hoped to consider, and since Judge Sneed had been a distinguished law professor before being appointed to the bench, I expected he could help me with this choice.

But a complication arose: In the course of my clerking duties I had the opportunity—if "opportunity" is the right word—for the first time to read large numbers of law review articles, which represent the kind of scholarship that law professors mostly produce. And these articles were typically both daunting and tedious. Though they often struggled ultimately to make quite a small point, they were nonetheless laden with learned footnotes citing hundreds of decisions and articles and books. These footnotes did little to advance understanding but, so far as I could tell, were essential to achieving the scholarly respectability necessary for the articles to be published and then taken seriously. All in all, I thought, the articles reflected a sort of obsessive academic overspecialization that would be difficult to reconcile with my own abiding commitment—supported, as I thought, by Emerson's vision of "the American Scholar" (not a "recluse, a bookworm, or a valetudinarian")—to being a wide-ranging, free-spirited dilettante. So I did not think I *could,* and I was quite sure I would not *want* to, write this sort of thing.

Then I ran across an article—or rather a review essay—criticizing Laurence Tribe's influential constitutional law treatise. It was written by someone whose name meant nothing to me and so did not at the time stick with me. Drawing on a study by the British political philosopher Michael Oakeshott, the essay suggested that Tribe's book was an unhealthy manifestation of a sort of rootless "rationalism." Maybe because I had picked up a battered copy of Edmund Burke at a used bookstore and had been reading it while taking BART to and from work, the argument caught my fancy. But even more I was encouraged by the essay's method or style: Unlike most of the academic literature I'd been reading, this essay was not padded with pretentious references or shows of superfluous learning, and its prose style had nothing of that enervated quality so typical of academic writing. The author had something important to say, I thought, and—wonder of wonders—he just came out and said it. It was altogether a very heartening encounter: This was the sort of thing I could aspire to write.

I had no idea at the time that Bob Nagel would later—almost a decade later—be a colleague; in fact, I don't think I even connected him with the Tribe review until after joining the Colorado faculty in 1987. But Bob's influence on this book will be evident to anyone who knows his work. The most obvious influence is in the central theme—or the concern with what reason, or "rationalism," means and with what the rationalist commitment has done to constitutional law. Bob's method and style will be less evident—unfortunately. I realized some time ago that for all I admire them, Bob's ways of perceiving and presenting are not mine. But I *have* tried—albeit with limited success—to follow his example of saying what one has to say without getting mired in academic discussion that serves more to demonstrate (or dissimulate) erudition than to advance understanding.

While at Colorado I've been fortunate to have other distinctive colleagues in addition to Bob who have engaged in a sort of perpetual and peculiar colloquium of which, for better or worse, this book is one expression. Pierre Schlag joined the faculty a year after I did; Paul Campos came a couple of years later. And when she is not in Tibet or Timbuktu, Rebecca French adds an unmatched exuberance and unconventional insight to the ongoing conversation. Each of these colleagues has read and commented on this book, and in a real sense they are all to one degree or another effective co-authors of the book, whether they agree with it or not.

Numerous other colleagues and friends have generously read and commented on all or part of the book in earlier versions. My thanks go to Kevin Reitz, Tom McAffee, Curtis Bradley, Henry Monaghan, Larry Alexander, Rick Collins, George Wright, Maimon Schwarzschild, Marci Hamilton, Phillip Johnson, Michael Perry, Dan Farber, Tom Berg, Robert George, Gerry Bradley, Cliff Calhoun, Dale Oesterle, Art Travers, Hiroshi Motomura, Richard Delgado, and Craig Callen. I have not been able to incorporate or respond to all of the suggestions or criticisms offered by these readers—they pointed in so many directions, any one of which would have been promising but not all of which could be pursued—but I have made some adjustments and have occasionally tried in footnotes to respond to criticisms or questions. Comments and questions from participants in faculty colloquia at Colorado, San Diego, and Samford, where I was fortunate enough to present versions of Chapters 5 and 6, were also very helpful. Before heading off for his first year of college, my son Nathanael read a draft and engaged me in a spirited discussion of the book, thereby proving among other things that the book is accessible to readers other than constitutional law specialists.

As always, my family patiently endured countless tedious dinner table ramblings on the subjects of this project. More important, they (and especially my wife Merina) are, for me, what make not only this project but all my projects meaningful.

I also must thank the faculty secretaries at the University of Colorado School of Law, and especially Kay Wilkie, for decoding the output of a computer illiterate and bringing it into readable form. And although not much of this book has appeared in print before, several short sections have been borrowed and adapted from earlier work; and I thank the following law reviews for the privilege of using the following essays:

- The Writing of the Constitution and the Writing on the Wall, 19 *Harvard J. Law & Public Policy* 391–400 (1996)
- Rationalizing the Constitution, 67 *U. Colo. L. Rev.* 597–621 (1996)
- Nonsense and Natural Law, 4 *So. Cal. Interdisciplinary L. J.* 583–604 (1995), with permission of the Southern California Interdisciplinary Law Journal

◼ Contents

THE CONSTITUTION AND THE PRIDE OF REASON

Introduction

The Constitution of Reason

*I*t was a confident, even a cocky age; and the founders did not feel themselves seriously constricted by the claims of modesty as they introduced their newly concocted Constitution to the world. Thomas Jefferson declared it to be "unquestionably the wisest ever yet presented to men." Although not perfect, the Constitution was "competent to render our fellow-citizens the happiest and the securest on whom the sun has ever shone." Like Jefferson, James Wilson conceded that the document was not perfect, but he nonetheless insisted that it represented "the best form of government that has ever been offered to the world." Hopefully contemplating the imminent adoption of the Constitution, Alexander Hamilton was moved to exclaim: "Happy will it be for ourselves, and most honorable for human nature, if we have wisdom and virtue enough to set so glorious an example to mankind!"[1]

These sanguine claims were corollary to another—that the Constitution was a manifestation of "reason." Past governments had always resulted either from violence or from blind accumulations of tradition, ambition, fortune, and fortuity. *This* Constitution, by contrast, was the product of conscious, mindful design—of deliberation guided by the newly improved science of politics. In the first paragraph of the first essay of what we now know as *The Federalist Papers*, Alexander Hamilton introduced the basic theme:

> [I]t seems to have been reserved to the people of this country, by their conduct and example, to decide the important question, whether societies of men are really capable or not of establishing good government from *reflection* and *choice,* or whether they are forever destined to depend for their political constitutions on *accident* and *force.*[2]

Several congenial ideas converged here. First, unlike earlier political communities, which had come into being through violent conquest or willy-nilly accretion, the people of the United States had enjoyed the good fortune of being allowed to *choose* their form of government. Second, because of this opportunity for choice, the people had been blessed with the privilege of fashioning a constitution on the basis of deliberation and conscious design. Third, this opportunity to design a government had presented itself at a time in history when, as Hamilton explained elsewhere in *The Federalist Papers*, "the science of politics . . . has received great improvement. The efficacy of various principles is now well understood, which were either not known at all, or imperfectly known to the ancients."[3]

James Wilson summarized the happy and unprecedented situation:

> Governments, in general, have been the result of force, of fraude, and accident. After a period of six thousand years has elapsed since the creation[,] the United States exhibit to the world the first instance . . . of a nation . . . assembling voluntarily, deliberating fully, and deciding calmly concerning the system of government under which they wish that they and their posterity should live.[4]

In short, a fortuitous conjunction of circumstances—contemporaries would have called it providential—had permitted the citizens of this country to create a constitution that would be the expression and embodiment of reason. As Paul Kahn has observed, the American founders in a sense attempted to do in action what over two millennia earlier Plato's *Republic* had attempted to do in words—that is, design a political constitution on the basis of self-conscious deliberation.[5] In constructing their new Republic, Americans "steered by the compass of Reason,"[6] as Henry Steele Commager puts it, and thereby founded, as Commager's title suggests, the Empire of Reason.

The Continuity of Constitutional Reason

If the law of the Constitution was the quintessential political manifestation of reason, then there seems to be a nice continuity from *The Empire of Reason* proclaimed by the founders and lauded by Commager to *Law's Empire*, as celebrated by Ronald Dworkin and other modern constitutional lawyers and scholars. So it seems fitting that in contemporary legal thinking, the genius of constitutional law—and the excuse for it—is thought to lie in the commanding role that reason plays in constitutional discussion. Such discussion, constitutional lawyers and scholars suppose, is the preeminent point at which reason exerts its influence on public policy.[7]

The vocabulary varies slightly, of course, but the essential theme runs through the work of leading constitutional scholars. Insisting that the Constitution and its interpretation are dependent on philosophy, Ronald Dworkin acclaims the "fusion of constitutional law and moral theory."[8] Bruce Ackerman has advocated a constitutional law based on what he has sometimes called "scientific policy-making"—an approach that would develop "a set of specialized and technical concepts" in order to explicate the Constitution in accordance with a comprehensive view informed by moral philosophy.[9] From a different political perspective Robert Bork denounces this reliance on moral philosophy,[10] but in a famous (albeit for him ill-fated) law review article he insisted on "the necessity of theory" in constitutional law and argued that decisions not derived from a consistent overall constitutional theory are illegitimate.[11] Suzanna Sherry maintains that the Constitution was, and remains, an Enlightenment document based on "a common epistemology of rationalism and empiricism."[12] Christopher Eisgruber asserts that "[t]he United States Constitution is dedicated to . . . bringing politics under reason's governance. . . ."[13] Paul Kahn understands that the point of the Constitution was "[t]o achieve a political order structured by reason and not by private passions."[14] Cass Sunstein declares that the Constitution established "for the first time, a republic of reasons."[15]

Nor can these declarations be viewed merely as self-congratulatory but inconsequential puffing; on the contrary, the assumption they express has important practical implications. For one thing, the understanding of the Constitution as an expression of reason provides the essential premise behind the modern defense of active judicial review—or the practice by which courts on a fairly frequent basis declare enacted laws or actions of other branches of government to be null and void. Robert Nagel observes that "through the years, the federal courts have made massive changes in our society; they have risked economic disaster, crime in the streets, presidential defiance, violence against schoolchildren, the breakdown of authority within prisons, and much more— all for the sake of what the supreme law is said 'to require.'"[16] And that law with its sometimes inconvenient or even exorbitant demands has achieved its status as supreme within our political culture in large measure because of its perceived association with "reason." Thus, in claiming the authority to call the nation to order over what may be the most traumatic and divisive issue of our time—abortion—Supreme Court justices explain that their decision foreclosing a wide set of political options is legitimate and worthy of the nation's respect because the decision is based on "reasoned judgment."[17] John Rawls confirms the justices' assumption: "[T]he court's special role makes it the exemplar of public reason."[18]

But the significance of the perceived link between the Constitution and reason is hardly exhausted in the practice of judicial review. In fact, constitutional thinking in this country extends well beyond the interventions of judges into the operations of what we might call "normal politics." Rather, these interventions are merely the most visible manifestation of, and the practical sanction supporting, a way of thinking that is an essential part of our normal politics. So in legislative debates we may confront "the spectacle of political representatives talking the arid language of law professors."[19] And even in casual political conversations at the office or over the dinner table, it is not uncommon for proposals or alternatives that some people might think attractive to be dismissed with the categorical observation: "But the Constitution doesn't allow that."

In short, the peremptory invocation of what "the Constitution says . . ." is hardly a habit exclusive to lawyers and judges. On the contrary, the practice is quite at home in American popular culture.

To an outsider, this practice of rejecting potentially attractive or beneficial political measures a priori might seem odd—something that needs explanation and justification. Insiders agree, it appears, that the practice requires justification; hence, for at least a couple of generations, constitutional scholars have labored to dust off or develop rationales for judicial review and, more generally, for the grip that constitutional thinking has on our political discourse. Typically those rationales seek, in a variety of ways, to identify the Constitution with reason.

One can imagine other sorts of justifications, of course. For instance, we might try to explain why courts sometimes invalidate statutes on more modest grounds of custom and tradition. ("There's no particular reason why constitutional law *needs* to work in this way. It's just how we happen to do things here. The practice seems to have worked okay, so we keep doing it.") Such justifications surface from time to time.[20] By and large, though, these more mundane accounts seem to lack appeal. Hence the marriage of the Constitution and "reason."

Troubling Questions

It is a happy union—or at least it looks happy in its public appearances. But as often happens when we consider a seemingly blissful marriage, suspicions inevitably arise. Some relationships seem too good to be true. So we proudly proclaim that the Constitution embodies reason—but then pause to wonder. What exactly does this proclamation mean? *How* does constitutional law express—or manifest, or embody—reason? And what exactly *is* "reason"?

To be sure, reason—or some thing or things that in the English language we name or translate as "reason"—has played well throughout history and in the most diverse political and philosophical environments. In classical antiquity, Plato and Aristotle regarded reason with deepest respect. So too, in a feudal and Christian age, did Thomas Aquinas. Centuries later, another Thomas of quite a different spiritual and political disposition dubbed his own time the "Age of Reason."[21] That was the age in which our own Republic was founded—and also the era in which French republicans, having converted the erstwhile church of Notre Dame into the "Temple of Reason," solemnly celebrated Reason in festivities replete with hymns, oratory, military parades and marching bands, an alluring and affectionate Goddess of Reason, and tumultuous shouts of "Long live reason! Down with fanaticism!"[22]

Later, in a much altered but no less enthusiastic cultural climate, Ralph Waldo Emerson disparaged the pedestrian powers of mere logic—what he called "understanding"—but placed his trust in a faculty that he called "Reason."[23] And in the less zesty prose of a contemporary political philosopher like John Rawls, the word (now appearing in demure lower case, and most often in its more subdued adjectival and adverbial forms) proliferates like measles on a sick child, as Rawls earnestly charts the course and contents of "public reason" by asking what reasonable people acting reasonably would find reasonable.

But could figures as historically separated and as temperamentally and intellectually diverse as Aristotle and Emerson, Aquinas and Paine, possibly have been talking about and commending the *same* faculty, or method, or intellectual virtue? It seems prima facie unlikely, and indeed studies by philosophers like Alasdair MacIntyre support the suspicion that "reason," or "rationality," has meant quite different things for different people and in different periods.[24] So what are we to make of the recurring contention that our own Constitution is a manifestation or expression of "reason"? Does the contention actually express a continuing commitment? Or is it merely an instance in which a variety of disparate claims can be presented under the heading of a common, commendatory term?

The Enemies of Reason

It would be premature to offer any answer to those questions here—they are, after all, what this book is about—and so I must frankly warn that to some extent "reason" will, of necessity, have to serve as a sort of floating term whose meaning or meanings will be supplied as the discussion proceeds. But even in an Introduction I need to say enough about the constitutional commitment to reason to give a sense of the subject that we will be investigating. So to begin with we can observe that whatever "reason" itself may turn out to mean, the evils for which reason is supposed to be a remedy have exhibited an enduring consistency. Those evils were alluded to in the statements quoted earlier from James Wilson and Alexander Hamilton. For present purposes, we can condense them into two principal "enemies of reason."

The first of these evils might be described as "chance" or "fortuity." "It is a common opinion, Machiavelli had remarked in *The Prince,* that "worldly events are so governed by fortune and by God, that men cannot by their prudence change them, . . . and for this they may judge it to be useless to toil much about them, but let things be ruled by chance."[25] Machiavelli himself, though somewhat less fatalistic,[26] ultimately could not deny the final, sovereign power of fortune—or "chance," or "God" (entities that in Machiavelli's observation seem to melt into each other). In a later work, Machiavelli acknowledged the "incontrovertible truth, proved by all history, that men may second Fortune, but cannot oppose her; they may develop her designs, but cannot defeat them."[27]

It was this same dark foe—that is, fortune or fortuity or, as Henry Adams would later put it, "the harsh brutality of chance"[28] tyrannizing over human affairs—that the American founders hoped to domesticate through the application of "reason." Hamilton and Wilson both observed the role of "accident" in the formation of earlier governments, and they presented the Constitution as a departure from this rule of fortuity. To invoke a more modern expression of the same aspiration, the Constitution was an effort to substitute human "mastery" for historical "drift" in the regulation of human affairs.[29]

But "mastery" has its own ominous connotations. After all, many past governments might well have been viewed as examples of human mastery—that is, of ruling groups exercising a self-serving mastery over less-favored classes. Thus, Hamilton and Wilson described previous political history as the product not merely of fortuity or "accident," but also of "force" and "fraude. "And the Constitution was offered as a remedy for that evil as well. The point, moreover, was not merely to replace government by and in the interest of elites with government by and in the interests of democratic majorities. On the contrary, the framers were acutely conscious of the danger of democratic abuses.[30] Their goal was to make government less the tool of self-interest and "passions" and "will"—of *force,* whether exercised by the few or the many—and more an expression of *reason.*

From a certain perspective, to be sure, mastery unguided by reason is no more than a mirage—the apparent master is himself the pawn of his own fortuitous passions—so that the second evil, force, is merely one particular manifestation of the first evil, fortuity. In Plato's *Gorgias,* Socrates argues that a tyrant who is not governed by reason does not even know how to pursue his own good. So tyrants, battered about by the whims of their own unruly passions, in fact "have the very least power of any in our cities."[31] In his searching political and theological reflection written in the dying days of the Roman Empire, Augustine observed a similar paradox; he described "the city of this world, a city which aims at dominion, which holds nations in enslavement, but is itself dominated by that very lust of domination."[32] Still, most people, like Socrates's interlocutors, will naturally find this perspective counterintuitive, and there is no need to insist on it here. For convenience we can follow Hamilton in separately describing the twin evils against which reason was to be counterposed as fortuity (or accident) and force.

In sum, in achieving independence and erecting a new Republic, the framers proposed to bring down the ancient despotisms of fortuity and force. Hence, although it may turn out that "reason" has meant different things to different people and in different periods, so that it would be futile to describe "reason" in terms of a particular epistemology or a specific procedure for gaining knowledge or answering questions, nonetheless within our constitutional tradition the term can be understood as expressing an ongoing political-moral aspiration. The constitutional project that the founders initiated, and that later generations have tried to maintain, has been the project of freeing politics from the control both of mindless fortuity and of self-serving force by bringing human affairs under the regulation of something that is opposed to those blind or malign powers—something called "reason."

The Unprecedented Constitution

We have so far noted one element of continuity in the constitutional commitment to reason: a continuing understanding of the evils for which reason is to serve as a remedy. We can now notice a second element that will give us some guidance in discerning what reason has meant. This element is the original and ongoing sense that the constitutional commitment to reason was, and is, in some sense without precedent—that the Constitution established a republic of reasons, as Cass Sunstein says, *"for the first time."*[33]

From a detached perspective, Sunstein's "for the first time" might seem recklessly presumptuous; but since his claim resonates with statements from the founding period it thereby serves to convey the audacity—indeed, the heroic quality—of the constitutional project. After all, the practice of discussion and debate—of giving and demanding and considering "reasons"—had hardly been unknown to past governments. And the founders, more avid students of classical history than we are, surely knew this. They knew of Periclean Athens, for example, and the Roman Senate, and the various councils and parliaments that had administered governmental business in European states. And they were intimately familiar with the English common law, and hence were acquainted with the claim of the common law to be, in its cautiously incremental way, the very perfection of reason.[34] But the founders evidently contemplated something different than this, and grander, when they described their new government as *the first* to be based on reason. Here, reason would not be peripheral or epiphenomenal, serving merely, as Machiavelli had put it, to "second Fortune" or to "develop her designs." Here, reason would somehow be in control.

Henry Steele Commager captures the aspiration. The American founders, he explains, "assumed—for the first time in modern history—that men were not the sport of Nature or the victims of society, but they might understand the one and order the other."[35] Their vision, in Suzanna Sherry's equally enthusiastic description, foresaw that "the human capacity to reason, in all its splendor, would control the future."[36]

In studying the constitutional project, it is important to keep the heroic quality of this aspiration in mind, in part because it is this quality that gives the project its distinctive authority and interest, and in part because it will help us to keep our sights on "reason" as the constitutional project has understood it. There are after all many sorts of mental or discursive operations or faculties or procedures—including within our constitutional tradition—that have been presented as forms of "reason" or "rationality." And of course no particular operation or procedure can claim any exclusive copyright in these terms. But the sort of "reason" that distinctively characterizes the constitutional project—and hence that provides the subject of this study—is one that aspires to free human affairs from the tyranny of fortuity and force in a way that no previous society or government had achieved.

The constitutional commitment to reason, in sum, amounts to an aspiration to free human governance, for the first time in history, from the powers of fortuity and force. But although this statement says what reason is supposed to *do,* we still do not know exactly what reason *is,* or how it might work, or indeed whether such a capacity exists at all. Perhaps there is no operation or faculty with the capacity to free us from fortuity and force. Perhaps the founders' vision—and that of their modern descendants—should be described not as heroic but rather as foolhardy, or deluded, or even incoherent.

These are the questions that this book seeks to investigate. What does "reason" mean within the constitutional project? In what sense is the Constitution an expression or embodiment of reason? And what does our constitutional experience teach us about the aspiration to live in accordance with "reason"?

The Purpose(s) of the Inquiry

The subject of this book, in sum, concerns the relation between the Constitution, or constitutional law and discourse, and reason. But a description of the *subject* of a book may still leave readers without any clear sense of what the book is really about. It is equally important to know *why* the author thinks the particular subject worth investigating, or what *purpose* he brings to the subject matter. After all, a legal historian might take up the subject of "Reason and the Constitution" and, driven by a particular set of historical concerns, write one sort of book. A philosopher primarily interested in theory of knowledge might start with the same subject and write an entirely different kind of book.

As it happens, I am neither a historian nor a philosopher; I am a law professor, and my interest in the relation between reason and the Constitution derives mostly from two kinds of problems familiar, but hardly limited, to law professors. The primary problem is that my duties as a law professor require that I try to account for, or somehow to make sense of, the assorted debates and decisions and doctrines that are lumped together under the heading of "constitutional law." A law professor, like a teacher or indeed any kind of presenter on any subject, cannot just report a mass of disorderly data: "The Supreme Court decided *Thomas v. Jones* in favor of Thomas, and the next year the Court decided *Able v. Nunes* in favor of Able." The professor is expected to organize and understand the data in some meaningful way—to illuminate the material, or to show how (to borrow Sellars's and Rorty's tolerant phrase) it all "hangs together."[37] And I describe this duty as a problem because for me—and I am surely not alone in this—the familiar accounts of how constitutional law all hangs together, whether offered by judges or scholars, often do not seem very believable.

I feel sleazy, frankly, standing in front of a room of law students and trying to convince them that they can usefully understand what the Supreme Court *has* done or what it *should* do in the name of the Constitution in terms either of notions like "original intention" and "plain meaning" or of concepts like "representation reinforcement," "equal concern and respect," or "human flourishing." But if these ideas have come to seem resoundingly empty, it is by now equally unhelpful to say simply that it is "all just politics." Against a certain backdrop of dominant assumptions and problems these notions may once have been illuminating and perhaps even radical; they do not seem so now. So my inquiry into the persistent claim that the Constitution is in some sense an expression of reason is primarily an effort to explore, in a more circuitous but hopefully more satisfying way, the question of how constitutional law hangs together.

In the course of this inquiry we will confront some standard constitutional law issues such as "originalism vs. nonoriginalism," federalism, and abortion; and I will offer some severe judgments regarding many of the familiar positions on these issues. I will not purport to have resolved the issues, however. And it is only fair to warn readers at the outset that the criterion of "hanging together" is attractive, I think, in part precisely because it does not prejudge the question of what sort of "hanging together" we can expect to find. More specifically, the term does not dictate that our account of constitutional law will be one that either in some sense "legitimates" what has been done in the name of the Constitution—scholarship calculated to produce *that* sort of "hanging together" will be the main subject of the final chapter—or that is practically helpful in telling the Court how to decide the next case. A satisfying account of how constitutional law and discourse came to be what they are *might* have those properties. Then again, it might not; it might even illuminate constitutional law and discourse in a way that highlights—perhaps without resolving—*new* predicaments that have gone largely unappreciated.

Most of what follows can be understood, in sum, as a response to a familiar, very basic challenge—one which professors face when they write about constitutional law but even more urgently when they try to teach students about constitutional law, and that students and citizens generally face when they try to understand constitutional law. But I would be less than candid—and readers might be puzzled both by what is included and what is omitted in the ensuing discussion—if I did not confess to an additional motivation growing out a different problem (or perhaps a different manifestation of the same problem). I can introduce this second difficulty by citing an observation of James Boyd White, who describes the "guilty dread" and the "expectation of frustration" that he feels as he approaches the professional literature that his job as a law professor obligates him to study.[38] Though White's judgments may seem harsh, in my own experience they are amply justified; indeed, "dread" almost seems too weak a word to describe the state of mind that I (along with, I'm confident, at least some others) at times experience when confronted with the prospect of a one-hundred-plus-page Supreme Court opinion, or a massively footnoted article by some young but up-and-coming constitutional scholar out to demonstrate his erudition by refining some already tedious constitutional doctrine, or a ponderous new book by a celebrated constitutional scholar earnestly presenting yet again, with only barely modified terminology, his view of how the Constitution *must* be interpreted. And this dread in turn provokes questions that are not simply pedagogical or academic but are more ethical or, some might say, existential in character. Is it worth reading the frustrating professional literature that one needs to read in order to produce a work of constitutional scholarship? Is this a valuable way to spend one's life? And what is the excuse for producing even more constitutional scholarship if others working in the field—some of whom are friends and colleagues, after all—will approach one's own scholarly output with the same dread and frustration?

My not entirely satisfying response to these questions is to pursue scholarly themes or questions that in some way reflect, or issue into, larger concerns of life that I and others must confront. This academic strategy would hope to generate scholarship that speaks to readers, perhaps not explicitly but at some level, not only as academicians or legal technicians, but as human beings with concerns and commitments that transcend the narrow confines of their job descriptions.[39] And the question of the relation between the Constitution and "reason" is inviting in this respect, because it indirectly but power-fully implicates the ethical commitment to living by reason; and that is a com-mitment whose validity and centrality have often been taken as axiomatic.

An aspiration to the "life of reason," in other words, is a common ethical commitment—and one that seems to have special or even irresistible appeal for lawyers and academicians. But what does such a life consist of, and is it in fact admirable and desirable? Some people confront ethical questions such as this one directly—in philosophy seminars, for example—but most of us ap-proach them more indirectly by pondering the meaning and consequences of different ethical values as reflected in the lives of real people (like Aunt Matilda or Richard Nixon), or fictional characters (like Hamlet or Huck Finn), or sometimes whole communities or cultures (like Sparta or the Trobriand Is-landers), or even fictional communities and cultures (Orwell's *1984* or More's *Utopia*). Thus, in Plato's *Republic,* after initial efforts to explain the meaning and claims of "justice" prove unsatisfying, Socrates suggests that it may be re-vealing to examine the virtue when writ large in a political community devoted to justice. Plato's ideal republic is then elaborated for at least the ostensible purpose of deciding whether and how Socrates and those conversing with him should themselves pursue justice in their individual lives.

In a similar way, the constitutional project has to a large extent been the work of people who were and are committed to the "life of reason"—and who have been determined to construct an entire political community dedicated to that ideal. So if the Constitution initiated the Empire of Reason, as Com-mager suggests, constitutional law can also be viewed as a sort of crucible for testing the commitment to reason.

It is this aspect of the constitutional project that, for me, gives the subject its special interest. What does our constitutional experience have to tell us, in other words, about the efficacy of a life that aspires to be ruled by reason? Ex-cept perhaps in the Epilogue, this secondary interest will work mostly beneath the surface. In the chapters that follow, I will not try to analyze the meaning or value of a commitment to reason except in connection with the Constitution and those who made it and those who speak for and about it. But it would be pointless to deny that my treatment of the specifically constitutional issues has been driven and influenced by my assumption that the Constitution is an es-pecially visible manifestation of, and thus perhaps a sort of object lesson re-garding, an ethical aspiration that can be traced back to the beginnings of hu-manity but that has come to pervade our post-Enlightenment civilization. And my underlying hope, in inspecting the claim that the Constitution embodies reason, is to learn something not only about the Constitution but also about the "life of reason," and perhaps even about that singular species that can be-come devoted to—and sometimes beguiled by—both.

PART I

THE FOUNDERS' REASON AND
THE LEGAL CONSTITUTION

The founders' aspiration was to embody reason in the Constitution in such a way as to initiate a new order for the ages—novus ordo seclorum—in which human affairs would finally be freed from the tyranny of force and fortuity. But was this vision so grandiose as to be implausible, perhaps even a bit ridiculous?

The people of the founding generation invoked "reason" so frequently, so confidently, and sometimes with such childlike naivete that it is tempting from a more modern and perhaps more weary perspective to view their enthusiasm with a mixture of suspicion and embarrassment. What are we to make of a class of people who wore powdered wigs and wrote in what would today seem an intolerably pompous dialect, who often developed "enthusiasms for silly practices and fatuous cults" like freemasonry, and yet who on encountering the most difficult political or philosophical problems—problems that had vexed the best minds for centuries—exhibited "a natural tendency to suppose that the answer would present itself in nothing above a week or two"? Might it be, as James Q. Whitman has suggested, that for the founding generation, "[t]he thrill of using one's free reason for the first time . . . often clouded the senses"?[1]

In short, was "reason" more than an exhilarating but ultimately vacuous slogan? Were the founders in their commitment to "reason" much different than other earnest and high-minded characters we sometimes encounter—the precocious high school student who reads a volume of Nietzsche or a book about the last days of Socrates and then announces that he has resolved to dedicate his life to "philosophy," or the grocery store clerk who is certain (perhaps from watching Carl Sagan on television or a special about Stephen Hawking) that "science" has, or at least soon will have, the answers to all the problems and mysteries of the cosmos?

There may be truth in this condescending depiction, but it is not the whole truth. Against such suspicions, I want to argue that for the founders "reason" was not *merely an empty slogan or a conclusory label to be attached to opinions they favored. Rather, the founding generation was in possession of a relatively fleshed out conception of "reason"—one that compares favorably in its sophistication with modern notions that typically accompany that term. Chapter 1 seeks to explicate what "reason" meant to the founders. Chapter 2 offers an account of their complex—or at least convoluted—strategy for embodying "reason" in the Constitution.*

The discussion in these chapters will suggest, I hope, that the founding of the constitutional republic was a remarkable accomplishment reflecting an enviable intellectual and political maturity. Still, the discussion is not offered as a nostalgic defense of the founders' vision and scheme. My intention is not to provide yet another apology for constitutional "originalism," for example. Rather, in Chapter 3 I argue that impressive though it was, the founders' strategy for bringing human governance under the sway of reason failed—and indeed by their own assumptions was bound to fail. This diagnosis will lead into an assessment in Part II of more modern efforts to salvage the project of embodying reason in constitutional law.

CHAPTER ONE

Old Bags and New Wine

The Reason of the Founders

*T*he founding generation's conception of "reason" resulted from the convergence of two traditions—one ancient, the other relatively modern. The ancient tradition was linked to what we might call the classical conception of Nature and the Great Chain of Being philosophy. The more modern tradition might be described as the antitraditional spirit of Cartesian rationalism.

The modern element is the more familiar one, and the one we typically associate with "the Enlightenment"; it is also, not surprisingly, the aspect of the founders' reason that we are inclined to regard as most worthy of celebration. Considered by itself, however, the modern element conveys a badly distorted image of what reason meant to the founding generation. In addition, if we are attuned only to the modern strand, we will likely perceive the important continuities but overlook the critical disjunctions between the founders' constitutional vision and our own. Hence, this chapter's discussion will begin by attempting an exposition of the more ancient, and more alien, component of the founders' reason. The discussion will then turn to the component that resonates with our own notions of "reason."

The Classical Theme: Reason and Nature

The ancient part of the founding generation's conception of reason might be imagined as a picture depicting two lovers locked in an intimate embrace. These lovers are identifiable. One is Nature. The other is the human mind. It is clear, moreover, that these partners have been painted by the same masterful hand. They are not incongruent, the way real lovers sometimes are—one willowy and the other oaken, or one elegant and the other gawky. Rather, the pair is beautifully complementary. These partners were manifestly made for each other.

Less metaphorically, we might describe the ancient part of the founding generation's conception of reason in three propositions. First, Nature is endowed with an inherent structure that has both material and ethical aspects. Nature comes to us not in naive innocence, much less in turbulent confusion, but rather already charged with design, order, and purpose. Second, the human mind has been constituted so that it is cognitively commensurate with Nature. So the mind is capable of grasping Nature's design. Third, underwriting both propositions—and providing an explanation for what might otherwise seem the miraculous congruity aligning the cosmic flow of Nature with the minuscule movements of the human mind—is the assumption that both Nature and the mind are the creations of an overarching, benevolent Providence.

These ideas were not born in the eighteenth century. From a religious perspective, their inspiration might be found in the first chapter of Genesis: "In the beginning God created the heaven and the earth. . . . So God created man in his own image. . . ."[1] From a more philosophical perspective, their lineage might be traced back at least to Plato. And since our project requires a grasp of this now somewhat alien approach to understanding the world, Plato's writings provide a natural introduction.

Mind over Matter

In the *Phaedo,* Plato has the character Socrates[2] describe his youthful excursions into the then undifferentiated field of science and philosophy. Socrates reports: "When I was young, Cebes, I had an extraordinary passion for that branch of learning which is called natural science. I thought it would be marvelous to know the causes for which each thing comes and ceases and continues to be."[3] Many of the pre-Socratic philosophers had investigated similar issues and had traced the causes of all phenomena to basic material elements—water (Thales), or air (Anaximenes), or earth, air, fire, and water (Empedocles).[4] Socrates himself was initially attracted to this sort of explanation.[5]

Later, though, he became disenchanted with these naturalist accounts. Then Socrates came across a book by Anaxagoras that suggested an entirely different explanation: "[I]t is *mind* that produces order and is the cause of everything."[6] To Socrates's disappointment, Anaxagoras himself failed to appreciate or develop this radical insight. Instead, "the fellow made no use of mind and assigned it no causality for the order of the world, but adduced causes like air and aether and water and many other absurdities."[7] Nonetheless, Socrates concluded that the account proposed but then neglected by Anaxagoras was the correct one. The cause of everything in the world is not natural elements and processes—these are "conditions," not "causes"[8]—but rather "mind."

These reflections point to a view of Nature that I will call the classical conception. This conception differs in fundamental ways from a view common both in Plato's day and in ours, which we might indicate with the terms "nature" (lower case) or "naturalism."[9] Plato discussed the differences in these views at greater length in his *Laws.* As the Athenian in that dialogue explains, the common view holds "that fire and water, earth and air, are the most primitive origins of all things" and that "the soul is a later derivative from them."[10]

By this view, the universe—the material elements, the heavens, the plants, and animals—are all produced "not . . . by the agency of mind, or any god, or art, but . . . by nature and chance."[11] These naturalist theories had been "widely broadcast, as we may fairly say, throughout all mankind." Propagated by "men who impress the young as wise, prose writers and poets," such views led to "youthful epidemics of irreligion."[12]

But the Athenian rejects the naturalist position in favor of a different account. By this view, something described as "soul" is "among the primal things, elder-born than all bodies and prime source of all their changes and transformations." In other words, "soul came first— . . . it was not fire, nor air, but soul which was there to begin with. . . ." And what people generally but misleadingly call "nature" is in fact "secondary and derivative from art and mind."[13]

In short, according to the naturalist view, nature is primary and mind or soul is derivative. The other position—the one favored by Plato—reverses this order. Mind or soul comes first and produces Nature.

The diametrically opposed worldviews described by Plato persist, in a variety of guises, throughout the course of Western thought. The naturalist view was typical, as Plato asserted, of much Greek thought, especially of atomists such as Democritus.[14] It also expresses the characteristic perspective of contemporary science. William Barrett describes this viewpoint, which he labels "scientific materialism":

[Scientific materialism] was the conviction that the ultimate facts of nature are bits of matter in space, and that all the varied phenomena of experience are to be explained by the movement and configuration of that matter. Moreover, these bits of matter had only the properties that accord with mechanics: mass, extension, solidity, and movement in space.[15]

The contrary position favored by Plato is manifest, in one form or another, not only in Plato's own philosophy but also in major religious traditions—Judaism, Christianity, Islam. Probably the philosophical and religious traditions have interacted in their influence. Early Christian apologists like Justin Martyr believed that Plato must have had access to the Hebrew scriptures[16] while, more verifiably, Neoplatonism heavily influenced Augustine[17] and, through him, Christian thought. In any event, Plato's basic conception persisted in the Western intellectual tradition described in Arthur Lovejoy's classic *The Great Chain of Being*. Lovejoy traced this view back to Plato, and he showed how in different versions it has appeared again and again throughout the history of Western philosophy, science, and religion.

The essential recurring ideas in this intellectual position can be stated briefly. First, the world was created by an originating mind—the demiurge or, more commonly, God—who by virtue of being perfectly good and self-sufficient could not know envy, and hence chose to confer existence on everything that it could conceive of.[18] Second, because everything that exists is the product of mind, not of chance, there is a reason why everything exists in just the way that it does. Following Leibniz, Lovejoy called this the "principle of sufficient reason."[19] Third, because the originating mind could not but choose to give existence to everything that it could conceive of, the universe is in fact rich with the greatest possible variety of entities—Lovejoy called this idea the "principle of plenitude"[20]—which together form a continuum from the lowest and most inanimate to the highest and most intelligent. This hierarchy is the Great Chain of Being.

Lovejoy showed how the core of Western thought through the eighteenth century consisted of the working out and the reworking of these themes. Not surprisingly, this view of Nature has important implications for the question of reason.

Nature and the Possibility of Reason

The critical point is that if Nature is the product *of* "mind," then it may be commensurate with or accessible *to* "mind." The "principle of sufficient reason" dictates the content and shape of Nature and also supplies the bridge between Nature and the human mind. To be sure, this observation must be made with caution. Surely there is no guarantee that the infinite mind which created the cosmos is commensurate with the decidedly finite minds of mortal human beings who study that creation. Still, the assumption of design gives cause for hope. That which is the product *of* intelligence just might disclose its secret workings *to* intelligence. So scientists like Galileo and Newton can act with the faith, or at least the hope, that Nature will be so charitable as to behave according to laws or regularities discernible to the human mind.

Moreover, it is not only natural scientists who have grounds to hope. If Nature is the product of intelligent design and if it was made for an intelligently conceived purpose, then the structure or design of Nature would have not only a physical or material dimension but also a purposive or normative dimension. Moreover, these dimensions would not be wholly distinct properties of Nature, but rather different aspects of the same overall design. Thus, a belief in Nature (as opposed to nature) suggests the possibility of a fusion, or at least a tendency toward convergence, of *is* and *ought*—of how the world *is* constituted and how the world *ought to be* constituted.

In Plato's *Phaedo*, Socrates emphasizes this convergence in his criticism of Anaxagoras. Having observed the primacy of mind over nature, Anaxagoras had promptly forgotten the point in his explanations of matters and happenings in the world. What Anaxagoras had failed to grasp, Socrates maintains, was that if the world is the product or creation of a mindful agent, then "mind in producing order sets everything in order and arranges each individual thing in the way that is best for it." This premise in turn supports a particular way of reasoning about the world: "Therefore if anyone wished to discover the reason why any given thing came or ceased or continued to be, he must find out how it was best for that thing to be, or to act or be acted upon in any other way."[21]

Socrates explains this point more clearly in his exposition of how Anaxagoras *should* have reasoned:

I assumed that he would begin by informing us whether the earth is flat or round, and would then proceed to explain in detail the reason and logical necessity for this by stating how and why it was better that it should be so. I thought that if he asserted that the earth was in the center, he would explain in detail that it was better for it to be there; and if he made this clear, I was prepared to give up hankering after any other kind of cause. I was prepared also in the same way to receive instruction about the sun and moon and the other heavenly bodies, about their relative velocities and their orbits and all the other phenomena connected with them—in what way it is better for each one of them to act or be acted upon as it is. It never entered my head that a man who asserted that the ordering of things is due to mind would offer any other explanation for them than that it is best for them to be as they are. I thought that by assigning a cause to each phenomenon separately and to the universe as a whole he would make perfectly clear what is best for each and what is the universal good.[22]

The Leap of Reason

Socrates' suggestion provokes profound questions—not only epistemological questions about whether and how mere mortals can comprehend God's design, but also philosophical questions about the existence of evil and about divine and human freedom—that have plagued philosophers and theologians through the centuries. Fortunately, the present discussion need not delve into these profundities. For our purposes, the essential point can be expressed as follows: If Nature is the product of mind, then there should be a relation between *is* and *ought*, or between *what is* and *what should be,* and this relation might support kinds of reasoning that would otherwise be unwarranted. One might reason from *ought* to *is*. ("The earth *should* be round; therefore, the earth *is* round.") Conversely, one might move from *is* to *ought*. ("Acorns grow into oaks; therefore, acorns *should* grow into oaks.")

So the classical conception of Nature, and the corollary convergence of is and ought, would seem to have significance both for what we would call science and for what we would regard as ethical and political inquiries. History bears out this surmise. On the side of science, for example, Lovejoy showed that the type of reasoning permitted by the classical view has been characteristic of much Western thought in areas such as astronomy and biology. Scientists like Kepler and Galileo deduced conclusions about how the world is from philosophical or religious premises about how it must be.[23]

Some quirky (to us) examples may be especially helpful in conveying the substance and flavor of this kind of reasoning (and, a little later, in illustrating the affinity between this classical tradition and the thinkers of the founding generation). The principle of plenitude—or the idea that God has given existence to everything He could conceive of—led many early modern scientists and thinkers to infer that there must be intelligent inhabitants of other worlds. After all, even *we* can imagine possible creatures that do not seem to exist *here*; so these creatures must exist somewhere else. Let us suppose, then, that there are intelligent beings on the moon; would they be just like earthly human beings? No, said Galileo. Although there are no "sure observations," it can be inferred through "primary intuition and pure natural reason" that they would be "entirely different and to us wholly unimaginable." Why? Because, Galileo explained, such variety is "required by the richness of Nature and the omnipotence of its Creator and Governor."[24]

Or consider Kant's argument for the infinite extension of the physical universe and the infinite plurality of worlds:

> [We must] conceive of the creation as proportionate to the power of an Infinite Being, . . . it can have no limits at all. . . . It would be absurd to represent the Deity as bringing into action only an infinitely small part of his creative potency—to think of that reservoir of a true immensity of natures and of worlds as inactive and shut up in an eternal desuetude. Is it not much more reasonable, or, to express it better, is it not necessary, to represent the totality of the creation as it must be in order that it may bear witness to that Power which is beyond all measurement?[25]

These were not isolated instances or aberrations. Lovejoy explained the premise that made such reasoning seem cogent:

> In so far as the world was conceived in this fashion, it seemed a coherent, luminous, intellectually secure and dependable world, in which the mind of man could go about its business of seeking an understanding of things in full confidence; and empirical science, since it was acquainted in advance with the fundamental principles with which the facts must, in the end, accord, and was provided with a sort of diagram of the general pattern of the universe, could know in outline what to expect, and even anticipate particular disclosures of actual observations.[26]

If scientific *is*-propositions could be derived from religious or philosophical *oughts,* the logic also ran the other way. For example, it was common to derive admonitions to humility from astronomical observations about the relative tininess of the earth in the vastness of the universe.[27] But the derivation of *ought* from *is* was not limited to these sorts of ad hoc moralisms or pieties. The connection could be much more explicit, careful, and thorough; the very foundation for morality lay in the world as created.

Moral reasoning, in other words, could be understood as a mapping out of one dimension—the purposive or teleological dimension—of the creator's design. Perhaps the clearest instance of this sort of reasoning—and an instance that shows the relevance of such reasoning to political and legal matters—occurs in classical natural law theory, as most fully developed in the thought of Thomas Aquinas. In this view, within the providential scheme everything has a natural end, or *telos.* Ethics consists of the rules or virtues that lead a thing to realize its *telos,* and politics is the application of ethics to the community as a whole.[28]

Such thinking continued into—or even, as Lovejoy argued, culminated in—the eighteenth century,[29] so it is hardly surprising to find that this way of thinking permeates the discourse of our own founding generation. To be sure, the American founders likely would not have rushed to claim Plato and

Aquinas as their intellectual fathers.[30] Nonetheless, the classical conception of Nature is pervasively manifest in their thinking on matters of science, ethics, and politics.

Nature and Reason in the American Enlightenment

The American Constitution, we are accustomed to thinking, was a product of "the Enlightenment."[31] The received wisdom simplifies, of course. For one thing, it understates the importance in American thought of religious, and specifically Protestant, assumptions and beliefs.[32] For another, it tends to gloss over the fact that "the Enlightenment" was not a single, unitary phenomenon,[33] and indeed that no one at the time realized that they were living in "the Enlightenment" at all.[34] For the moment, though, these qualifications to the received wisdom are not critical. It seems sufficient for now to depict the broad notions of Nature and reason that most heavily influenced those who wrote and supported the Declaration of Independence and the Constitution—notions associated with what Henry May calls "the Moderate Enlightenment" and with the overlapping "Jeffersonian" worldview described by Daniel Boorstin. And as it turns out, those notions are very much an expression of themes pervasive within the classical conceptions of Nature and the Great Chain of Being philosophy.

In a study of the underlying "mindscape of ideas" that informed the Jeffersonian worldview, Daniel Boorstin shows that Jeffersonian thought was firmly anchored in the Great Chain of Being philosophy.[35] The worldview associated with Plato and later elaborated in a variety of ways by both Neoplatonic and Christian thinkers is pervasively manifest, both explicitly and implicitly, throughout Jefferson's thinking on subjects ranging from religion and science to history and politics.

THE CENTRALITY OF PROVIDENCE. Boorstin points out, as Jefferson himself did, the central importance of God-as-Creator in the Jeffersonian worldview.[36] Boorstin notes that "Jefferson on more than one occasion declared 'the eternal pre-existence of God, and his creation of the world,' to be the foundation of his philosophy."[37] In a similar vein, Henry May observes that "Jefferson's universe was as purposeful as that of [Yale president and aggressive Protestant] Timothy Dwight and presupposed as completely the existence of a ruler and creator. The world was intelligently planned, benevolently intended, and understandable."[38]

To be sure, Jefferson's Providence was not the wholly transcendent, dread-inspiring deity of Calvin; and precisely for that reason God could play an even more important role in the everyday world for Jefferson than for the Calvinists. For Jonathan Edwards, the Calvinist philosopher and preacher, God was inscrutable. Human knowledge, unless assisted by divine inspiration, was worthless. And although John Adams early rejected Calvinism, he retained a Calvinist mindset: "As deeply as any of his Calvinist ancestors, he believed in a God beyond human understanding."[39] The Jeffersonian God, by contrast, was not distant or alien; rather, He was benevolent and, most important, eminently intelligible.[40] Because the general Jeffersonian orientation was above all pragmatic or utilitarian,[41] the Jeffersonian God was of necessity a very useable deity; and the Jeffersonians made constant use of him in all branches of their thinking.

THE CONVERGENCE OF IS AND *OUGHT*.   If the world was the product of a supremely wise and benevolent Providence, then there could be no radical divergence between *is* and *ought*. Hence, the Jeffersonian cosmology worked by "blending the world as it is with the world as it ought to be. . . ." In this cosmology, "[a]ll facts were endowed with an ambiguous quality: they became normative as well as descriptive."[42]

Given their "conviction that the processes of nature were universally good—having been conceived by a supernatural power," the Jeffersonians could not explain or even acknowledge the existence of any radical or deeply entrenched evil in the world.[43] And indeed, Boorstin observes that "[h]ow thoroughly the Jeffersonian had emptied his universe of dramatic conflict between good and evil" was a manifestation of "the vast distance by which he had separated himself from the Calvinist. . . ." Apparent evils were attributed to the "inability of individual men to comprehend the divine scheme. . . ."[44] And the Jeffersonians took delight in elucidating this scheme by revealing the hidden value or usefulness in supposed evils.

For example, Adam Seybert, a contributor to the American Philosophical Society over which Jefferson presided and which served as a clearinghouse for the ideas and discussions of Jefferson and his friends, explained that unhealthy and uninhabitable swamps, though seemingly an obstacle to human flourishing, were in fact necessary to maintain the proper level of purity in the atmosphere. Seybert concluded that "ere long marshes will be looked upon by mankind as gifts from Heaven to prolong the life and happiness of the greatest portion of the animal kingdom."[45] Though one suspects that Socrates might have subjected this position to some skeptical and incisive questions, still this seems to be precisely the *kind* of explanation endorsed by the Socrates of the *Phaedo*.

In a similar vein, Benjamin Rush, another member of the Society and a prominent American thinker as well as a signer of the Declaration of Independence, maintained for a time that in the providential scheme every disease must have a natural remedy and that medicinal plants would necessarily be located in the same geographic areas as the diseases they served to remedy. Recalcitrant empirical evidence eventually forced Rush to relinquish his thesis of geographical coincidence; he then explained that Providence had wisely separated remedies from their corresponding diseases in order to stimulate human activity and commerce.[46] On a larger scale, the Jeffersonians concluded that mankind's evident propensity to warfare helpfully served in the divine scheme to prevent overpopulation.[47]

These complacent accounts of evil could earn Jeffersonians the contempt of less optimistic contemporaries.[48] But the Jeffersonians' attitude toward evil was a natural corollary of their view of the world as the creation of a benign Providence, and the consequent linkage of *is* and *ought*. And this view also determined the Jeffersonians' understanding of both the natural world and the human world of ethics and politics.

NATURE AND SCIENTIFIC REASON.   For American thinkers of the late eighteenth century, the facts of Nature conformed to, and hence must be understood by reference to, the providential plan. Henry May explains that despite significant diversity among the members of the American Philosophical Society, "[o]ne and all . . . saw nature as designed by a wise creator for the use and edification of man."49 Nor was this view of Nature merely an abstract proposition; it informed the Jeffersonian method of reasoning about specific scientific questions. For example, Jefferson believed that the world had been created in a single, brief creative period; the creator would not have needed thousands or millions of years to accomplish his ends.50 Moreover, since the world as originally created already conformed to the divine design, it could not change in fundamental respects. Thus, reacting to the contention that the earth had evolved slowly and in response to natural agents such as steam, Jefferson objected:

> I give one answer to all these theorists. . . . They all suppose the earth a created existence. They must suppose a creator then; and that he possessed power and wisdom to a great degree. As he intended the earth for the habitation of animals and vegetables, is it reasonable to suppose, he made two jobs of his creation, that he first made a chaotic lump and set it into rotatory motion, and then waited the millions of ages necessary to form itself? That when it had done this, he stepped in a second time to create the animals and plants which were to inhabit it? As the hand of a creator is to be called in, it may as well be called in at one stage of the process as another. We may as well suppose he created the earth at once, nearly in the state in which we see it, fit for the preservation of the beings he placed on it.51

In a similar spirit, in his *Notes on Virginia* Jefferson addressed the question whether mammoths still exist. Although fossils of mammoths had been found, might they not in more recent times have become extinct? But Jefferson rejected this possibility a priori: "Such is the economy of nature, that no instance can be produced, of her having permitted any one race of her animals to become extinct; of her having formed any link in her great work so weak as to be broken."52 Given this necessary inference from the order of Nature, Jefferson considered possible empirical evidence inconsequential.53 In making this deduction, moreover, Jefferson was hardly eccentric; other thinkers (such as Spinoza) working within the Great Chain of Being framework had likewise found this sort of argument to be compelling.54

MORAL AND POLITICAL REASONING.   Their belief in a providentially created and governed world also guided the Jeffersonians' thinking about ethics and politics. They believed, Boorstin explains, that "uniform and objective moral principles" were inherent in human biology itself. Moreover, God impresses these principles on the human heart; they are equally known to the ploughman and the professor by means of a moral sense that God gives to every human being.[55]

With respect to the government of society, likewise, the Jeffersonians believed that God ordains principles for society and that the purpose of political theory is to discover "the plan implicit in nature."[56] The proper ends of society are not for human beings to choose; they are given in the divine plan, and the duty of government is simply to ascertain and conform to that plan. Thus, the Jeffersonian theory of government amounted to little more than deference to the Creator's plan.[57] As Henry May notes: "A benign God, a purposeful universe, and a universal moral sense are necessary at all points to Jefferson's political system."[58]

The notion of individual rights, so central to the Declaration of Independence and to Jefferson's political legacy, was for Jefferson likewise grounded in the divine scheme. As the Declaration itself said, "rights" are conferred on humans by "their Creator." In Jefferson's usage, Boorstin explains, "[t]he word 'right' was always a signpost pointing back to the divine plan of the Creation."[59] For similar reasons, modern worries about conflicts between rights, or about balancing competing rights against each other, or about the excessive or corrosive character of rights,[60] did not afflict Jefferson. "Faith in the Creator's design was what saved the persistent iteration of 'rights' from seeming an anarchic individualism."[61]

To be sure, Jefferson himself was in some ways not entirely representative of the thought of his time. He personified what Henry May calls the "Revolutionary Enlightenment." By contrast, most of the signers of the Declaration of Independence as well as most of the delegates to the Philadelphia Convention—Jefferson, of course, was not in this group—were adherents of the "Moderate Enlightenment." James Madison, who played such a crucial role in the creation of the Constitution, was the "very symbol of the Moderate Enlightenment." And May argues that the spirit and assumptions of the Moderate Enlightenment were enduringly embodied in the Constitution itself.[62]

In the next chapter we will take a closer look at the some of the political assumptions of Madison and the delegates to the Philadelphia convention. For now, it is enough to observe that the differences between the radical and moderate versions of the Enlightenment do not affect the particular conclusions suggested here. Moderates like Madison differed from radicals like Jefferson in their temper and tone, and also in some of their specific political positions. As we will see, moderates tended to be less optimistic than Jefferson was—especially with regard to human nature.

Nonetheless, like Jefferson, moderates believed not in the fearsome, inscrutable God of Calvin but rather in a beneficent, intelligible God whose design was readily accessible to human understanding. Proponents of rational religion, they had little patience for or interest in theological dogmas such as predestination or the Trinity, nor were they fond of spiritual "enthusiasm" such as that exhibited by the Quakers. In their more dispassionate faith, Providence upheld a world of calm order and balance.[63] Thus, the moderates shared with Jefferson the classical assumptions about Nature and reason.

The Modern Theme: a Declaration of (Epistemic) Independence

The discussion thus far may suggest that founding era thinking about Nature and reason was nothing more than a rehearsal of centuries-old themes. The basic idea—that Nature was created by God with an inherent structure or design discernible by human intelligence—had been presented and re-presented at least since the time of Plato. But although this account may be accurate as far as it goes, the account fails to capture something that seems vital to the founders' incessant invocations of "reason." After all, if they were merely restating ideas that had been loitering around for centuries, then why did the founders seem to regard themselves as some sort of philosophical and political Columbuses announcing the discovery of a whole new continent? And why did they talk about their commitment to reason as if they were engaged in an untried experiment?

In part, perhaps, such talk reflected a kind of naivete.[64] There is no cause for condescension here. History offers ample examples of thinkers, and movements of thinkers, who become intoxicated with what they suppose to be their own intellectual discoveries and who congratulate themselves on having broken free from the benighted past—all the while failing to realize that their ostensible innovations have already been thoroughly hashed over by earlier generations or other cultures. "Is there any thing whereof it may be said, See, this is new? it hath been already of old time, which was before us."[65] This is a recurring spectacle, and there is no reason to suppose that our own intellectual conceits will escape the embarrassment. The point is simply that we *know*, as Carl Becker powerfully and entertainingly demonstrated earlier in this century, that the thinkers of the Enlightenment failed in important respects to appreciate their indebtedness to—and their continuing imitation of—their intellectual ancestors.[66]

Still, there does seem to be something distinctive in Enlightenment ideas about reason—or at least in Enlightenment attitudes toward reason. I will suggest that this distinctive element reflected the infusion into the classical tradition of the spirit, though perhaps not the substance, of Cartesian rationalism.[67]

The Cartesian Spirit

The Cartesian attitude is one of intellectual self-confidence, but it had its origins in despair. Descartes's intellectual world is remote from our own and yet strangely familiar: In the aftermath of the decay of medieval scholasticism, Descartes found nothing but conflicting schools and clashing opinions, none of which could establish itself against its rivals. Regarding philosophy in particular he observed despondently "that it has been studied for many centuries by the most outstanding minds without having produced anything which is not in dispute. . . ."[68]

A like despondency has often led erstwhile truth-seekers into a general discouragement and skepticism. Plato discussed the dangers of "misology"—or the hostility to reason that affects many who conclude from the perpetual conflict of contradictory opinions that "there is nothing stable or dependable either in facts or arguments, and that everything fluctuates just like the water in a tidal channel. . . ."[69] Alasdair MacIntyre's modern classic *After Virtue* gives a comparable depiction of contemporary moral discourse.[70]

Closer to home (for constitutional lawyers, at least), Robert Bork evinces a similar sentiment. Speaking of the moral philosophy that figures in much contemporary constitutional theorizing, Bork asserts:

> It seems not to occur to most . . . academics that they are undertaking to succeed where the greatest minds of the centuries are commonly thought to have failed. . . . If the greatest minds of our culture have not succeeded in devising a moral system to which all intellectually honest persons must subscribe, it seems doubtful, to say the least, that some law professor will make the breakthrough any time soon. It is my firm intention to give up reading this literature. There comes a time to stop visiting inventors' garages to see if someone really has created a perpetual motion machine.[71]

Most of us probably have felt this sort of despondency at times. In Descartes's case, the discouragement and doubt became so severe that he expressed distrust about the existence even of the objects before his own eyes.[72] But Descartes's intellectual journey culminated not in resigned skepticism, but rather in a remarkable self-confidence, because of a method he hit upon that seemed calculated to produce certain knowledge. It is not important here to review his method in detail or to revisit the specific steps in the argument by which he convinced himself that *he* existed ("I think; therefore I am"), that God existed, and that God guaranteed the accuracy of his perceptions.[73] For our purposes, what matters is Descartes's basic orientation toward knowledge and reasoning.

More specifically, Descartes concluded that in order to achieve real knowledge he should begin by doubting everything—by repudiating everything he and others had previously believed and starting fresh. With respect to all existing opinions, he must "reject them completely" so that they could be replaced by beliefs grounded in "a rational scheme." In particular, he must distrust "example and custom"—unreliable teachers that had generated "many errors which could obscure the light of nature and make us less capable of correct reasoning." And in building his intellectual world anew, Descartes resolved to trust nothing except his own understanding—to believe nothing "unless it presented itself so clearly and distinctly to my mind that there was not reason or occasion to doubt it."[74]

Descartes had high hopes for this approach. Given time and patient inquiry, all knowledge might be ours.[75] Moreover, the exercise itself promised to be exhilarating: "What pleased me most about this method was that it enabled me to reason in all things. . . ."[76]

Much in Descartes's argument has come in for criticism—and even, in recent times, for reviling. The Cartesian quest for foundational certainty and the Cartesian split between mind and body have sometimes been viewed as principal sources of error and even evil in modern thought. And between Descartes and the American founders there intervened philosophers like John Locke who criticized much of the substance of Descartes's position. But as Charles Taylor remarks, "loud denunciations of Descartes are not of themselves a sign of a writer's having escaped Descartes's baleful influence."[77] Indeed, the contagious *spirit* of Descartes's enterprise has infected many a thinker who may be either innocent of or hostile toward the philosopher's specific ideas. Ernest Gellner describes this persistent orientation:

> One of the central themes, perhaps indeed the central obsession, of Cartesian rationalism is the aspiration for autonomy. There is the overwhelming desire for a kind of self-creation, for bringing forth a self and a world not simply taken over from an unexamined, accidental, contingent inheritance. Rationalism is the philosophy of the New Broom. Man makes himself, and he does so *rationally*. Cultural accumulation is irrational: it is a blind process. If our thought and valuation are its fruits, they are unworthy of our trust. . . .[78]

Although Gellner appears as a celebrant of reason, he acknowledges that this "Promethean aspiration to autarchy and self-creation" cannot be fully realized.[79] But it does not follow that we should disavow the aspiration, or even that we *can* disavow it. On the contrary, an aspiration to reason is by now central to our very identity.[80]

Reason versus Authority

A consequence of this Cartesian orientation is that reason comes to be seen as the antithesis of tradition and authority.[81] This perceived opposition distinguishes Enlightenment reason from its forerunners. For instance, the *Summa Theologica* of Thomas Aquinas can be viewed as a monument of, and to, human reason. Indeed, the work can be (and has been) *condemned* precisely on the ground that Aquinas trusted inordinately in the power of reason. Still, the *Summa* reflects a careful interweaving of reason, tradition, and authority. Aquinas is ever respectful of Aristotle, Augustine, scripture, and other authorities; he tries to reconcile his own thinking with theirs, not to ignore or reject or overthrow them. The work supposes harmony, not hostility, between "reason" and "authority."[82]

Once the Cartesian repudiation of custom and example has become established, however, this apparent marriage of reason and authority comes to be perceived as a sort of sin against nature. The hostility of reason and authority is a notion that has been pervasively absorbed into the general culture, and indeed that helps define the contours of the so-called culture wars in contemporary America.[83] Gellner observes:

[T]he really big battle with which the wider public is familiar is one which pits Reason against Authority, with Tradition usually acting as a subsidiary, and sometimes important, ally of Authority. The picture contrasts the man who in the end respects only his own reason, who heeds only the evidence and rational conviction available to him, with the man who defers to Authority and Tradition.[84]

The Self-Made Mind in America

The Cartesian spirit of intellectual independence—of "thinking for yourself"—was abundantly manifest in the Enlightenment; indeed, according to Kant's well-known dictum, it was the very essence of enlightenment.[85] Not surprisingly, it was conspicuous in the thinking of American figures like Jefferson. The Jeffersonians insisted that "reason" is a faculty we must exercise *for ourselves,* not trusting to the supposed wisdom of past generations. Indeed, though contemporary scholars like Morton White try to spell out in a more positive way what the founders meant by "reason,"[86] it sometimes seems that for the founders themselves reason was consciously understood primarily in terms of what it *was not.*[87] And what reason was not, specifically, was trust in tradition, authority, or (what for Jefferson seem to have been interchangeable notions) "monkish ignorance and superstition."[88] Suzanna Sherry nicely, and approvingly, captures this component of the founding generation's thinking. The Enlightenment, she explains,

> was a repudiation of "the millennium of superstition, other-worldliness, mysticism, and dogma known as the Middle, or Dark, Ages." Personal revelation and institutional power were no longer valid sources of authority. Instead, the human capacity to reason, in all its splendor, would control the future.[89]

This aspect of American thought is faithfully reflected in Henry Steele Commager's *The Empire of Reason.* Although Commager perhaps does not offer the most balanced or insightful *analysis* of the Enlightenment in this country, by wholly succumbing to the Jeffersonian enthusiasm he does manage to achieve a certain *resonance* with the self-styled "Age of Reason." Thus, it might at first seem odd that in a book-length celebration of the employment of "reason" in the founding of this country, there is never any deliberate effort to set forth just what "reason" consists of, how it works, or why it is entitled to such unreserved deference. But perhaps this omission in Commager's treatment is consonant with the times he writes about. In any event, what Commager does communicate clearly, as did the men he studies, is a notion of what reason stands in opposition to.

So Commager tells us, on page one, that reason means emancipation from "ignorance, credulity, and superstition."[90] The American founders, he explains with perceptible satisfaction (although not with complete accuracy), refused to credit scripture, miracles, or revelation.[91] They insisted on "freedom from the trammels of religious superstition"—on finding answers in Nature rather than scriptures.[92] Commager quotes Jefferson's account of the "animating principle of his age": "We believed," Jefferson said, "that men, habituated to thinking for themselves, and to follow their reason as guide, would be more easily and safely governed than with minds nourished in error and vitiated and debased . . . by ignorance."[93] The Cartesian spirit is unmistakable.

Jefferson explained his view at greater length in an avuncular letter offering advice about education to the youthful Peter Carr. After brief notes about the Italian language (not advisable as a subject of study because it "will confound your French and Spanish"), Spanish (highly recommended), and moral philosophy (a waste of time, since everyone can apprehend moral truths directly through a God-given "moral sense"), Jefferson reached the subject of religion, and here he became more expansive:

> [S]hake off all the fears and servile prejudices, under which weak minds are servilely crouched. Fix reason firmly in her seat, and call to her tribunal every fact, every opinion. Question with boldness even the existence of a God; because, if there be one, he must more approve of the homage of reason, than that of blindfolded fear.

After a discussion of matters such as the historicity of scripture and the relation between religious belief and virtuous conduct, Jefferson returned to this theme:

> In fine, I repeat, you must lay aside all prejudice on both sides, and neither believe nor reject anything, because any other persons, or description of persons, have rejected or believed it. Your own reason is the only oracle given you by heaven, and you are answerable, not for the rightness, but uprightness of the decision.[94]

Or, as Thomas Paine put the matter with characteristic pithiness:

> I do not believe in the creed professed by the Jewish church, by the Roman church, by the Greek church, by the Turkish church, by the Protestant church, nor by any church that I know of. *My own mind is my own church* [my emphasis].[95]

A Peculiar Union

The notions of reason that prevailed at the founding were, as we have seen, a compound of old and new. The founding generation embraced—or at least took for granted—classical notions about a Nature created and governed by Providence and exhibiting a design accessible to human intelligence. The founders also manifested—indeed, were intoxicated by—the Cartesian spirit of independence and repudiation of tradition and authority.

There is of course nothing inevitable about this particular alignment of ancient and modern traditions. Powerful and influential thinkers have often accepted the notion of a cosmic order without supposing that the best way to discern that order is to throw off traditional teachings and resort to what Gail Heriot has called "[r]igorous 'starting from zero' analysis."[96] The discussion has already mentioned Aquinas, to note just one example. Edmund Burke would be another obvious instance. Or, leaving the Western intellectual tradition for a moment, consider the perspective of Confucius:

Confucius had a strong belief in a natural order that was also a moral order. Heaven for him was a guiding Providence, and one's fulfillment as a man came from acting in accordance with the will of Heaven. This will, however, could be best understood through the study of history. In the traditions, customs, and literature of the past, in the collective experience of mankind, there was objective confirmation of the moral law written in the heart of man.[97]

It hardly seems self-evident that the eighteenth-century conjunction of the classical belief in a cosmic order with the modern disdain for inherited wisdom is a more natural or more inherently plausible position than the traditional orientation reflected in different ways by thinkers like Aquinas, Burke, or Confucius. Indeed, from a detached perspective the Enlightenment conception of reason may seem an odd and unstable mixture. How could the founding generation so confidently embrace an ancient philosophical tradition while at the same time declaiming so fiercely against the embracing of ancient traditions? And why didn't—and why *don't*—partisans of the Enlightenment more scrupulously apply their demand that every faith be interrogated and vindicated before the tribunal of reason to their own faith in the power of free and fresh human intellect to trace out the grand design of Nature?

However contingent and even paradoxical, though, the union of old and new that made up the eighteenth-century conception of reason had—and continues to have—an undeniable power to inspire grand, or perhaps grandiose, visions.[98] Indeed, the newly declared independence of the human mind could produce a slightly giddy sense of undreamed of possibilities, much in the way that the political declaration of independence had opened up exhilarating visions for America itself.[99] Once again, Commager captures this spirit of the Enlightenment:

> There was a prodigality about them; they recognized no bounds to their curiosity, no barriers to their thought, no limits to their activities or, for that matter, to their authority. They took the whole earth for their domain and some of them the cosmos, for they were not afraid to extend their laws to the universe.[100]

Of course, we need not suppose that all Americans were so carried away. Jefferson and Paine were surely more susceptible to rationalist enthusiasm than most. So the picture sketched out above reveals only part of the reality. Most of the framers of the Constitution were, as May explains, at least more moderate in their projections regarding a world remade according to reason. And there were those among the framers—John Dickinson, for instance—who soberly advised against trusting unduly in reason, and who repeatedly recommended the virtues of experience and tradition and the course of incremental adjustment.

But, as we shall see, Dickinson's was not the dominant voice in the council that constructed the Constitution.

CHAPTER TWO

The Special Dispensation of Reason and the Legal Constitution

Suppose that without initially knowing anything about the matter you happen to hear the sorts of laudatory claims, such as those described earlier in this book, declaring that the Constitution is the political expression or embodiment of "reason," or that, in Cass Sunstein's words, the Constitution established "for the first time, a republic of reasons."[1] Curious and hopeful, you resolve to do something that lawyers, law professors, and judges themselves rarely do—that is, actually go and read the document. What will be your reaction?

The Preamble may seem promising. In it you encounter commitments to forming a more perfect union, establishing justice, and securing the blessings of liberty for a people and its posterity. These are lofty aspirations, worthy of a document presented as the manifestation of political reason.

Almost immediately, though, you find yourself inundated by a flood of petty details. "The number of Representatives shall not exceed one for every thirty Thousand. . . ." "No Person shall be a Senator who shall not have attained to the Age of thirty Years, and been nine years a Citizen. . . ." "The Times, Places and Manner of holding Elections for Senators and Representatives, shall be prescribed in each State by the Legislature thereof. . . ." And you are barely into Article I. You quickly scan Articles II through VII. More of the same.

Is this any way to go about achieving the quintessential expression of political "reason"? If one simply reads over its dry text, the Constitution surely feels more like a set of corporate by-laws—albeit for a very large and somewhat byzantine corporation—than like a historically unprecedented manifestation of reason. So if you came to the document anticipating something that would exude Confucian sagacity or Platonic wisdom, you might be sorely disappointed.[2] (In fairness, Plato was capable of prescribing a political constitution with a degree of tedious detail that makes the American framers seem like lyric poets by comparison.)[3]

Your disappointment would be misconceived, perhaps, but it is also instructive; it points us toward a central feature of the framers' thinking about how reason should guide the making of a constitution. The Constitution they wrote is on its face a nuts-and-bolts legal instrument—not a collection of grand political ideas or a direct expression of noble political principles. This is to say that the Constitution as originally designed and drafted does not appear to be the sort of document that, as we will see, contemporary theorists have wanted it to be, or have imagined that it is. Indeed, the Constitution does not overtly either *express* or *appeal to* "reason" at all—or to ideals discernibly grounded in "reason."

How then could its authors have issued such lavish claims in behalf of this dull, studiously technical piece of work? This chapter proposes an answer to that question. The discussion is in two stages. I will begin by arguing that in drafting the Constitution the framers tried to employ and give effect to reason in two ways, which happen to correspond to the ancient and modern components of the founding generation's conception of reason, as discussed in the previous chapter. This initial discussion, however, will not fully account for the technical and legalistic quality of the Constitution; in addition, the discussion will reveal problems and paradoxes, some quite familiar and some less often noticed, in the framers' project.

The second stage of the discussion will focus more directly on those problems and paradoxes. In the course of this discussion I will try to explain why the framers chose to adopt the facially uninspiring document that is the Constitution, and how they could regard that legalistic document as the unprecedented and quintessential manifestation of political reason.

The Constitution and Eighteenth-Century Reason

Start with an obvious threshold question: What might it even mean for a political constitution, or a government, to be in accord with reason? For the founding generation, as we have seen, reason had both an ancient, affirmative component and a more modern and skeptical component. The affirmative component consisted of the belief in an orderly, purposeful Nature accessible to the human mind. The skeptical or negative component entailed a rejection of tradition and authority in favor of the fresh application of human intellect. Both themes were evident in the making of the Constitution.

Nature and the Constitution

Nature, as we have seen, was not for the founders what "nature" is within a scientific materialist framework. On the contrary, Nature contained not only an intrinsic physical order but also a normative dimension that included, among other things, ethical principles and human rights. Thus, by contrast to previous governments that had arisen out of force or fortuity and had served mainly to promote the interests of some dominant party or class, a government based on reason would be one consciously designed to respect principles of justice and to protect the rights that Nature confers on human beings.

The framers understood their constitutional project in just this sense.[4] The delegates to the Philadelphia convention repeatedly emphasized that in creating a government capable of promoting the public good, the Constitution must at the same time protect rights and respect principles of justice. George Mason declared "the preservation of the rights of the people" to be the "pole-star" and the "primary object,"[5] while Gouverneur Morris wanted "a Govt instituted for protection of the rights of mankind."[6]

To be sure, the pragmatic political negotiations in Philadelphia were not the appropriate setting for a philosophical seminar on the ontological foundations of rights and principles in Nature. And in any event, classical assumptions about a Nature designed and governed by Providence were so widely shared that such a discourse would likely have seemed superfluous.[7] Roger Sherman observed at one point that "[t]he question is not what rights naturally belong to men"—the answer to *that* question, it seems, was already clear enough for practical purposes—"but how they may be most equally & effectually guarded in Society."[8] Still, although this aspect of the relation between Nature and the Constitution remained in the background of the discussions, it was the crucial presupposition on which the framers' project was founded.

Thus, Morton White's investigations reveal that there was little change in the notions of "reason" that informed the Declaration of Independence, with its eloquent commitment to self-evident truths like human equality and inalienable rights, and those that influenced the construction and defense of the Constitution.[9] With respect to "Publius," the pseudonym collectively used by James Madison, Alexander Hamilton, and John Jay in defending the proposed Constitution, White explains:

> [Publius] also believed in the existence of man's essence . . . and he thought that the law of nature was a law of nature's God. Man's nature or essence was presumably created by an omnipotent, wise, and beneficent being; and it was from this nature or essence that both Hamilton and Madison derived man's duties and corresponding rights in some of their writings. . . . [A] view of this kind is present in some of Hamilton's earliest writing on natural law as well in Madison's. And although the view was not made very explicit in *The Federalist*, I do not think that the authors could have defended their version of natural rights without some appeal to a Creator of man's essence even though the references to God in *The Federalist* are quite exiguous and perfunctory.[10]

Building a Government from Scratch

But how would a convention, or a people, go about designing a government that would protect the rights conferred by Nature? The previous chapter suggested that when people of the founding generation referred to "reason," they meant among other things to emphasize the possibility, and indeed the duty, to "think for yourself"—not to defer to the ostensible wisdom of the past. "Reason" connoted the opposite of accepting, following, and perhaps adding incrementally to a received tradition. The man of reason in America would not be the scion of an intellectually aristocratic lineage; he would be a self-made man.

This sort of self-help, ground-up orientation powerfully affected the deliberations of the Philadelphia convention, which determined that the United States would be governed not by an inherited or even an adjusted scheme but rather by a newly made constitution. So the convention started from first principles and produced a Constitution, as Bruce Ackerman observes, "whose few thousand words contained a host of untried ideas and institutions."[11]

This course was hardly foreordained. The delegates might have chosen merely to tinker with the existing constitution—the Articles of Confederation—so as to remedy its most patent defects. After all, that is what they had been appointed to do—indeed, the states probably would never have agreed to a convention to consider overall revisions in the government[12]—and it is what delegates who became dissatisfied with the course of the proceedings often suggested they *should* do. Or the convention might have tried to import, with necessary modifications, the British constitution which had evolved over a period of centuries in the mother country and under which the colonists had been governed until the Revolution. Some delegates, notably John Dickinson, repeatedly urged this approach. The convention as a body chose to do neither of these things, however, but instead chose to fashion a new government through, to borrow Rufus King's phrase, "recurrence to first principles."[13]

An intention to build from the ground up was manifest from the outset. No sooner had the preliminary business of choosing officers and agreeing to rules of order been completed than Edmund Randolph rose and, in the convention's first substantive speech, proposed a comprehensive agenda for discussion and a new overall plan of government to be considered.[14] In a slightly condescending gesture of diplomatic deference to political predecessors, Randolph already manifested the confidence in fresh reason that would drive the discussions: "In speaking of the defects of the confederation," Madison's notes report, Randolph "professed a high respect for its authors, and considered them, as having done all that patriots could do, in the then infancy of the science, of constitutions, & of confederacies. . . ."[15] The implication was plain enough: Political science had advanced and, with all due respect, there was now no reason to accept or treat with reverence the political arrangements of the less-enlightened past.[16]

Not all the delegates agreed. Oliver Ellsworth observed at one point that "[w]e are razing the foundations of the building, when we need only repair the roof."[17] John Lansing complained that the system being devised was "too novel & complex."[18] Representatives of the less-populated states especially favored an approach that would merely reform the acknowledged defects in the Articles of Confederation. Their position was not wholly disinterested, of course. Under the Articles, each state had been equally represented in the national government without regard to population; not surprisingly, the small states were anxious to resist a plan in which representation would be made proportionate to the various states' populations. A reformist as opposed to a start-from-scratch approach was more conducive to their interests. So their delegates tirelessly pointed out that the pressing problems of the Articles of Confederation, which the convention had been commissioned to address, did not derive from equal state representation.[19] Consequently, the convention had no call to tamper with that aspect of the existing regime.

But leading supporters of the Constitution such as James Madison and James Wilson (both, perhaps not coincidentally, large state representatives) showed no patience for this argument. Again and again they declaimed on the importance of adopting a constitution based on sound "fundamental principles." The problem with the existing government, Madison maintained, was that it was grounded in "improper principles." Wilson agreed that in a constitution there could be "nothing so pernicious as bad first principles."[20]

Their opposition to mere tinkering reformism also disposed such delegates against deferring to the British model. John Dickinson, who represented Delaware (a small state), respected the wisdom embodied in tradition. He repeatedly urged the convention to model the new government after the British constitution.[21] But James Wilson objected that the situation here was unprecedented, and it was accordingly necessary to construct a government for this country's unique needs. "The British Government cannot be our model." In a similar vein, John Rutledge deplored "blind adherence to the British model."

Charles Pinckney added that in any event the composition of the British government "was perhaps as much the effect of chance as of any thing else." And cringing before chance was precisely what proponents of reason could not abide. "We ought to be governed by reason," Rufus King observed, "not by chance."[22]

To observe that the convention adopted a "first principles" approach is not to say, of course, either that the delegates *succeeded* in freeing themselves from the past or that they were uninterested in the past. It is surely true, as James Stoner has perceptively argued, that both in its inception and in its subsequent development "the Constitution . . . somehow combines the scientific reason of the modern political theorists and the common law reasoning of lawyers and judges."[23] Indeed, it could hardly have been otherwise: The conceit that we can ever actually set aside the past and truly start from scratch is, as modern philosophers like William James have persuasively argued,[24] little more than an enticing self-delusion. Holmes made the point, characteristically, in a grim paradox: "[C]ontinuity with the past is only a necessity and not a duty."[25] So it is not surprising that the Constitution is permeated with features traceable to the state constitutions, to English political history, or to the common law.

Nor is it clear that the framers would have been embarrassed by this fact, or would have regarded it as inconsistent with their claim to have constructed the Constitution on first principles. Trusting in reason emphatically did not mean *ignoring* the past, or refusing to learn from it. On the contrary, history provided the empirical data that reason could work upon. So the delegates frequently discussed the political lessons to be drawn from other governments and federations both in the recent past and in classical antiquity.[26]

But *learning* from past experience is one thing—*following* or deferring to past precedent quite another. In fact, the framers were unwilling to adopt any model of government presented in history, not only because the circumstances in this country were unique but also because, as James Wilson noted, the classical confederacies had been "formed in the infancy of political Science,"[27] and were therefore defective. With the benefit of improvements in political science and with the application of their own reason, the founders believed they could do better.[28]

The Conundrums of Nature

The discussion thus far suggests ways in which the framers' project reflected both the ancient and modern strands of the founding generation's conception of reason, but it does not yet account for the prosaically technical, legalistic quality of their end product. Instructed to start largely from scratch and to design a government that respects natural human rights, a convention might proceed to produce a wholly different kind of document—a comprehensive list of the most important human rights,[29] perhaps, with an institutional mechanism for enforcing those rights. Or the convention might have adopted the strategy embraced three-quarters of a century later by the framers of the Fourteenth Amendment who, according to William Nelson, "understood constitutional politics as a rhetorical venture designed to persuade people to do good, rather than a bureaucratic venture intended to establish precise legal rules and enforcement mechanisms."[30] But what in fact emerged from Philadelphia was singularly short in idealistic rhetoric, and it did not so much as provide a list of basic rights. Indeed, the Constitution did not even explicitly provide for judicial enforcement of constitutional provisions through invalidation of unconstitutional laws (though such enforcement was later to be inferred).

Instead of idealism and abstract principle, the original Constitution was a technical document devoted largely to institutional structure and procedure. Why? In short, nothing in the discussion thus far directly addresses the question noticed at the outset of this chapter: How did the founding generation's aspiration to embody "reason" in the Constitution culminate in this sort of legalistic end product?

The Constitution and Human Nature

In addressing this question, we must take into account a different aspect of Nature—*human* nature—to which the framers devoted considerable attention. "What is government itself," Madison asked, "but the greatest of all reflections on human nature?" A sound constitution must be responsive not only to Nature in a cosmic sense, that is, but also to the nature of its citizens and subjects, and these happened to be human beings. Moreover, the founding generation's study of history seemed to provide, as Robert Wiebe reports, "proofs of an immutable human nature."[31]

But what *is* the nature—or the essence and structure—of human nature?

One component of human nature as the founding generation conceived of it has already been discussed: Human beings have the capacity to reason. So they have a potential for goodness and virtue. But in the framers' view, the power of reason was not the whole, or even the dominant characteristic, of human nature. There is also a darker side. More specifically, it is human nature to crave, and to exercise, power.[32]

Alexander Hamilton put it succinctly to the convention: "Men love power." Having gained power, they fight to keep it. "From the nature of man we may be sure," George Mason warned, "that those who have power in their hands will not give it up while they can retain it." And those who gain and retain power will inevitably misuse it. Commenting on the danger inherent in the admission of new states, Elbridge Gerry expressed the basic assumption: "They will if they acquire power like all men, abuse it."[33]

Their recognition of this more menacing dimension of human nature complicated the framers' task in two ways. First, and perhaps most obvious, it meant that they could not count on those who in the ensuing years and decades would administer the newly created government to behave as reason might dictate. Consequently, a constitution made *in accordance with* reason could not simply *express* or *appeal to* reason. Indeed, to attempt to employ reason in this straightforward way would be, paradoxically, contrary to reason. "[T]he people never act from reason alone," Gouverneur Morris observed,[34] and it would therefore be irrational to form a government on the assumption that they do. So if human affairs were to be governed by reason rather than by force or fortuity, then some other, more subtle strategy was needed.

Less obvious but just as important, the framers' recognition of the darker side of human nature rendered their own proceedings problematic. Acting from self-interest rather than impartial reason was an entrenched feature of common human nature. So what basis did the framers have to exempt themselves from this generalization? Political maneuvers and arguments, however disinterested they may appear, are usually designed to gain or consolidate—or abuse—power: Why should not the convention's own deliberations and decisions be tainted by this observation (as in some later historiography they *would* be[35])?

Taken together, these two problems might seem to show that the framers' project was doomed from the start. How could human affairs be rescued from the rule of force and fortuity, thereafter to be placed under the dominion of reason, when neither the men who were constructing a frame of government nor the persons who would administer it in the future could be expected to act in accord with reason? Nonetheless, the framers proceeded on the faith that these problems of human nature were surmountable. We must now consider their responses to each problem.

Institutionalizing Reason

Of the two problems, that of ensuring that future officials and citizens not innately disposed to act according to reason would nonetheless do so received by far the most explicit attention. The framers' response to that problem is familiar, and so we can deal with it briefly.

The response had two parts. First, the framers tried to construct a government in which public-spirited reason, meager though the supply might be, would tend to flow to the centers of power. This was not—and, given their assumptions about human nature, could not be—the framers' primary strategy.[36] Nonetheless, their Constitution authorized processes through which reason might hope to percolate upward and achieve influence, and it created institutions in which persons capable of reason and virtue might be expected to congregate. For example, the delegates hoped that the Electoral College might be a process for bringing wisdom to bear on the choice of the chief executive, or at least that it would avoid the most dangerous obstacles—intrigue and "cabal"—to the exercise of disinterested reason.[37] And they hoped that the Senate, because of its lengthy terms of office and its method of appointment, might attract persons of "wisdom & virtue."[38]

Still, given the irrepressible tendency of human beings to acquire and then abuse power, it would be rash simply to trust in the possibility of governance by the virtuous and wise. "Confidence," Elbridge Gerry warned, "is the road to tyranny."[39] So although the delegates largely agreed on the immediate need to strengthen the powers of the national government—it was that need, after all, that had called the convention into being—they also did not trust the national government with these soon-to-be-bestowed powers. On the contrary, the delegates were obsessed with preventing the expansion and abuse of governmental powers.

The view that majorities have a natural tendency to oppress minorities was frequently expressed.[40] As an institutional matter, consequently, the founders' fears focused primarily on the legislative branch, where majorities would control. James Wilson warned that "[t]heory and practice both proclaim . . . [the] danger of a Legislative despotism. . . ."[41] Gouverneur Morris worried about "Legislative tyranny."[42] So did Madison.[43] But the other branches were not beyond suspicion either. Edmund Randolph saw danger in "the unqualified power of the President to pardon treasons."[44] In response to the suggestion that executive powers be strengthened in order to resist legislative usurpation, Roger Sherman questioned whether one man could be trusted more than many. And for good measure he added a caution against "Judges meddling in politics."[45]

Sometimes the fears were not differentiated by branch, but instead were expressed in composite terms. Randolph could not support "a plan which he verily believed would end in Tyranny." George Mason condemned the convention's creation as "exceptionable & dangerous." There would be no remedy "if the Government should become oppressive, as he verily believed would be the case."[46]

So how was such despotism to be prevented? It was at this point that the framers' trust in what they regarded as an improved political science came most conspicuously into play. Political science had discovered methods for structuring government so as to defuse power by diffusing it.[47] In this way, the ambitions and selfish interests of individuals, without being actually reformed, could nonetheless be directed to the public good. "Vices as they exist, must be turned against each other," Gouverneur Morris asserted. "We must take man as we find him," Alexander Hamilton explained, "and if we expect him to serve the public must interest his passions in doing so."[48] In short, the effort to structure government so that even in pursuing their own self-interest officials and citizens would serve the public good represented the framers' principal response to the problem of human nature in future generations.

Consequently, nuts-and-bolts issues about what political science more specifically taught—or about what exact methods and institutions would be best calculated to channel self-interest into the service of the public good—were the questions to which the discussions in Philadelphia and in the ratifying debates were largely devoted. What offices should be created? How should their occupants be chosen? For what terms? How should powers be allocated between the state and national governments, and among the different branches of the national government?

Fortunately, we need not review the debates on these specific questions here. It is enough to note what is by now a commonplace: The framers' political science led them to conclude that the diffusion of power was the principal means for combating the irrepressible human inclination to seek, and then abuse, power. In short, the framers' primary answer to the first problem presented by human nature—that is, that future governors would likely pursue power and self-interest rather than acting under the direction of reason—was to divide and subdivide governmental power.

But this answer to the first problem—that is, that future generations would be composed of self-serving human beings—serves to underscore the difficulty of the second problem: The framers themselves happened to be human beings. Dividing up power, after all, is a delicate business. Put a little too much power in one branch or at one level of government, and it will likely overwhelm the other branches or levels. Make the national government too strong and it will subjugate the states; leave the national government too weak and the states will dominate *it*. Give the large states too much influence and they will oppress the small states. The framers were well aware of these perils, and they spent much of their time in Philadelphia discussing just these kinds of issues, trying to convince each other that some particular set of arrangements would avoid oppressive imbalances.

But given their own assumptions about human nature, why should they have trusted each other?[49] What grounds did they have to suppose that their own discussions were animated by impartial reason, rather than by self-interest and a desire to accumulate power?

Dissonance in the Constitutional Deliberations

The question was, understandably, a delicate one that partipants in the convention were loathe to address directly. Much of the time they studiously avoided any overt discussion of the problem, in effect acting and talking as if the normal operations of human nature had somehow been suspended for purposes of the convention itself. Although they did not expect that citizens and politicians generally would act on the basis of public-spirited reason, nonetheless they supposed that *they themselves* could and would do what is contrary to normal human nature—that is, act on the basis of disinterested reason.

Sometimes delegates were a bit more direct, pleading with each other to set aside self-interest (even while expressing views that would have made this plea seem vain). Gouverneur Morris, for example, described the human proclivity to act from self-interest in terms that suggested immutability. He observed that "[t]he Rich"—a class, incidentally, that certainly included Morris himself, as well as many others in the convention[50]—"will always strive to establish their dominion & enslave the rest. They always did. They always will." Yet the delegates themselves, Morris implored, must be devoted to the public interest and guided by "the language of Reason"[51]—and in a situation, moreover, where their own and their states' self-interest was more significantly at stake than in almost any ordinary political controversy.

The apparent inconsistency in this position could not be entirely suppressed, and at times the difficulty of maintaining both that humans generally do not act from disinterested reason but that precisely such behavior was to be expected in this situation led to embarrassing contradictions. Perhaps no one exemplified this dissonance more vividly than Gouverneur Morris himself. He repeatedly admonished delegates to set aside narrow personal and state interests and to act for the good of the country and even the world,[52] and he eloquently proclaimed his own ability to do just that.

> He came here as Representative of America; he flattered himself he came here in some degree as a Representative of the whole human race; for the whole human race will be affected by the proceedings of this Convention. He wished gentlemen to extend their views beyond the present moment of time; beyond the narrow limits of place from which they derive their political origin. If he were to believe some things which he had heard, he should suppose that we were assembled to truck and bargain for our particular States. He can-not descend to think that any gentlemen are really actuated by these views. We must look forward to the effects of what we do. These alone ought to guide us.[53]

While claiming for himself the role of "Representative of the whole human race," though, and imploring his fellow delegates likewise to extend their concerns "beyond the narrow limits of place from which they derive their political origin," Morris did not expect such catholic characters to occupy the government created by the Constitution. Nor did he lament their anticipated absence; on the contrary, he considered them dangerous. So Morris advocated long national residency requirements for Senators, "urging the danger of admitting strangers into our public Councils."[54] And when it was suggested that shorter residency requirements would be acceptable because newcomers could be counted on to act for the public good, he protested. Apparently forgetting his own earlier self-description, Morris objected:

As to those philosophical gentlemen, those Citizens of the World as they call themselves, He owned he did not wish to see any of them in our public Councils. He would not trust them. The men who can shake off their attachments to their own Country can never love any other. These attachments are the wholesome prejudices which uphold all Governments.[55]

Though Morris may have been an especially vivid personification of the inconsistency, no one really found a satisfying resolution to the tension between the delegates' assumptions about human behavior generally and the expectations they imposed on themselves. The disjunction naturally provoked suspicions of hypocrisy, and the suspicions sometimes overwhelmed constraints of courtesy. On one occasion, after listening to small state delegates insist that equal representation in Congress was essential to the preservation of liberty, Alexander Hamilton lost patience. He bluntly indicted their motives (and perhaps, inadvertently, his own): "The truth is it is a contest for power, not for liberty."[56] Gunning Bedford of Delaware conceded the point but turned it against Hamilton and the large state representatives by identifying the self-interested motives behind the various states' positions, one by one. The implication of Bedford's speech was that all of the delegates' pious protestations of disinterested concern for reason, justice, and the common good were a sham:

> If political Societies possess ambition[,] avarice, and all the other passions which render them formidable to each other, ought we not to view them in this light here? Will not the same motives operate in America as elsewhere? If any gentleman doubts it let him look at the votes [in the convention]. Have they not been dictated by interest, by ambition? Are not the large States evidently seeking to aggrandize themselves at the expense of the small? They think no doubt that they have right on their side, but interest had blinded their eyes. . . . Will it be said that an inequality of power will not result from an inequality of votes. Give the opportunity, and ambition will not fail to abuse it.[57]

This momentary outbreak of frank political realism led Bedford to threaten that the small states would "find some foreign ally of more honor and good faith, who will take them by the hand and do them justice."[58] But such candor strayed too far beyond the bounds of civility. Expressing his sorrow at "the language of the honorable gentleman from Delaware," Rufus King "was grieved that such a thought had entered his heart. He was more grieved that such an expression had dropped from his lips."[59] And the next week a chastened and somewhat becalmed Bedford backed off. While protesting that he "had been misunderstood," Bedford, a lawyer, also asked the delegates to remember "the habits of his profession in which warmth was natural & sometimes necessary."[60]

There is nothing unusual, of course, in such threats and retractions, or in politicians first clinging to and then angrily or opportunistically rupturing the pretense of disinterestedness. Such inconsistencies are standard fare in political debate. But the dissonance had a peculiar significance in the context of the Philadelphia convention because it was a specific manifestation of the fundamental conundrum: How could the convention expect reason and concern for the public interest to prevail within its own deliberations while believing that such qualities were contrary to human nature as manifested in virtually all other contexts?

Their vacillations and vagaries may suggest that in the end the framers had no answer to this question. And perhaps they didn't. They would not have been the first advocates, and certainly not the last, to purport to be exercising a kind of reason even while denying the possibility of that kind of reason. Indeed, a good deal of modern thought, with its frequently materialist or determinist suppositions, reflects just this tension in one way or another.

In this case the matter is more complicated, though. That is because some statements made in the convention suggest that the framers, or some of them, had a different, more audacious take on this matter—one that sheds light on (but may ultimately point to a debilitating flaw in) their idea of the relation between reason and the Constitution.

The Founding as a Special Dispensation

In expecting that they themselves could do something that is contrary to normal human nature, the framers may have been guilty of inconsistency. But they were not simply and unreflectively inconsistent; rather, they seem to have consciously regarded their own situation as in some important sense uniquely privileged. Fate or providence had conferred on them an unprecedented opportunity—the opportunity of sitting for a brief moment outside the vicissitudes of politics and history in order to design a government on the basis of reason. In short, the framers had somehow found themselves situated, as it were, in a sort of evanescent, political Archimedean point. So it was up to them to rise to the occasion by struggling against baser motives in order to act not from self-interest, but from public-spirited reason.[61]

Their sense of their own situation as uniquely privileged was not necessarily a manifestation of arrogance; it might have been simply a reluctant, even humble, acknowledgment of what seemed to be the plain facts. We can appreciate and perhaps pardon the framers' sense of their special position if we recall that modern historians sometimes find it hard to avoid drawing a similar conclusion—that there was something peculiar, perhaps something bordering on providential,[62] in the framers' situation. Even the resolutely unsuperstitious Bruce Ackerman observes that the content of (and perhaps the very possibility of) the Constitution resulted from the fact that "[b]y some uncanny accident, Washington, Madison, and the other American revolutionaries convening in Philadelphia chose the last possible moment at which their deliberations would be unaffected by the events that shook Paris, and the world, in 1789."[63]

In any event, if the Philadelphia delegates occupied a unique place in history, as they believed, their situation brought with it both a downside and an upside. The downside was that if the convention failed in its purpose, then the country—and indeed the world—would probably not have another chance. As Lance Banning observes, the delegates thought the constitution they were trying to fashion represented "possibly the final hope for liberty on earth."[64] Their sense of their singular and portentous situation is evident in Madison's early warning that "it was more than probable we were now digesting a plan which in its operations would decide for ever the fate of Republican Government." Hamilton immediately agreed. Rufus King "conceived this to be the last opportunity of providing for [the country's] liberty & happiness." Charles Pinckney expressed a like view. Elbridge Gerry forecast the global consequences of failure: "Something must be done, or we shall disappoint not only America but the whole world."[65]

The convention's sense of its peculiar and indeed providential situation is reflected in a famous if somewhat befuddled speech by Benjamin Franklin. At a particularly desperate moment in the proceedings, and on the premise *"that God Governs in the affairs of men"*—Franklin's emphasis is duly recorded in Madison's notes—the venerable delegate proposed prayer. Then, and without any apparent sense of inconsistency, Franklin prophesied that if the convention's project should fail, "mankind may hereafter from this unfortunate instance, despair of establishing Governments by Human wisdom and leave it to chance, war and conquest."[66] The present moment was, in short, the last chance to rescue human affairs from those perennial enemies—force and fortuity, or "chance, war, and conquest"—and to secure the rule of reason. And although Franklin's allocation of responsibility variously to God, chance, human wisdom, and force may not lend itself to any crystal clear schematization (a shortcoming hardly unique to Franklin), his speech nonetheless conveys the convention's sense of its unique and portentous place in history.

Though ominous, the framers' distinctive situation also had an upside: The delegates had an unprecedented opportunity to use reason, as Madison said, in "framing a system which we wish to last for ages." James Wilson was in full accord: "We should consider that we are providing a Constitution for future generations, and not merely for the peculiar circumstances of the moment." Likewise John Rutledge: "As we are laying the foundation for a great empire, we ought to take a permanent view of the subject and not look at the present moment only."[67]

So the convention had a once-in-history chance, and it was imperative that the delegates exert themselves, resisting their normal self-interested proclivities, in order to take advantage of it. Alexander Hamilton expressed both the unparalleled potential and the dreadful urgency of the situation: "It was a miracle that we were now here exercising our tranquil & free deliberations on the subject. It would be madness to trust to future miracles."[68]

The Once, Not Future, Reign of Reason

In sum, providence or history had somehow conspired to provide a brief, one-time opening through which reason might exert itself to shape the enduring structure of American government. The opportunity would soon pass, and it would not present itself again. So the convention was in "a grim race against time."[69] To be sure, the framers knew that adjustments might be necessary, that details would need to be filled in.[70] They provided a mechanism—an unwieldy one, evidently not fashioned for frequent use—for amendment. But they also believed that there would not be another chance to deliberate effectively in crafting the overall design and essential features of a constitution. So the constitution of reason needed to be fixed *now*. Reason, so to speak, would probably have only one real shot.

This blend of present hopefulness and projected distrust was manifest in an exchange between James Madison and Gouverneur Morris regarding the issue of periodic censuses. The delegates knew that the states' representation in Congress would need to be adjusted as state populations grew at different rates and as new states entered the union. But should the Constitution contain specific prescriptions about how these adjustments must be made—how often censuses should be taken, for instance—or would it be wiser to entrust these matters to the judgment of future legislatures? After listening to conflicting views, Morris advocated the latter alternative. "If we can't agree on a rule that will be just at this time, how can we expect to find one that will be just in all times to come." And Morris added an observation that, taken seriously, would seem to cast doubt on the convention's whole project: "Surely those who come after us will judge better of things present, than we can of things future."[71]

Madison's notes report his own response:

> Mr MADISON, was not a little surprised to hear this implicit confidence urged by a member who on all occasions, had inculcated so strongly, the political depravity of men, and the necessity of checking one vice and interest by opposing to them another vice & interest.[72]

The requirements for adjusting representation needed to be fixed in the document, Madison went on to argue,[73] because future legislatures could not be counted on to behave in a reasonable or disinterested fashion.

Madison's response reflected his exasperation with Morris's vagaries but, more important, it also quietly disclosed an essential assumption underlying the convention's proceedings. On first inspection, Madison's argument might seem obtuse. After all, the question of representation was just as contentious in 1787, and just as critical to the various states' interests, as it would be in the future. Indeed, the often acrimonious debates about representation in the convention itself provided powerful evidence of that fact. Why then should "the political depravity of men" count in favor of resolving questions of representation now rather than in the future?

Madison's speech is cogent, however, on the assumption that the framers had been privileged to participate in a unique moment in history in which reason was being allowed to shape the form of government. The moment was in a sense a dispensation from the usual rule of human nature and human affairs, in which reason plays a distinctly subordinate part. So it was imperative to exercise reason *now* in order to obviate the need for it *later*.

Reason and the Legalistic Constitution

We are now in a position to appreciate how the framers' project conceived of the relation between the Constitution and reason. The framers wanted a constitution congruent with Nature—one in which natural rights and principles of justice would be respected. More specifically, a sound constitution would need to guard these natural rights and principles against human nature, with its perpetual craving for power. So the purpose of the Constitution, in a sense, would be to protect the human dimension of Nature from the predations of human nature. This purpose might be achieved, the framers believed, by diffusing power among a variety of different governmental institutions. But the division of powers was all important. And the task was especially tricky because the Philadelphia convention was working within a unique and momentary window of opportunity in which public-spirited reason might be brought to bear on the framing of governmental institutions.

If this was the framers' sense of their situation and task, then perhaps we can understand why they adopted the kind of legalistic and structural constitution they did, rather than opting for a more idealistic or inspirational listing of basic human rights and principles of justice. More specifically, we can understand their heavy reliance on two particular features evident in the Constitution: the enumerated powers doctrine as the central substantive strategy, and the implementation of that strategy through a technical, *written* document.

The Centrality of the Enumerated Powers Strategy

The enumerated powers strategy reflects the framers' belief that the way to prevent power from being abused is to diffuse it. This point is commonplace, but it is nonetheless important to appreciate that the enumerated powers strategy was not just one feature of a complex constituting document. Rather, it represented the framers' principal response to *all* the kinds of constitutional problems with which we are familiar.

Most obviously, the strategy dealt with what we call "separation of powers" questions; it allocated powers among the organs of government at the national level. In addition, because the framers believed and maintained that national institutions would have only the limited powers actually granted them by the Constitution and that other powers would remain with the states, the listing of national powers was their response to questions of "federalism"; no separate inventory of state powers was deemed necessary.

Finally, the enumerated powers strategy was also the framers' principal method of protecting individual rights—a matter which in modern times has become the major constitutional concern. This last point is perhaps less obvious, and so may deserve a brief explanation. Although the delegates understood that the creation of a national government inevitably would have important consequences for state governments, still the overriding purpose of the constitutional convention was to frame a government for the nation, not to reorganize or improve government at the state level. With respect to individual rights, consequently, the framers were primarily concerned to protect such rights against the new national government. And by insisting that the national government would exercise only the limited powers granted it, the framers believed they had effectively provided such protection.[74] There was no need to list rights in the way state constitutions typically did because the authority conferred on the national government did not encompass the power to invade individual rights anyway. Thus, in response to a proposed provision "that the liberty of the Press should be inviolably observed," Roger Sherman objected: "It is unnecessary. The power of Congress does not extend to the Press." And a sizable majority of the delegates agreed.[75]

So the Philadelphia delegates considered adopting a bill of rights, but concluded that the measure would be superfluous;[76] and they vigorously defended this position in the ratification debates.[77] It was not that they denied the importance of individual rights. Rather, the enumerated powers method was fully capable, they thought, of protecting such rights.

The Written Constitution

If the enumerated powers strategy describes the *substance* of the original Constitution, its *form* or means of implementation consisted of a careful, legalistic listing of these powers. What institutions of government may exercise which powers, and what procedures must they follow in wielding those powers? These are the questions to which the dry, technical prose of the Constitution speaks.

The legalistic form reflects the framers' assumption that reason could not or would not routinely characterize political life. They had been given a unique privilege to exercise reason in the construction of a government but, ironically or not, the actual and intended *result* of their application of reason was to forestall future generations from exercising reason—or at least from exercising it in the same full-blown, ground-up way that *they* had done. The framers did not expect this sort of reason—the sort of foundational reason that sweeps away the past and truly starts from "first principles"—to be a recurring phenomenon. So they tried to construct a constitution which future generations could interpret and follow, not rethink or reinvent.[78] As John Patrick Diggins observes: "The Constitution itself was deliberately designed in mechanistic rather than in moral terms so that after its enactment it would as a system function apart from human agency."[79]

This conception of the relation between reason and the Constitution might be described by means of an analogy drawn from the framers' own period. The function of reason in the constitutional project was much like the role of God in the standard depiction of deism: Just as God creates and winds up the cosmic clock and then retires, letting the clock run on its own, reason would create a governmental structure that would then operate according to the usual workings of politics and human nature. The Constitution would exert itself not by calling on citizens and officials to exercise reason in any full-blooded "first-principles" sense, but by limiting them to the application of what we might call "legal reason" in discerning and carrying out the Constitution's commands.[80]

John Marshall understood the point perfectly when a few years later he observed, in the most famous of all cases interpreting the Constitution, that the establishment of principles of government "is a very great exertion; nor can it, nor ought it, to be frequently repeated." Once established, such principles "are designed to be permanent."[81] And the device for making them permanent was the reduction of the framers' conclusions to writing in a legal document. So Marshall stressed, again and again, that this was a *written* Constitution. He emphasized that "a written constitution" was "the greatest improvement on political institutions" developed by the citizens of this country.[82] And the whole thrust of his opinion was to show that the genius of a written constitution lies precisely in its *legal* character; unlike the more ethereal and elusive constitutions of countries such as England, our written and legal Constitution can be enforced just like other legal instruments such as statutes or contracts.

The Original Originalism

The framers' attempt to consolidate reason in the Constitution left future generations with an awkward choice. Suppose, for sake of argument at least, that we respect and desire to follow the wisdom of the founders. Which part of their wisdom should we follow—the part that tried to determine and fix the political teachings of reason in a concrete constitutional structure, or their more general notion that reason means "thinking for yourself"? In a very rough way, that choice indicates the difference in spirit that divides what we have come to call "originalism," which leans to the former alternative, from the various strains of "nonoriginalism," which gravitates toward the latter.

If the framers themselves did not exactly resolve this tension, their conception of their own situation as a unique opportunity for the exercise of disinterested reason inclined them toward fixing or stabilizing the conclusions of reason.[83] It may be, as Jefferson Powell has argued, that the framers were by and large *not* originalists of a particular kind; they may not have favored the variety of originalist interpretation that tries to seek out and follow the subjective intentions-behind-the-words of the enactors.[84] But the framers' view of the relation between reason and the Constitution, and their effort to fix the conclusions of reason by consolidating those conclusions in a written constitution, made their project inherently originalist in its basic orientation.[85]

To say this, however, is not to say that originalism supplies *us* either with a satisfactory overall understanding of the constitutional enterprise or with a binding imperative to administer the Constitution in an originalist fashion. On the contrary, it seems clear by now that for all of its sophistication, and for better or worse, the framers' particular strategy for embodying reason in the Constitution was doomed from the start—and not only by the unfathomable and ungovernable flow of history, but by a fatal internal contradiction. How the framers' strategy failed, and why it was in fact destined to fail, are subjects for the next chapter.

CHAPTER THREE

The Framers' Fatal Flaw

The framers used reason in constructing the Constitution, and when they had finished that job they turned to reason again in order to convince their fellow citizens to accept the Constitution. To be sure, the supposition that the general citizenry would be governed in the matter by reasoned argument may have been in tension with the framers' "special dispensation" notions about reason and the convention. And indeed, the Federalists were well aware of the near impossibility of the ratification decision being determined by dispassionate reason. Still, given the advisory and probably *ultra vires* nature of their proceedings, there was little other than reasoned argument that they *could* turn to.[1]

Their opponents, the so-called Antifederalists, likewise resorted to reason in an effort to defeat the proposal. The quality of the resulting debate can still elicit admiration, or even awe. William Nelson notes that although *The Federalist Papers* constitute "one of the greatest examples in human history of the use of reasoned analysis to achieve a political end," that work was not a unique achievement but rather was "one of many similar efforts by both proponents and opponents of the Constitution to persuade the public by reason."[2] Lawrence Sager observes that "[i]n embarrassing contrast to the rhetoric of modern national politics, the remarkably rich literature pro and con ratification, of which *The Federalist* is only a piece, was serious, sophisticated, and addressed to a broad population."[3]

And yet for all of our appreciation, with the benefit of hindsight we can also detect a deep irony in the ratification debates. Despite their displays of eloquence, learning, and critical analysis, both the supporters and opponents of the Constitution seem to have badly misjudged their situation and prospects. Indeed, they seem to have gotten things exactly backward.

Both the Federalists and the Antifederalists agreed—or at least they purported to agree[4]—that a consolidation of general governmental power on the national level would be a very bad thing. So both sides employed their full repertoire of argument and rhetoric to persuade the citizenry either that the Constitution would *not* permit such a consolidation of power (the Federalist argument) or that it *would* (the Antifederalist argument). This debate culminated in the ratification of the Constitution, and so we might infer that the citizens who participated in the decision—or at least the dominant part of them—ultimately found the Federalist argument more persuasive.

In retrospect, though, we can also see that they were wrong: The accumulation of national power that the Antifederalists predicted has in fact occurred—many times over. The Constitution has been interpreted, as Richard Epstein remarks, "to create a federal power that, if candidly acknowledged at the Framing, would have scuttled the new constitution of 1787 even before the ratification debates began."[5] And yet we do not lament the founders' decision to ratify the Constitution; rather, for the most part, we celebrate it.

We can put the point differently: The founding generation's sustained experiment in reason led it to adopt an evaluative judgment (A concentration of power in the national government is *bad*) and also a predictive judgment (The Constitution will prevent a concentration of power in the national government). These two judgments combined to support the conclusion that the Constitution should be ratified. From *our* standpoint, by contrast, the founders' *conclusion* was right—but only because *both* their evaluative judgment and their predictive judgment were wrong.

Lucky for us that the founding generation was mistaken across-the-board. If Americans of that period had been better predictors, who knows what might have happened? Would we still be living under the Articles of Confederation? Would the new and fragile nation have split up into a sort of eighteenth century Bosnia, as essays five through eight of *The Federalist* predicted? Or would unity have been achieved anyway but under less salutary conditions, the way it has been achieved in countless other countries—through collapse into political turmoil followed by military consolidation, for example?

We will never know the answers to these questions, of course, and so it may be just as well that we hardly ever ask them. All's well that ends well. For practical purposes it makes little difference, perhaps, whether the framers in their wisdom actually designed a good constitution or in their ignorance merely stumbled into one.

It would be inappropriate for us to leave the matter here, though, for at least two related reasons. First, even if the Constitution is a fait accompli and there is no movement today to rescind the ratification of the Constitution, a diagnosis of how and why the framers' scheme failed to work out according to plan is still relevant to issues that *are* controversial—such as the seemingly interminable debate between so-called originalists and nonoriginalists. Second, and for our purposes most important, we cannot really appreciate the more contemporary understanding of how reason relates to the Constitution without first considering how the framers' conception of that relationship proved unsatisfactory.

The Framers' Big Blunder

The framers, as we have seen, tried to implement reason in careful legalistic fashion; and so it may seem ironic that the most obvious defect in their plan can plausibly be viewed as a technical flaw, or a failure in practical legal judgment. Central to their constitutional strategy was a misplaced trust in the enumerated powers doctrine—the idea that government powers could in practice be confined by listing such powers in a written document and specifying that the national government would have only those powers actually conferred on it.

As discussed in the previous chapter, the enumerated powers doctrine was the framers' principal response to *all* of the major types of constitutional concerns that still engage us today—concerns of separation of powers, federalism, and individual rights. The framers believed that by enumerating the powers of the different branches of the national government they could allocate and diffuse powers on the national level, hedge in national powers as against the states, and insulate individual rights against intrusions by the national government. Thus, in the ratifying discussions the Federalists argued with energy and apparent conviction that a bill of rights was unnecessary because the powers of the national government were so limited that there could be no danger to state or individual rights.

The Collapse of the Enumerated Powers Strategy

In retrospect, we may wonder how they could have been so myopic. Their confidence in the enumerated powers device seems, as Leonard Levy argues, "a colossal error of judgment."[6] From our standpoint it is easy to appreciate the prescience of Antifederalist arguments predicting the expansion of implied powers, and of course subsequent events have vindicated these arguments.[7] We may point to the New Deal period, with its validation of sweeping national powers, as providing confirmation of Antifederalist prophecies.[8] But in fact, the writing on the wall was already legible much earlier—indeed, within Washington's first term.

The specific issue then—revealingly, one that from our vantage point seems distinctly quaint—concerned the power of Congress to charter a national bank. The Constitution said nothing about banks per se. But Alexander Hamilton, Secretary of the Treasury and a strong proponent of the bank, argued that this could not be dispositive of the question. In an argument that could hardly have been better calculated to corroborate the Antifederalist predictions that he had earlier resisted, Hamilton contended that to give Congress the power to accomplish a particular *end* necessarily meant that Congress had power to adopt *means* to that end. So "[t]he only question must be, in this as in every other case, whether the mean to be employed . . . has a natural relation to any of the acknowledged objects or lawful ends of the government."[9] And in this case, that question was easily answered. Chartering a bank would be helpful in the achievement of not merely one but several constitutionally authorized ends: collecting taxes, borrowing money, regulating interstate commerce, and maintaining the military forces.[10]

An alarmed James Madison countered by reemphasizing

> the peculiar manner in which the Federal Government is limited. It is not a general grant, out of which particular powers are excepted; it is a grant of particular powers only, leaving the general mass in other hands. So it has been understood by its friends and its foes, and so it was to be interpreted.[11]

The problem with a position like Hamilton's, Madison insisted, was that it left essentially no practical limits on national power. And though not given to shrill rhetoric, Madison issued an ominous warning: If Hamilton's view of implied powers prevailed, then "[t]he *essential characteristic of the Government*, as composed of limited and enumerated powers, *would be destroyed*. . . ."[12]

Despite this warning, Hamilton's argument carried the day in 1791, and except for occasional periods of attempted but unsuccessful retrenchment it has carried the day ever since. The major chapters in the story are well known. In *McCulloch v. Maryland*,[13] the Supreme Court embraced a broad view of implied powers. In *Gibbons v. Ogden*,[14] the Court gave an expansive construction to the commerce clause—a clause, incidentally, that in the ratification debates had been described by Madison as "an addition [to national powers] which few oppose and from which no apprehensions are entertained"[15]—and in the New Deal and civil rights movement periods this clause was read as authorizing far-reaching national legislation regulating the economy and the practices of private employers.[16] Occasionally the Court has endeavored to circumscribe the commerce power, but these efforts have proven futile and in most cases have been explicitly abandoned.[17] To be sure, we may at this moment be in the middle of another attempt at retrenchment.[18] If so, the fate of like efforts in the past should provoke serious doubts about the long-term prospects of the current effort.[19]

This brief story may be misleading insofar as it seems to suggest that the framers expected enforcement of their legalistic strategy to rest largely or entirely with the courts, so that the responsibility for the failure of that strategy belongs mostly with the judiciary. Although the framers probably anticipated the possibility of some sort of judicial review,[20] the ideas of a legalistic, written Constitution and of aggressive judicial enforcement of that Constitution were not so inseparable in their minds as those ideas have come to be in ours. Madison's argument against the constitutionality of the bank was directed to the House of Representatives, not to the Supreme Court. And indeed, in *McCulloch* and the New Deal decisions and the 1960s decisions like *Heart of Atlanta Motel*, the Court did not *compel* Congress to assume greater powers; the expansive interpretation of the commerce clause was made first by Congress, not the courts. But the essential point remains unchanged: Over the decades, a series of decisions not only by the courts but by other branches has expanded the commerce power to the point where it can provide a basis for virtually any legislation that Congress might desire to enact, at least if Congress makes the effort to record the requisite findings connecting the legislation to matters involving commerce.

And of course the commerce power is only one of the ways in which the national government exercises sweeping authority. Congress also wields broad powers under section 5 of the Fourteenth Amendment,[21] for example, as well as under the taxing and spending and treaty clauses.[22] Lawrence Lessig points out that "[a]s a practical matter there are no real federalism limits on the federal power to spend."[23] By attaching conditions to the receipt of vital federal funding, Congress can achieve, indirectly but effectively, virtually all that it can do through direct regulation. So even if the courts should manage to confine the scope of the commerce clause, it seems likely that congressional power would simply be redirected through other channels.

Nor is it only Congress's powers that have grown well beyond early expectations. Presidents issue executive orders and make executive agreements that in effect differ little from statutes and treaties.[24] The accumulation of such powers, Martin Flaherty maintains, has turned the executive, not Congress, into "the most dangerous branch."[25] But judicial powers have also grown to dwarf those of founding era courts. Federal courts supervise entire state and local institutions such as prisons and school districts; they occasionally have even ordered communities to raise taxes in order to support improvements in school systems.[26] George Carey observes that the Supreme Court is today "an institution of immense powers, far beyond anything dreamt of by the Founding Fathers."[27]

But by far the largest aggregation of power has occurred in a set of institutions that the original Constitution did not provide for at all—administrative agencies, sometimes referred to as the "Fourth Branch." The administrative state, though now taken for granted, departs so dramatically from the original constitutional design[28] that Bruce Ackerman argues it can only be accounted for by supposing a major (albeit unwritten and, prior to Ackerman, undetected) constitutional amendment that was effectively adopted sometime around 1936.[29]

In short, while we may still piously recite the proposition that the national government is one of limited powers or limited jurisdiction—and indeed, the Supreme Court does continue to intone these pieties[30]—in reality the actively enforceable constitutional limits on national powers are few and frail. To be sure, Congress still leaves many areas mostly to the states, but the lines of jurisdiction are now based more on loose tradition, policy, and convenience than on binding constitutional restrictions.[31] The situation in which Congress might earnestly desire to do something but find itself unable to do it on grounds of lack of constitutional power rarely if ever arises.[32]

So it seems that Hamilton's position has triumphed, perhaps beyond his own wildest imagination. But if Hamilton was right, it does not follow that Madison was wrong. Hamilton's triumph may have been inevitable, and it may also be laudable—this view, of course, remains at least somewhat controversial—but that triumph *does* mark the failure of the original design and strategy. And Madison accurately described the consequence: "The essential characteristic of the Government, as composed of limited and enumerated powers," *has* been, for practical purposes, and for better or worse, "destroyed."

The Rights Strategy

Typically, of course, lawyers and citizens do not grieve over the demise of the enumerated powers doctrine, or even pay much attention to it. At first glance, our serenity in this matter might seem odd; one might suppose that the failure of a doctrine that the framers viewed as the centerpiece of the constitutional design would have catastrophic consequences. Yet in constitutional law casebooks the framers' reliance on the enumerated powers doctrine is commonly noticed in passing; and the failure of the strategy, at least as a legally viable limit on government, is treated as an incidental consequence of changing constructions of the commerce clause—most likely in a triumphalist presentation of the Supreme Court's New Deal "switch in time" that in the conventional understanding brought the benighted *Lochner* era to an end.

One reason why the failure of the enumerated powers device for limiting national power is not mourned is that we have come actually to prefer, by and large, a central government that takes a more active role in the economy and in the protection of various rights and interests than the original Constitution contemplated. But the framers' oft-expressed fears of "tyranny"—fears that from our perspective may sometimes seem to border on paranoia—also fail to resonate with us because of a common account of the Bill of Rights.

According to this account, the founders soon perceived the flaw in the original constitutional design—that is, its unwarranted reliance on the enumerated powers strategy—and corrected this mistake by adopting the first ten amendments. In doing so, they supplemented the initial enumerated powers strategy with a fallback, "rights" strategy—one that was later augmented with the addition of further constitutional rights, especially those associated with the Fourteenth Amendment. And as things have turned out, the fallback strategy has borne virtually the entire burden of holding government in check: Enforceable limitations on government power have commonly been developed through the judicial elaboration of individual rights—freedom of speech, freedom of religion, due process of law, equal protection, and so forth—*not* through the confinement of government to the specific powers listed in Articles I, II, and III. It is revealing that in the writings of prominent constitutional scholars like Ronald Dworkin and Robin West, the original Constitution virtually disappears; almost all the attention is paid to subsequent amendments—in particular the First and Fourteenth Amendments—that create individual rights.[33]

From our perspective it may seem quite obvious that the "rights" approach was always more promising than the "enumerated powers" approach. So it is difficult to fathom how the framers could have misjudged the matter so badly.[34] Still, the important point is that they *did* adopt the fallback strategy, and their adoption of a list of rights has given later generations a useable device for limiting governmental power. So the framers' initial misplaced reliance on the enumerated powers strategy amounts to a curious, slightly embarrassing, but ultimately not very consequential wrinkle in our constitutional fabric.

In assessing this familiar account of the founding period, it is important for our purposes to distinguish between two questions. One question asks whether the founders' decision to supplement the original text with a list of rights has, as things have turned out, provided later generations with a mechanism for using reason to define and enforce appropriate limits on government. For the moment, that question can be deferred. An importantly different question—and one more directly pertinent to our discussion of the founding period—is whether *the founders* understood the adoption of the Bill of Rights to represent a significant adjustment in their conception of how reason relates to the Constitution, or of how reason might be used to direct and limit the power of government.

To put the matter crudely: If we were asked to grade the founders on their prescience and performance, should their decision to adopt the Bill of Rights excuse or mitigate to any significant degree the "colossal error of judgment," as Levy describes it, that their initial confidence in the enumerated powers doctrine seems from our standpoint to have represented? Or was the Bill of Rights more in the nature of a lucky accident?

The Casual Bill of Rights

In addressing this issue, we need to remember some familiar facts about the Bill of Rights.[35] Although James Madison had not supported a bill of rights in the Philadelphia convention, he was obligated by ratification and campaign commitments to introduce some such measure in the First Congress.[36] Those whose curiosity runs to the counterfactual might pause for a brief moment to speculate on what might have happened had Madison persisted in his initial position. Would he have been defeated in the first congressional election by his opponent, the future president James Monroe, and then have passed from prominence in the formative period of the Republic? Would a different bill of rights—or none at all—have been adopted?[37] Might the failure to adopt a bill of rights have led to the second constitutional convention that Antifederalists were agitating for, and that Madison was desperately seeking to forestall, and what would the outcome of a second convention have been? Suppose a different bill of rights *had* eventually been adopted—perhaps a meatier one more in accord with Antifederalist wishes: What effect, if any, would the difference have had on our subsequent constitutional history? In sum, has the vast unfolding history of American constitutional liberty hinged on a bit of late eighteenth-century electioneering in a district in backstate Virginia?

In any event, Madison *was* induced to support a bill of rights, and perhaps partly as a result of this change of heart he was elected to the House of Representatives. But when he proceeded to propose a bill of rights in the First Congress, Madison was forced to coax and cajole—to "beg the House to indulge him"—in order to persuade his colleagues even to consider the matter. They felt they had more important business. Noting Madison's anxiety, Representative John Vining of Delaware agreed to postpone discussion of his own bill for establishing a land office, but Vining added with respect to the land office bill that "in point of importance, every candid mind would acknowledge its preference."[38] Legislators, it seems, just couldn't work up much interest. Many of them regarded the provisions as "a few milk and water amendments," "trash," "nonsense," "an anodyne to the discontented," "little better than whip-syllabub, frothy and full of wind, formed only to please the palate."[39] Of course, some of these disparaging sentiments were expressed by Antifederalists who wanted something much stronger. Their position reflects an irony in the situation: Those who had contended most ardently for a bill of rights contributed little to its substance and often opposed it,[40] leaving its content to be dictated largely by people who had argued just a year or so earlier that a bill of rights would be unnecessary and perhaps even pernicious.

In this situation, little attention was paid to the actual content of the proposed rights. For example, with respect to the religion clauses, which in recent years have been the focus of vast outpourings both of popular passion and of scholarly and judicial analysis, Leonard Levy explains:

> [The debate in the House] was apathetic and unclear: ambiguity, brevity, and imprecision in thought and expression characterized the comments of the few members who spoke. That the House understood the debate, cared deeply about its outcome, or shared a common understanding of the finished amendment is doubtful.
>
> Not even Madison himself, dutifully carrying out his pledge to secure amendments, seems to have troubled to do more than was necessary to get something adopted in order to satisfy popular clamor and deflate Antifederalist charges. Indeed, he agreed with [Roger] Sherman's statement that the amendment was "altogether unnecessary. . . ."[41]

If debate on the religion clauses seems lackluster, however, the discussion was lavish compared with the interest paid to some of the other rights. Consider, for example, the cruel and unusual punishment clause, which in modern times has been the locus for voluminous and wrenching judicial and scholarly debates regarding the permissibility of capital punishment. When this provision was read in the House, only two representatives troubled themselves to comment on the measure. William Smith of South Carolina thought the words "cruel and unusual punishment" were "too indefinite." Samuel Livermore of New Hampshire agreed; the measure expressed "a great deal of humanity," but "it seems to have no meaning in it" because the terms were undefined. For example, "villains often deserve whipping, and perhaps having their ears cut off," but there was no way to tell whether the amendment would prohibit this salutary kind of punishment. No one bothered to answer these objections and questions; the House simply proceeded to pass the amendment "by a considerable majority," and then moved on to the next amendment. It appears the discussion cannot have taken more than about five minutes.[42]

What should we make of such complacency? We might (and some scholars do, as Levy's tone suggests) react with dismay or even anger, blaming the founders for what looks to us like unconscionable apathy in such momentous matters. And indeed it *is* unsettling to discover that provisions that we regard as the bedrock of our constitutional order—and that have generated libraries of commentary and exposition by judges and scholars, editorialists and Independence Day orators—were in fact adopted hastily, casually, virtually without interest or reflection.

Viewed in context, though, the founders' apparent indifference seems more understandable. What their attitude shows, I suggest, is that they were still counting on the enumerated powers strategy to define and limit the powers of government.[43] In short, the founders evidently viewed the Bill of Rights not so much as a serious and independent fallback position, but rather as a way of *reinforcing the enumerated powers strategy* by making its premises more explicit, or as a cosmetic addition calculated to appease opponents of the Constitution, or both.

More specifically, the founders apparently viewed some of the provisions in the Bill of Rights simply as explicit reaffirmations that Congress had only the powers actually given it. I have argued elsewhere that this was true of the religion clauses of the First Amendment.[44] The enactors of those clauses were not adding new substantive rights or principles to the Constitution; rather, they were merely reiterating what they had asserted all along—that is, that the national government had no power over religion because the regulation of religion was within the sole jurisdiction of the states. Opponents of the Constitution had worried because this jurisdictional division, although repeatedly affirmed by the Federalists, was not made explicit in the text; so the First Congress obliged by putting the restriction on national jurisdiction in writing. There was no change of strategy here—no revision in the way in which reason was thought to inform the Constitution, or to operate in governance—but merely an agreement to make more clear what the Federalists had maintained and the Antifederalists had wanted from the start.

Akhil Amar's observation that the very wording of the First Amendment shows that it was understood as a sort of "necessary and proper" clause-in-reverse suggests that a similar assessment may apply to that Amendment as a whole, including the free speech clause.[45] And indeed, when later in the decade Madison opposed the Sedition Act of 1798 (a law that today seems a plain violation of the right to free speech[46]), he seems to have understood the clause in just this way—that is, as a constitutional provision asserting clearly that the regulation of speech was a matter within the jurisdiction of the states, not the national government. Thus, although the sixth article of the Virginia Resolutions, authored by Madison in opposition to the Sedition Act, *does* refer to the First Amendment, the reference follows and is evidently intended mainly to reinforce earlier articles asserting that the Federal Government is one of limited, enumerated powers formed by a compact among the states, and deploring "a spirit [that] has in sundry instances been manifested by the Federal Government to enlarge its powers by forced constructions of the constitutional charter which defines them." This expansionist tendency was working, the fourth article asserted, "so as to destroy the meaning and effect of the particular enumeration which necessarily explains and limits the general phrases [in the Constitution]."[47]

Other parts of the Bill of Rights look more like enactments of substantive rights or principles. For example, the Eighth Amendment's proscription of cruel and unusual punishments seems substantive in nature. After all, Congress *did* have power to adopt criminal laws on some subjects and to impose penalties, so the Eighth Amendment seemingly did more than merely reaffirm limits on congressional power that were already implicit in the original Constitution anyway. Nonetheless, whether because they were confident that the national government's powers were too limited to be seriously threatening or because they just were not paying much attention to the matter, the First Congress apparently regarded such provisions as window dressing[48]—and consequently devoted virtually no thought to the substantive meaning of the rights or principles in question.

In sum, the adoption of the Bill of Rights does not seem to have been understood by its enactors as reflecting any significant departure from or addition to the original constitutional design,[49] which indeed they had viewed as already constituting a bill of rights for practical purposes.[50] To acknowledge this is not to deny the crucial importance of the decision to enact the Bill of Rights. Many a casual decision that seems inconsequential when made, and that accordingly elicits little or no reflection, comes over time to have vast significance. Because you decided, at the last moment and almost without thought, to take Section Two of English 100 instead of Section One, you met the person to whom you have been married for the last quarter-century. Or you decide there's time to wait for the hotel shuttle instead of taking a taxi, and thereby avoid a fatal auto accident. The Bill of Rights may be the consequence of a similar, albeit more magnificent, fortuity; or it may reflect, as we sometimes say in these instances, a "providential" occurrence. But we cannot credit the people who enacted it with having comprehended its far-reaching consequences. They put *their* trust in a different strategy—the enumerated powers strategy—which subsequent events rendered (or rather showed to be) almost wholly ineffectual to achieve its purpose.

A Technical Failure?

The discussion thus far has suggested that the failure of the founders' scheme for limiting the power of government reflected a merely technical error. Assuming their sincerity (as not everyone does[51]), their error shows that they were, at least in that crucial particular, short-sighted lawyers. But is this a completely satisfactory account? Was the failure of the original constitutional scheme merely the result of bad lawyering? Even if the account of the demise of the enumerated powers doctrine given above provides a tolerably accurate description of what in fact has happened, the account may provoke doubts of various kinds.

In the first place, even if the enumerated powers strategy *did not* work out as planned, it does not necessarily follow that the strategy *could not* have worked. Perhaps with greater will and ingenuity, later generations could have found ways to carry out that strategy. Indeed, as noted, a few scholars and even a few current justices seem intent on reviving the strategy.[52] Even if they fail—and the futility of such efforts in the past does not bode well for the current campaign—the failure might only show that *we* lack the understanding or commitment needed to implement the enumerated powers doctrine, *not* that the doctrine itself is flawed, or that the framers somehow blundered by embracing it.

A different sort of uneasiness arises from the seeming incongruity of attributing the default of an epic political project to a merely technical error of judgment. Perhaps this objection reflects nothing more than aesthetic frustration; it may express a need to believe that history is at least a minimally competent artist with some decent sense of proportion. Still, despite our occasional recitation of the "For want of a nail . . ." proverb, we may wish to suppose that grand developments in history can be traced to more dignified causes. So it seems incongruous to suppose that the failure and subsequent transformation of the framers' grand constitutional strategy should be the consequence of something as mundane as a lawyerly miscalculation.

The historian might note these doubts but then set them aside as beyond the scope of her jurisdiction. We cannot dismiss them so quickly, though, because they bear directly upon the central question we are pursuing—that is, the question of what the constitutional project tells us about the possibility of bringing human governance under the rule of reason, and thereby liberating human affairs from the tyranny of force and fortuity. So it is worth thinking again about the basic question. Why did the framers' legalistic constitutional strategy fail—fail, that is, in terms of their own expectations?

In the remainder of this chapter I want to consider two familiar but different accounts—we can call them the "changed circumstances" and the "interpreter infidelity" accounts—of the failure of the framers' strategy. Before we consider these accounts, though, it may be well to remind ourselves of just how the framers attempted to embody reason in the Constitution. The framers' basic idea, as the previous chapter has described, was to protect Nature against nature—or to guard natural rights and principles of justice from the ravages of self-serving and power-craving human nature—by consolidating the teachings of reason in a written legal document which later generations could read and follow. As noted, the framers believed they had made a great discovery in political science in recognizing the advantages of a *written* constitution. The exercise of governing reason itself had been made possible by a sort of special dispensation from the usual irrational forces of history and human nature; but it was the possibility of reducing to writing the conclusions reached during that special dispensation that permitted the framers to project their exercise of reason onto future generations. In short, fixing the conclusions of reason was possible only because of, and through the use of, a *written* legal text. This conception of the Constitution, authoritatively set forth in *Marbury v. Madison*, was what I have been calling the framers' "legalistic" strategy; and our question is why that strategy did not work out as they intended.

Changed Circumstances

The "changed circumstances" account of the failure of the legalistic strategy asserts that the framers' enumerated powers doctrine lost its efficacy simply because American history unfolded in ways that the framers did not foresee and that rendered the doctrine obsolete. As an example of this view, consider a recent essay by Lawrence Lessig. Early in his essay, Lessig calls attention to a seeming paradox: The tremendous expansion in national power that has occurred under the commerce clause, he thinks, is at the same time plainly inconsistent with the framers' *intentions* and yet plainly authorized by the *text* that the framers adopted.[53] The chasm that divides what was intended from what was authorized, Lessig argues, primarily reflects changes in the basic character of the national economy. At the founding, most commerce was local in nature, and thus would not have fallen within Congress's power to regulate commerce "among the several States." But especially in this century the economy has become increasingly integrated, so that most or all activities now have an effect on the national economy as a whole, and hence have become subject to national regulation.[54]

By this view, the expansion of national power cannot be attributed to any judicial misinterpretation of the constitutional *text*. On the contrary, Lessig insists that "it is not that the Court can simply 'enforce' affirmative limits on federal regulation—such limits simply don't exist out there to be found. . . ."[55] Nor does Lessig fault the framers for bad drafting. Given the nature of the economy in that era, as well as other "conventions and understandings" presupposed by the framers,[56] the text they wrote was adequately crafted to support their project in the founding period. The difficulty is simply that the world—in particular, the economy—has changed. That is why their text is no longer serviceable for carrying out their project: "For the plain language of our Constitution today abstracted from the context of the founding yields a Constitution quite inconsistent with the vision of the framers."[57]

The "changed circumstances" account largely absolves the modern Supreme Court of blame for the failure of the legalistic strategy;[58] it also absolves the framers, but only in part. The framers, by this view, may have had an essentially sound vision of government. And they were competent legal drafters. But the framers were also fallible prophets who forgot about, or at least did not sufficiently appreciate, their own fallibility. As the previous chapter has explained, the framers viewed the work of reason as essentially a one-act play. Taking advantage of the special dispensation from the usual historical determinants of force and fortuity, *they* themselves would exercise reason and protect natural rights by constructing a legalistic constitution which subsequent generations could follow, not perpetually rethink. Lessig's analysis suggests that this project was misguided for a quite obvious reason: Absent an ability to foresee the future, a legal text that operates to produce particular effects at one time will produce entirely different (and unintended) effects at a different time as circumstances change. And since *any* human constitution-maker will be fallible in just this way, Lessig's analysis implies that the one-shot, legalistic approach to bringing reason into governance could never be viable.

Interpreter Infidelity

A different rendering of our constitutional history, which we might call the "interpreter infidelity" view, tries to be kinder to the framers and more affirming of the legalistic strategy they adopted. By this view, if the original legalistic strategy has failed, the reason is not that the text adopted by the framers (supplemented by later amendments, understood legalistically) either was or is deficient. The problem is that later interpreters, and especially the modern Supreme Court, have carelessly or perhaps willfully distorted the Constitution in order to advance their own agendas or political philosophies. In this vein, and on the premise that "clear language has the capacity to resolve critical cases," Richard Epstein argues that "difficulties of interpretation cannot explain the current malaise of modern American constitutional law. The remorseless and enormous expansion in government power can only be explained by the systematic repudiation of the basic principles of limited government which informed the original constitutional structure."[59]

This sort of diagnosis—which since the time of the Warren Court is usually thought of as a "conservative" criticism, but can just as well be a "liberal" complaint[60]—is common. Perhaps the most forceful contemporary advocate of an "interpreter infidelity" view is Robert Bork. Like Epstein, Bork argues that the Constitution provides enforceable limits on congressional power and that the Supreme Court's abandonment of those limits in the New Deal period was a politically motivated "manifestation of judicial activism."[61] More broadly, Bork assails justices and legal scholars for twisting the Constitution "because they have moral and political agendas of their own that cannot be found in the Constitution. . . ." The result of this self-serving distortion, Bork contends, is that "innovations are announced in the name of the Constitution—though they have little or nothing to do with it."[62]

Though not necessarily incompatible, the "changed circumstances" and "interpreter infidelity" accounts diverge in several important respects. Most obviously, they disagree about whether many modern political developments and judicial doctrines are truly authorized by the text of the Constitution. This disagreement might naturally lead into a debate about which among a range of readings of the commerce clause—or the "necessary and proper" clause, or the Fourteenth Amendment—is in some sense the proper or correct interpretation. But I will perhaps be pardoned for not entering into that sort of debate here. For one thing, the debate seems endless. As we have seen, the basic interpretive positions were staked out by Madison and Hamilton almost before the ink on the Constitution was dry; and although after two centuries the vocabulary of the debate has become more esoteric, the essential arguments seem not to have changed very much. As old adversaries (Hamilton-Madison; Marshall-Roane; Frankfurter-Black) grow weary and then die, new combatants (Brennan-Scalia; Dworkin-Bork) simply rush in to hold the lines. It hardly seems likely that any Johnny-come-lately will supply the argument that will bring this perpetual skirmish to a conclusion.

More fundamentally, some recent theorizing may give us cause to wonder whether debates about the "correct" interpretation of the constitutional text are not only interminable but also, on a deep level, incoherent. One sort of criticism suggests that arguing about the true meaning of the constitutional text—or of any text—is like arguing about the true color of a mermaid's tail;

the argument goes nowhere because the ostensible thing being argued about does not actually exist. This criticism will turn out to be overblown, I think, but it also points us to the most basic flaw in the framers' constitutional scheme. So we must consider it more closely.

Challenging Textual Trust

We can begin with a rough statement of the criticism. In essence, the objection asserts that the framers' belief (and to a considerable extent *our* own belief) in the power of writing, or of words, to capture and convey meaning is a false faith. Words have no inherent meaning. Rather, they can have meaning only *to someone*. But people who read words always do so in a particular context and with particular purposes; context and purpose control the reader's attribution of meaning to an arrangement of words. And an author cannot control the contexts and purposes that will govern the reading of words. Consequently, there is no way to *fix* meaning in words.

Legal scholars sometimes operating under the title of "deconstructionism"[63]—it is not for me to say whether the title, borrowed from a body of European criticism, is deserved[64]—have pressed this sort of argument to radical extremes, arguing that even what seem the clearest of constitutional clauses have no definite meaning. In this vein, the clause that has perhaps received the most attention in the scholarly literature—though not, for excellent reasons, in the case law—is the provision in Article II, section 1, clause 5, which provides with respect to the office of President that "neither shall any person be eligible to that Office who shall not have attained to the Age of thirty five Years. . . ." Many lawyers and scholars have supposed that however vague or ambiguous some parts of the Constitution may be—the due process or equal protection clauses, for example—nonetheless the meaning of provisions like the presidential age requirement is beyond serious dispute.[65]

But the deconstructionists deny even this. For example, several scholars have argued that the provision might be understood to signify a level of maturity rather than a precise numerical age.[66] More imaginatively, Anthony D'Amato affirms that under some circumstances it might be plausible to read the presidential age requirement merely as disqualifying candidates afflicted with acne.[67]

Arguments like D'Amato's probably strike most people (who after all are not deeply immersed in deconstructionist literature) as profoundly wrongheaded or goofy.[68] One commonsensical counterargument asserts that the deconstructionist position can be rebutted simply by observing that we *do* often manage to communicate in writing. If the radical deconstructionist position were correct, and if writing were really as perilous and inherently indeterminate an enterprise as the deconstructionists seem to suggest, then seemingly it should not be possible for deconstructionists even to argue for their views. They do after all write—sometimes prolifically, and apparently on the assumption that people will be able to read what they have written and understand at least roughly what they are trying to say. Doesn't their very behavior contradict—doesn't it show that even *they* do not actually believe—the point they purport to make?

In this vein, Richard Kay notes an objection to originalist interpretation which suggests that "linguistic communication is impossible," but he replies that this objection is "wildly counterintuitive." Kay argues that "[t]he most telling response to this objection is simply that no one really believes it, not even the writers who make the objection. If they did, they would not use language to advance the argument."[69]

Where Deconstruction Goes Wrong—and Right

Kay's observation seems cogent as far as it goes, but it does not quite identify the underlying flaw in what I am calling the deconstructionist objection. What exactly is the error? It may be helpful to list several ideas or propositions associated with the deconstructionist view that seem correct in order to isolate both the merit and the mistake in the objection.

To begin with, it is true that the sounds or marks we call "words" do not have inherent meaning. Nearly everyone will admit this, I think, when the issue is baldly presented. Language, most people agree, is conventional. "Cow" doesn't just naturally or inherently mean a four-legged beast that gives milk and says "moo"; the word has that meaning only because, and only to the extent that, speakers or writers use it to convey that meaning and listeners or readers understand what the speakers or writers intend.

It is also true that what listeners or readers understand will be governed by their contexts and purposes. Consequently, one *can* imagine contexts and purposes that will lead people to attribute to words different meanings than those we would ascribe to them given our own more familiar or assumed contexts and purposes, or than those that as speakers or writers we might have intended the words to convey. Indeed, we have all experienced this possibility directly; we have misunderstood, and we have been misunderstood.

More radically, a person *can* deliberately repudiate as an interpretive purpose the goal of discerning what the speaker or author was trying to communicate. I *can*, if I choose to, deliberately misunderstand what you say, or attach to your words a different meaning than the one you intended. Again, most of us have known (or, perhaps, have *been*) people who do just that—not merely postmodern literary theorists, or even lawyers, but your junior high school pal who creatively misread some hilarious (to him) sexual innuendo into everything anyone said. So it seems undeniable that "creative misreading" of the kind described by D'Amato *is* always a possibility.

Nor can it be said that such misreadings are simply and objectively wrong on the ground that the words themselves just don't mean what the deconstructionist interprets them to mean. To say *that* would be to suppose that the words themselves have an inherent or natural meaning. If they did have such a meaning, then the deconstructionist's reactions to the words would amount to a simple mistake of fact; he would commit the same kind of error that a person commits if she thinks, for example, that a pig is a cucumber. But as noted above, it is implausible to suppose, and hardly anyone believes, that words have a natural or inherent meaning in that way.

So the deconstructionist objection calls our attention to a number of facts about texts, or about words, that are both true and important. If the objection nonetheless seems a bit kooky, that is because it appears to overlook another fact that is also true and important: Although creative misreading is always a possibility, it is not the *only* possibility. I *can* choose to misunderstand you. But I can also do the opposite—that is, try to understand what you intend to communicate. Even with the best of intentions, of course, communication often breaks down. But the fact that attempts at communication also frequently succeed seems to demonstrate that understanding, like misunderstanding, is a possibility—and indeed a possibility that is often realized.

In sum, the deconstructionist objection serves to remind us that language has no inherent or natural meaning. This may seem an obvious observation, but it is one that in practice is often forgotten (by, among others, deconstructionists).[70] The deconstructionist objection also identifies and illustrates one very real possibility—that is, creative misreading. The flaw in the argument is that it seems to infer that because misreading is *an* alternative, it is the only alternative. But to demonstrate that A is possible is not to demonstrate that B is *not* possible.

So it seems the deconstructionist argument fails to show that the framers' (and the originalists') notion of conveying meaning by means of a text is a priori impossible or incoherent. But the argument is helpful in a different way: It makes clear that the possibility of conveying meaning through words *is* dependent on certain assumptions. Most important, that possibility assumes a certain kind of reader with a particular purpose—the purpose, that is, of discerning the semantic intentions of the author or speaker.[71]

More specifically, the framers' constitutional project of fixing the conclusions of reason in a written document presupposed that the future interpreters of the constitutional text would be readers who would attempt to read and understand the meaning the framers intended to convey, not readers who would seek to creatively misread that text. The authors of the constitutional text had no power (as authors never have power) to *compel* readers to approach the text in a particular spirit or with a particular purpose; the framers could only *hope* that later interpreters would engage with their construction in the spirit necessary to carry on their project.

But this observation leads to a troubling question: Did the framers have good grounds to expect this kind of reader?

Human Nature Again

The answer to that question, at least given the framers' own view of human nature, seems to be "No." As the previous chapter suggested, in the framers' view human beings have the capacity for reason and virtue, but their dominant characteristics are selfishness and love of power. The delegates to the Philadelphia convention repeatedly stressed that they were designing a constitution for just that kind of person. Indeed, it was precisely because future citizens and officials could not be counted on to act from reason and virtue that the conclusions of reason needed to be fixed in a written, legalistic Constitution.

But of course it would be these same self-serving citizens and officials—or some subset of them—who would be reading and interpreting the Constitution.[72] So if human beings are the sort of creatures that the framers insisted they are, what basis could there be for supposing that in reading the Constitution these human beings would approach the text with the disinterested purpose of trying in good faith to determine what the words originally meant, or what the authors of those words were trying to communicate? On the contrary, one would expect that these readers should be powerfully inclined to "creatively misread" the text, not playfully or perversely in the manner of deconstructionist academicians, but in order to further their own interests and enhance their own power.[73]

To be sure, this depiction of human nature may put the point too simplistically—and in terms more cynical either than the framers, hard-headed realists though they were, would have accepted or than our knowledge of modern judges and interpreters seems to warrant. But the depiction can be significantly qualified without altering the conclusion. Let us say that human beings, including politicians and judges, are not simply the kind of characters that popular opinion often takes lawyers to be—that is, self-serving hypocrites who constantly and consciously manipulate words solely to serve their own interests. Instead, humans at least have the capacity to use reason in a more disinterested way, and they have a desire to seem—and even, perhaps, to *be*—virtuous.

Even so, the domination of self-interest and the craving for control will normally seize the faculty of reason and bend it to the service of self. Madison put the matter gently: "As long as the connection subsists between [man's] reason and his self-love, his opinions and passions will have a reciprocal influence on each other. . . ."[74] More bluntly, people may convince themselves that they are following the dictates of reason and virtue, but in fact their reason is largely in servitude to their interests. Or as Gunning Bedford said with respect to large state delegates like Madison and Wilson who had argued passionately that justice required proportional representation, "They think no doubt that they have right on their side, but interest had blinded their eyes."[75]

If we take this somewhat more complex and more charitable view as expressing the framers' understanding of human nature, then it still seems that their hopes for the sort of interpreters needed to carry out their project were, on their own assumptions at least, destined to frustration. Rather, the judges, politicians, lawyers, and scholars who would argue over constitutional meaning might in many cases convince themselves that they were acting according to reason and virtue; but in reality these advocates would often be using reason to enhance their own power, interests, and political views.

So it seems that in the end the framers' particular project was doubly inconsistent with regard to human nature. They drafted a constitution on the assumption that human beings are driven primarily not by reason and virtue but by self-interest and the love of power. But as we have seen, they strayed from that assumption, in the first instance, when they suspended the assumption *for themselves*—by supposing that *they* could act on the basis of disinterested reason for the good of the country and even the world. And they strayed from it again when, by supposing that they could fix the conclusions of reason in a written legal document, they tacitly presupposed the existence of future interpreters who would themselves rise above human nature as the framers understood it. The framers accounted for the first inconsistency by invoking the notion of a special dispensation from history; their own proceedings were, in Hamilton's characterization, a "miracle."[76] But they did not expect the miracle to be a perpetual one; hence, their excuse for the first inconsistency merely underscores the magnitude of the second inconsistency.[77]

It turns out, in sum, that although the "interpreter infidelity" account of constitutional history given by Bork and others means to be charitable to the framers and critical mostly of their successors, especially the modern Supreme Court, in fact the account inadvertently points to a vitiating flaw in the framers' own scheme for putting reason in the governing seat. By the "changed circumstances" account, the framers' deficiency was simply that, like other mortals, they could not foresee the future; as a result, their text came to have different consequences than the ones they intended. The "interpreter infidelity" account, by contrast, reveals a deeper incoherence in the framers' conception. In order to work as planned, their legalistic strategy required their successors to have precisely the sort of qualities that the framers did not expect them to have, and the presumed absence of which was the very reason for adopting a legalistic Constitution in the first place.

To put the point differently, critics like Bork may be right that lawyers, justices, scholars, and politicians have twisted the words of the Constitution in order to advance their own values and interests. But then, that is precisely what one would have expected if human nature is what the framers believed it to be. This observation serves to highlight a fatal inconsistency in the framers' project of making a legal constitution commensurate with reason. The inconsistency was merely latent in 1787; but by our own time it is glaringly revealed in the long-accomplished collapse of the framers' enumerated powers strategy for limiting the scope of national government.

An Apology

The framers do not come off very well in the preceding discussion. That is unfortunate, and unfair, because in fact the Philadelphia convention and the ensuing ratification debates surely represented both the most heroic and the most careful, sustained, and public-spirited effort to apply reason to constitutional governance that our country's history can exhibit.[78] I would venture that, by comparison, neither the deliberations that produced the Reconstruction amendments[79] nor the modern ruminations of constitutional scholars have come close to equaling the framers' achievement. Take your pick of current Supreme Court justices or constitutional scholars and place him or her alongside James Madison: The comparison is at once comic and tragic.[80] So if it is nonetheless true that the framers blundered, or that with benefit of hindsight we can see that they were guilty of inconsistencies fatal to their constitutional strategy, perhaps there is a lesson to be learned about the prospects of managing human affairs on the basis of reason.

It seems likely, moreover, that nothing presented in the discussion thus far would come as much of a shock to men like Madison. Indeed, anyone inclined to suspect Madison of any naive faith in the power of reason, or of undue confidence in the wisdom or virtue of the Philadelphia convention, need only read Federalist 37—a document whose gloominess is all the more remarkable because it appears in the middle of a set of generally upbeat essays seeking to promote the Constitution. So if we could call Madison back and ask him to read this chapter, one can imagine the Father of the Constitution explaining, with a paternal sigh and then a chuckle: "It is true, children, that history did not unfold as we anticipated. But then, we never really expected that it would."

It is revealing that early in the Philadelphia proceedings, Madison already had a premonition about the fate of the enumerated powers device on which the framers placed so much hope:

> Mr Madison said that he had brought with him into the Convention a strong bias in favor of an enumeration and definition of the powers necessary to be exercised by the national Legislature; but had also brought doubts concerning its practicability. His wishes remained unaltered; but his doubts had become stronger. What his opinion might ultimately be he could not yet tell.[81]

Madison might well have repeated this comment more than once in his long political career. He supported the Constitution, of course, and he dutifully argued for the virtues of the enumerated powers strategy (although a similar ambivalence about the efficacy of that strategy can also be detected in Madison's contributions to *The Federalist Papers*). Later, as noted, he vigorously resisted a broad reading of implied powers—even a reading broad enough to justify what from our standpoint seems the picayune measure of chartering a bank—warning that such a construction would mean that "the essential character of the government" would be "destroyed." But when his argument was rejected he did not throw a tantrum or conscientiously withdraw from political office; and when a quarter of a century later a second bank was authorized, President James Madison calmly treated the constitutional issue as settled.[82]

But if Madison understood the fragility of the enumerated powers approach, why did he persist in supporting a constitutional scheme that seemingly relied so heavily on that approach as a device for limiting national power? Two different though not inconsistent possibilities are worth considering. First, it is well to keep in mind that although Madison and the other framers gave much attention to preventing a consolidation of power at the national level, their faith in the enumerated powers doctrine was surely affected by their belief that in any event the centrifugal forces of decentralization and destabilization were stronger than the centripetal forces tending toward a strong national government. And in this belief they were probably right. Despite judicial decisions (like *McCulloch*) *authorizing* greater national powers, the political forces throughout the antebellum period pointed more in the opposite direction. Thus, half a century after the Philadelphia convention Tocqueville remarked on the declining power of the central government,[83] and he opined, with eerie foresight, that ultimately nothing but "some extraordinary event" such as "an internal crisis, or a war"[84] could reverse this tendency.

To be sure, if these historical observations serve at least partially to excuse the framers' misconceived assumption that the enumerated powers strategy could serve to limit national power, still they do little to redeem the founders' aspiration to bring human governance under the rule of reason. On the contrary, one might plausibly argue that the eventual dominance of the national government was influenced less by either the framers' strategy for reducing the conclusions of reason to a legal document or by decisions like *McCulloch* that read that document expansively than by that most stark antithesis of reason—an unspeakably brutal Civil War. And of course the war itself was to a large extent a consequence of the incapacity of reasoned deliberation—even as practiced by that most sanguine partisan of enlightenment, Thomas Jefferson, or by those blessed to participate in the special dispensation of the Philadelphia convention—to deal with the abomination of slavery.

A different exonerating observation might suggest that although Madison *hoped* the constitutional design would work out cleanly and rationally in something like the way outlined in the famous Supreme Court decision that bears his name, he also had a fallback strategy. That strategy was not the Bill of Rights—another "parchment barrier"[85]—but rather the grim, glorious realities of pluralistic politics.

Such reliance is discernible in Madison's famous analysis of factions in Federalist 10, reiterated more summarily in Federalist 51. Madison tied the problem of political factions to selfish, passionate, quarrelsome human nature:

> The latent causes of faction are thus sown in the nature of man. . . . So strong is this propensity of mankind to fall into mutual animosities that where no substantial occasion presents itself the most frivolous and fanciful distinctions have been sufficient to kindle their unfriendly passions and excite their most violent conflicts.[86]

So what is the remedy for such conflicts? More precisely, what will prevent a faction from gaining power and oppressing the rest of society, thereby suppressing the natural rights that republican government is supposed to protect? The solution, Madison argued, does not lie in wisdom or virtue. The people in general typically do not exhibit such qualities. "If the impulse and the opportunity [to carry into effect schemes of oppression] be suffered to coincide, we well know that neither moral nor religious motives can be relied on as an adequate check." And although Madison hoped that the national government might attract persons of "enlightened views and virtuous sentiments," he placed no great confidence in that prospect. "It is in vain to say that enlightened statesmen will be able to adjust these clashing interests and render them all subservient to the public good. Enlightened statesmen will not always be at the helm."[87]

Instead, Madison argued that in a large Republic, the very variety of factions would prevent any of them from gaining dominance.

> Extend the sphere and you take in a greater variety of parties and interests; you make it less probable that a majority of the whole will have a common motive to invade the rights of other citizens; or if such a common motive exists, it will be more difficult for all who feel it to discover their own strength and to act in unison with each other.[88]

What is conspicuous here by its absence is any discussion of, or any significant reliance on, the specific legalistic mechanisms established by the Constitution.[89] To be sure, those mechanisms were discussed at length and argued for elsewhere in *The Federalist Papers*. Nonetheless, Federalist 10 can be understood to suggest that in the final analysis the best protection against tyranny lies not so much in these specific legal devices, but rather in the people themselves as they pursue complex and competing interests and visions in an extended Republic.

In a similar vein, although Madison argued at length in Federalists 45 and 46 that power would not gravitate from the state governments to the national government, he also quickly and quietly conceded that such a development just *might* occur. But if a shift in power should happen, that would be because the people favored the change; and the people would adopt such a position only if it turned out that the accumulation of national power was in fact desirable:

> If, therefore, . . . the people should in future become more partial to the federal than to the State governments, the change can only result from such manifest and irresistible proofs of a better administration as will overcome all their antecedent propensities. And in that case, the people ought not surely to be precluded from giving most of their confidence where they may discover it to be most due.[90]

In sum, although Madison may have believed that the specific features of the Constitution were in accordance with reason, he also understood that the best laid plans often go astray. More than most of his fellow Fedralists, Madison could frankly acknowledge that the Constitution partook of the manifold imperfections of all human endeavors. But the crucial practical question was whether the Constitution was better than the alternatives; Madison believed that it was.[91] More generally, Madison appears as a man who admires the notion of governance in accordance with reason as an enlightened ideal, who dutifully does what he can to give substance to that ideal, but who is also resigned to the fact that human nature is not so constituted as to permit any very strong confidence that anything worthy of the name of "reason" will in fact rule. In the final analysis, the safety net in which he trusted with genuine hope, though hardly with absolute confidence, was the unruly give-and-take of partisan, pluralistic politics.

Given Madison's and the founders' acute consciousness of the dark side of human nature, what else could they realistically expect? The framers tried in a cautious way to consolidate the conclusions of reason in a legal document they called the Constitution. But it would take a forgetting—or a repudiation—of the framers' grim awareness of human nature, and indeed of their notions about Nature itself, before "reason" could expand to claim its full dignity, or to manifest its full pretensions. How that expansion came about is the subject to which we turn now.

PART II

REASON IN MODERN CONSTITUTIONAL DISCOURSE

The principal actors at the Philadelphia convention viewed their effort to embody reason in the Constitution as an experiment that had no predecessors and, if it should fail, would probably have no successors. One might surmise, therefore, that the breakdown of the framers' central strategy would lead to the abandonment of their aspiration to bring human affairs under the governance of reason, at least within this constitutional system.

But the surmise would be badly mistaken. On the contrary, modern constitutional discourse exhibits, at least on the surface, an essential continuity with the framers' project and document. The discourse still invokes, and claims to be constrained by, the constitutional text. Most important, it still consistently purports to be guided by "reason." Indeed, especially in legal scholarship, modern aspirations for and claims about the essential role of reason in constitutional law, far from receding, have become even more expansive.

These more capacious claims are natural enough, and at least in one sense they may seem plausible and perhaps inevitable. For the Enlightenment, as we have seen, "reason" implied "thinking for yourself"—shaking off the shackles of authority and tradition. But from our standpoint the framers' conception of their constitutional project may seem to have fallen short of that ideal—or even to have betrayed it—in two different ways. The first has already been noticed: The framers' effort to codify reason in a text that later generations would for the most part simply follow, not perpetually rethink, meant that full-blooded reason was to be banished from active participation in governance almost as soon as it had been admitted. Later generations were not to partake of the immediate presence of reason.

Second, and even more fundamental, the founding generation's notion of reason as a capacity for discerning the plan implicit in Nature may strike modern observers as a singularly modest and even servile conception—not to mention an untenable one. Desiring and grandly proclaiming intellectual autonomy, the generation of Jefferson dared go only half-way. The highest goal that generation could conceive of was to comprehend and conform to a preestablished providential plan. The founders thus repudiated Authority and Tradition but bowed before Nature. Abjuring religious superstition, they remained abject before God.

So there is something ironic, maybe even unseemly, in Jefferson's denunciations of "servile prejudices under which weak minds are servilely crouched."[1] The modern thinker is likely to demand a kind of "reason" that is not so fettered. In the exercise of reason we cannot be bound by any preexisting plan handed to us by Nature; we must be free to design and construct for ourselves.

In short, in its commitment to reason modern constitutional discourse amounts to both a continuation and an extension of the framers' project. Like the common law that "works itself pure," modern constitutional thinkers are even more purely devoted to the framers' aspiration than were the framers themselves. Or so it may seem.

It would nonetheless be a mistake to conclude that the relation between the framers' project and modern constitutional law has been one of placid continuity, or of stable and steady maturation. In fact, in pursuing the ideal of governance by reason, modern constitutional discourse has encountered serious obstacles. The principal challenges are associated with two major difficulties, which might be described as the legalistic text *and the* collapse of Nature, *and each has left its mark on modern constitutional discourse.*

The first of these challenges is in one form or another a constant topic in constitutional debates, and so for all of its importance and intricacy, it can be dealt with summarily here. The textual problem and the modern response to it will thus be the subject of the brief chapter that immediately follows.

The second difficulty presents more serious and more subtle problems. These will be the focus of discussion in the ensuing chapters.

CHAPTER FOUR

From the Legalistic Constitution to the Constitution of Principle

*A*s we have seen, the framers' ideas about the role of reason in governance led them to draft a document with a particular character: Their Constitution was legalistic, reflecting a focus on institutional structure with the end of carefully defining and limiting the *powers* of various governmental institutions. As the legalistic, limited powers strategy proved ineffectual, however, it was natural for constitutional thinking to shift to different strategies, often more oriented to the elaboration of fundamental *rights* and *principles*. But the document that judges, lawyers, and citizens had inherited was not designed for such strategies. So a major challenge to the constitutional project has been to pursue one set of strategies for bringing reason into governance while attempting, or at least purporting, to adhere to a document self-consciously designed with a different strategy in mind. A good deal of modern constitutional theory and controversy arises out of this disjunction.[1]

A New Constitution?

Perhaps the most straightforward response to the difficulty might have been to do what the founders did in 1787 when the then-existing constitution—the Articles of Confederation—seemed inadequate; the nation might have chosen to design and adopt a new constitution more suited to the newer approaches that now seemed more promising. This time around, more than a few impatient hours might be devoted to selecting the rights that would receive special constitutional protection and to designing remedies and enforcement mechanisms for these rights; and the conclusions of such deliberation might be expressed in terms that would not leave subsequent generations forever baffled about just what *this* constitution's framers were trying to do. For example, the novel and monumental institution whereby a handful of unelected judges—or even one— can nullify laws enacted by a large body of duly elected representatives would not be left to be inferred from an unobliging text and then perpetually argued about by jurists and constitutional theorists. Instead, the validity and scope of the practice would be explicitly provided for.

For all its abstract simplicity, though, this alternative was never realistically possible. Designing and adopting a new constitution would be a gargantuan political task—one that would make goals such as balancing the federal budget seem minuscule by comparison. There is no likelihood that our political community could carry out this task at all, much less do so calmly and wisely. The closest we have come, in fact, is in adopting several amendments establishing new rights and, most important, one amendment—the Fourteenth, of course—with language sufficiently supple, or sufficiently obscure, that it has been able to supply the raw material for the judicial development of numerous rights and principles. But a deliberate overhaul from the foundations, though often proposed,[2] has never been seriously attempted. Indeed, the Fourteenth Amendment itself was ratified during a unique historical period in which a decisive number of states could be forced more or less at gunpoint to accept it, and even then the amendment was adopted on the strength of repeated assurances (now most often studiously forgotten) that it would *not* alter the federalist structure of government in any fundamental way.[3]

In short, the framers were almost surely right about one thing: The opportunity to deliberately design a constitution from scratch amounted to an unprecedented historical privilege that later generations would not enjoy.

Reconceiving the Constitution

So in the absence of a new constitutional text, we have simply had to work with the old one. But in order to support new strategies, constitutional lawyers and judges have found it necessary to reconceive the Constitution.

Common Lawyers and Philosophers

Not surprisingly, they have reconceived it in different ways. One sort of reconception tends to view the Constitution more or less as a starting point for familiar kinds of incremental or common law reasoning. A more ambitious reconception—and one to which we will be paying closer attention—regards the Constitution essentially as an authoritative source of moral and political values to be developed through more philosophical reasoning.[4]

These reconceptualizations are not inevitably antithetical; indeed, they might even complement each other, as James Stoner suggests they did in the Philadelphia convention itself.[5] Still, the different conceptions reflect fundamentally different visions which in turn lead to different conceptions of constitutional reason. The first strategy prescribes the kind of unpretentious reasoning that common lawyers have long practiced—primarily arguing from precedent and analogy—and typically contemplates a gradual, almost imperceptible development of constitutional law. Judicial decisions often adopt this method of presenting their conclusions, largely limiting themselves to discussion of what the precedents are said to require. The second reconceptualization, by contrast, is markedly more ambitious; it makes constitutional discourse less a kind of reasoning distinctive to lawyers, and more a branch or subset of philosophical reasoning generally.[6]

Despite these seemingly radical differences in orientation, however, the divide between "common law" and "philosophical" constitutional discourse is also elusive, in part because many judicial decisions and scholarly writings are a blend of both. And it might be that these styles of reasoning are not so much opposites, but rather opposing ends of a continuum.

Even so, different judges and scholars plainly gravitate to different ends of that continuum. In *Bowers v. Hardwick*,[7] for example, in which by a 5–4 vote the Supreme Court upheld a Georgia statute that the state construed as prohibiting homosexual conduct, both the Justices in the majority and those in dissent talked about precedents as well as about the broader unifying themes or political-moral principles that ostensibly ran through those precedents. But the majority opinion by Justice White was plainly more cautious about venturing beyond the narrow holdings of earlier cases, whereas the dissenting opinion by Justice Blackmun was much more eager to leap from those precedents to a more general "right to be let alone."[8]

Similar differences, even if they are only differences in degree or direction, are evident in constitutional scholarship. Some scholars defend a careful, incremental, common law approach to the Constitution.[9] Others are impatient with such reasoning. They may regard it as practically unhelpful: Although moving slowly—small step by small step—may *seem* prudent, how can we know without a vision of the overall landscape whether our small steps are taking us in a desirable direction? Thus, in *Private Property and the Constitution*, Bruce Ackerman devoted his first few critical pages to demonstrating the incoherence and inefficacy of "takings" conventions and precedents before going on to advocate a more ambitious discourse based on "scientific policymaking" informed by a "comprehensive view."[10]

Critics of the unpretentious common law approach may also argue that it is unworkable, and indeed hypocritical. In order to decide whether the instant case is in relevant respects more like Precedent A, cited by the plaintiffs, or Precedent B, cited by the defendants, isn't it necessary to be clear about the comprehensive philosophy or package of principles that informed (or, more to the point, *should have* informed) those earlier decisions?[11] Isn't a judge who refuses to acknowledge this essential element simply fooling his audience—and perhaps himself? In this vein, Ronald Dworkin argues not only that judges *do* rely on moral reasoning in reaching decisions but that "they have no real option but to do so"; judges who try to disguise their moral convictions in the modest language of text and precedent are guilty of "a costly mendacity."[12]

Fortunately, we need not resolve the dispute between constitutional common lawyers and constitutional *philosophes* here. The point of drawing attention to the distinction is to explain that the following discussion will concern itself mostly with the "moral reasoning" strand of constitutional thought, albeit for a reason different than those given by scholars like Ackerman and Dworkin. We are interested in the moral reasoning strand not because it is self-evidently either preferable or inevitable, but because that approach is the one most expressive of the aspiration that is the subject of this book—the aspiration to liberate human affairs from the tyranny of force and fortuity and subject those affairs instead to the governance of reason.

This is not to say, of course, that analogical arguments and lawyers' debates over which precedent is more like the instant case are unworthy of the label "reason."[13] Whether such argumentation constitutes "reason" presents a question that might easily degenerate into a sterile semantic dispute. The important point is only that this is not the kind of governance by reason that, at least in its sanguine moments, the constitutional project has aspired to establish. From the perspective of Cartesian rationalism, as Ernest Gellner explains, "[c]ultural accumulation is irrational; it is a blind process."[14] And what is important for our purposes is not to approve or disapprove that judgment, but merely to note that it *is* the judgment adopted by the Enlightenment aspiration to "reason." But the incremental, analogical reason of the common law is, at its core, a process of cultural accumulation.

To put the point differently, the framers were perfectly familiar with the common law system; many of them were in fact common lawyers. And the Constitution did not abolish the common law system, even if, as Craig Klafter argues, American lawyers of the period were in the process of transforming the common law to make it more in accord with notions of science and reason.[15] But the crucial point is that when the founders claimed that the Constitution was the most perfect form of government ever offered to the world, and that by means of the Constitution human governance would be regulated by reason *for the first time*,[16] they evidently intended to announce something more than a peaceful continuation of the common law system. It was not the incremental, case-by-case method of the common law that they counted on to redeem human affairs from force and fortuity. The framers contemplated a new reign of reason in some grander sense.[17]

Prudently or not, proponents of a modest, common law constitutionalism decline to join in this grander vision. Conversely, scholars like Ronald Dworkin, Bruce Ackerman, and Robin West evince a commitment to reason that resonates more fully with the Enlightenment aspiration. And if Dworkin, Ackerman, and West are especially vivid or extreme representatives of that aspiration—caricatures, some might say—still they are hardly unique. Constitutional law casebooks and classrooms rarely devote the bulk of their attention to tracing the links between all of the precedents that might arguably have been relevant to the case under consideration. And the landmark cases that dominate modern constitutional law—*Brown, Miranda, Griswold, Sullivan, Roe*—cannot plausibly be understood simply as natural products of the common law method, even if their subsequent elaboration and application have owed much to that method. So with all due respect to common law constitutionalism, it is the more philosophical or "moral reasoning" dimension of constitutional discourse, with its special emphasis on the elaboration of constitutional *rights* and *principles*, that will occupy our attention.[18]

The Constitution as a Repository of
Rights and Principles

In order to support the more ambitious style of reasoning, the Constitution cannot be merely a mundane legal document; it needs to be something more like a source of broad moral principles. Thus, in much contemporary thinking, the Constitution appears not so much as the technical legal instrument that its framers contemplated and that *Marbury* described, but rather as a source of, or a safe harbor for, broad constitutional values, norms, or rights. Textual details recede and give place to dialogue about underlying purposes and principles.[19] Robert Nagel observes that "[i]n large measure, constitutional interpretation has come to be the identification of a trace of some grand value in a particular provision and then the explosion of the meaning of the provision so that it stands for the grand value itself."[20]

In short, we have reconceived the Constitution to be just the kind of idealistic and explicitly aspirational document that its framers opted not to adopt. Just how this transmogrification was effected makes for a fascinating story— but one that is already quite familiar and need not be rehearsed in detail here.[21] One chapter of the story would tell about shifting interests or changing conversations: In this century, the primary attention of judges, lawyers, and theorists has been redirected to the most apparently open-ended of the Constitution's provisions. The shift is by now so ingrained that from our perspective it can be sobering, and sometimes puzzling, to remember that for well over a century the free speech clause lay essentially dormant,[22] that the establishment clause was effectively a dead letter from its inception until midway through the twentieth century,[23] and that in 1927 Holmes could refer to the equal protection clause as "the last resort of constitutional arguments."[24] Today these clauses and others conspicuous for their apparent lack of precise legal content—the due process clause, the Ninth Amendment—are overwhelmingly the focal points of attention in the constitutional community.

One is reminded of the man described by Lon Fuller who after eating a pair of shoes said that the part he had liked best was the holes.[25] But the shift in focus to the most vacant, or at least the most delphic, provisions of the text has helped modern lawyers and scholars to break loose from the older, legalistic Constitution. The more open-textured a provision is, after all, the more amenable it is to the view that it "speaks the language of fundamental principle,"[26] or that it "patently cannot be understood other than as an abstract moral principle."[27]

The reconception of the Constitution has also been assisted by distinctions worked out by scholars that permit modern decisions to be simultaneously connected to and detached from original notions and intentions. Ronald Dworkin's well-known distinction between the general *concept* embodied in the text and the specific *conception* that the enactors may have entertained but did not make authoritative is one such rationale.[28] Michael Perry accomplishes much the same result by distinguishing between two different phases of constitutional adjudication: *identifying a directive* contained in a constitutional text, and *specifying the meaning* of the directive in a concrete case.[29] In Perry's view, a constitutional directive represents a decision by the enactors "to privilege . . . some political-moral value or values. . . ."[30] And although Perry insists that judges are bound by the enactors' directive,[31] or by the "political-moral value" the enactors chose to privilege, judges are *not* bound to carry out the directive in precisely the way the enactors might have contemplated that it would be carried out. For instance, the fact that none of the enactors of the Fourteenth Amendment ever imagined that the provision would prohibit gender discrimination does not mean that a modern interpreter cannot properly construe it to have that consequence.[32] On the contrary, a constitutional directive leaves room for—indeed, requires—specification, which is a task that text and history cannot perform for us.[33]

These distinctions are by now so accepted that for some it is almost impossible to understand the Constitution *except* as a repository of basic principles-to-be-elaborated. Bruce Ackerman is hardly averse to controversy, but when he describes the Constitution as "a rich lode of principle"[34] he evidently does not intend to be provocative; on the contrary, he is simply reporting what everyone now understands. The by-now axiomatic character of this conception is manifest in Michael Perry's observation that "[t]he fundamental reason any part of the Constitution . . . was ratified is that the ratifiers wanted to establish . . . a particular principle or principles: the principle(s) they understood the provision to mean or to communicate either directly, by naming the principle, or *indirectly, by referring to it without naming it* [emphasis added]."[35]

The transformation of the Constitution is perhaps most clearly manifest in the writings of Ronald Dworkin and Robin West. Dworkin has long advocated a "vision of the Constitution as principle."[36] It is not that Dworkin cannot conceive of a different, more legalistic Constitution. He refers disparagingly to those who regard the Constitution as "a document with the texture and tone of an insurance policy or a standard form of commercial lease."[37] And he concedes that some constitutional provisions—the Third Amendment, for example, with its prohibition against the quartering of soldiers—might be merely legal rules rather than expressions of broad principle.[38] But Dworkin's attention flows almost entirely to those provisions which, precisely because they lack definite legal content,[39] can only be understood, he thinks, as expressing "broad and abstract principles of political morality"—principles whose "scope is breathtaking."[40]

Dworkin is also insistent about the kind of reasoning that is needed to interpret this Constitution of principle. Constitutional reasoning does not consist of "technical exercises in an arcane and conceptual craft,"[41] as in traditional common law argumentation; rather it requires interpreters to engage with "fundamental questions of political morality and philosophy."[42] Like it or not, no interpreter can avoid employing this kind of moral reasoning; judges who pretend otherwise are, as noted, guilty of "mendacity."[43] Still, judges are only the "princes" in law's empire. The more exalted role of "seers and prophets" must belong to philosophers, "if they are willing,"[44] because of their superior expertise in working out the meaning of the law's abstract principles.

Dworkin recognizes the less pivotal role of the text in this new conception. For instance, he expresses impatience with efforts to locate a "textual home" for controversial rights like the right to abortion. If a right is fundamental, then it is safe to assume that it can be hung on at least one textual hook, and probably several, in the Bill of Rights.[45] So if the Constitution *ought to* protect a particular right, then the Constitution almost certainly *does* protect that right.[46]

In a similar spirit, Robin West stresses that the Constitution is less a legal instrument than a "repository of the 'glimpses,' 'memories' and 'dreams' of the culture's moral ambitions."[47] Progressive constitutional faith must rest primarily on the Fourteenth Amendment,[48] which West regards as "a source of moral insight and a vision of the just society," or as "a tool for dismantling society's racist, misogynist, homophobic, patriarchic, and economic hierarchies."[49] This understanding transforms the constitutional text from a legal document—one whose "existence frustrates more than facilitates normative debate"[50]—to a far less authoritarian but more facilitative text. The facilitative Constitution is valuable primarily as a "source of insight"; it guides us in much the same way as "the writings of Aristotle, John Stuart Mill, John Rawls, and Roberto Unger."[51]

Is the Constitution Really "Principled"?

Of course, one can easily imagine objections to this view of the Constitution as a source of moral insight or as a repository of latent principles waiting to be elaborated by judges and other interpreters. Possible historical objections are apparent from the preceding chapters; it seems clear that the framers did not think they were adopting a set of abstract principles. Forrest McDonald observes that "[t]he notion that the design of the Constitution was to achieve a certain kind of society, one based upon abstract principles of natural rights or justice or equality or democracy or all of the above" is an idea that "has come into fashion only in the last few decades and has all but destroyed the original Constitution."[52]

Moreover, it is not obvious that even the most open-textured provisions *must* be read as expressing broad principles. Modern scholars like Bruce Ackerman or Ronald Dworkin often suppose otherwise; the Fourteenth Amendment especially is for them simply incomprehensible except as a statement of abstract principles. But compare that amendment's equal protection clause, for example, with the Declaration of Independence, a document with which the Reconstruction Congress was certainly familiar. "We hold these truths to be self-evident, that all men are created equal. . . ." No room for quibbling there: The Declaration stated "principles" if any political document ever did. Now look at the comparable provision in the Fourteenth Amendment: "[N]or shall any State . . . deny to any person within its jurisdiction the equal protection of the laws." The equal protection clause at least *sounds* like a different sort of expression—tamer, hedged, more lawyer-like, more merely practical. Such reflections might lead one to wonder whether after all the real difference between the First or the Fourteenth Amendments and other, more mundane provisions (such as the nine-year citizenship requirement for Senators, or the 35-year-old age requirement for the president) is not that the former in any discernible way state a different order or kind of proposition (*principles* as opposed to mere *rules*) but only that, whether from necessity or inept drafting or linguistic change, these clauses are today simply more obscure.[53]

Indeed, from a more detached perspective the modern inclination to suppose that if a constitutional provision is vague and without precise legal content then it must be stating a "principle" seems odd, to say the least. We would not normally conclude that because Bob is a bit fuzzy and Mary is articulate, Bob is therefore more "principled" than Mary. So why should that conclusion become valid if for Bob we substitute the equal protection clause (or the Reconstruction Congress) and for Mary we insert Article II, section 1, clause 5 (or the Philadelphia convention)? With all due respect, it seems clear that John Bingham, leading drafter of the Fourteenth Amendment, was neither as learned nor as lucid as James Madison. William Nelson makes the point tactfully but effectively: "Bingham also spoke with clarity on some occasions, although not in the debates on the Fourteenth Amendment itself."[54] Should Bingham be blessed for his muddledness by being elevated to the status of father of our leading constitutional principles?

On a more philosophical plane, one might question the ontological status or even the existence of the entities that constitutional lawyers and scholars so freely invoke for the purpose of loosening up the constitutional text. In what sense does a "concept" or a "conception" exist at all, such that a legislator or framer can enact one without approving the other? And what sort of thing could a "principle" be such that a legislature can approve a particular principle without understanding its content or its implications? What exactly has the legislature enacted in this situation? A Platonic form, or a partially charted chunk of "moral reality"?[55] Or is a "principle," or a "concept" or "conception," something more on the order of a psychological fact or "mental state"? Perhaps these entities are even less attached to an actual time and place than mental states are; they might be merely words. When we say, for example, that we are applying the same "principle" of religious freedom adopted by the framers even as we condemn practices that they embraced, what exactly is going on? Are we just playing a complicated language game, or engaging in a bizarre verbal subterfuge?[56]

The Necessity of the Principled Constitution

These sorts of historical and philosophical doubts—quibbles, perhaps—might serve at least to test the almost child-like faith in constitutional principles that many contemporary lawyers and scholars seem to exude. Ultimately, though, such questions probably will not dissuade the devotees of the model of principles; and perhaps that is after all as it should be. In a sense, such doubts merely reaffirm a point already made—that the Constitution as originally conceived, and subsequent amendments made in the spirit of the original conception,[57] were not designed to provide topics for an ongoing *discourse* of reason. They were intended, rather, to consolidate in writing the practical *conclusions* of reason.

But if the original strategy for employing reason in constitutional governance has largely broken down, as I have argued, then it may seem that a new strategy is indicated. And if that new strategy requires a different sort of constitution than the Constitution the framers designed, then perhaps we have no choice but to redirect the document we have to other uses, awkward though the adaptation may be. A person may in a pinch use a wrench to pound a nail, and if there is no other tool available then it may be accurate but also pointless to remark that the wrench was not actually designed for pounding. In fact, modern legal experience arguably proves that the Constitution *can* be treated as an open-textured repository of concepts and rights and principles, even if that was not exactly the function its framers contemplated.

So if history itself does not give us a Constitution of principles, then too bad for history. In this spirit, Bruce Ackerman revealingly acknowledges that it is only as "lived experience" gives way with the passage of years to "book learning" that the "particularistic" understandings held by the enactors of a constitutional provision fade from memory, thereby permitting the provision to be elevated to the status of a repository of general principles.[58] One can almost imagine a crew of modern constitutional theorists and judges returning from a hard day's work of battering the Constitution into a form suitable for contemporary use and reporting: "It isn't a pretty job; in fact, it's an awful mess. But the job has got to be done."

The overriding role of practical necessity in the transformation of the Constitution is acknowledged in Lawrence Lessig's recent call for "translation." Lessig argues that in order to maintain fidelity to the framers' overall vision, we must abandon cramped commitments to the constitutional text and engage in "translation"—that is, "construction aimed at fidelity to an original value rendered helpless by changed circumstances."[59] Translation entails departure from the legalistic Constitution: "[T]o be faithful to the constitutional structure, the Court must be willing to be unfaithful to the constitutional text."[60] Thus, Lessig castigates the modern Supreme Court for failing to see that fidelity to the framers' constitutional values may require "a kind of radicalism in interpretation,"[61] and he proposes what he regards as more promising doctrines for shoring up federalism.[62]

There is, to be sure, an irony in Lessig's criticism of the Court for failing to imagine new ways of preserving federalism. One might argue that the Court has long appreciated Lessig's "translation" insight more fully than he himself does, and has already adopted more creative and radical remedies than those he has thought to propose. After all, federalism per se was not the point of the Constitution, as Madison made clear enough.[63] The ultimate value, rather, was sound government that would protect natural rights. And as discussed in this chapter, the Court has already attempted—we need not say here whether it has succeeded—to "translate" *that* value by reconceiving the Constitution as a very different type of document—that is, as an open-textured repository of rights and principles. Nonetheless, Lessig's discussion of "translation" correctly points to the real basis—practical political necessity—for the transformation of the framers' legalistic Constitution into something more like a locus for constitutional discourse.

Proof of this point can be found in the fact that even those who resist such developments often end up by succumbing to the same necessities that drive their opponents. For instance, Robert Bork criticizes his opponents for extracting broad principles from the Constitution and then using these principles to justify results the enactors never contemplated.[64] The characterization is surely accurate, and perhaps Bork's adversaries would not even care to contest it. But in seeking to explain decisions that he himself favors but that deviate from historical intentions—*Brown v. Board of Education,* for example—Bork inevitably resorts to the same interpretive maneuvering.[65]

More forthrightly, Gerard Bradley defends originalist interpretation against what he regards as more present-oriented, less-constrained approaches, but the kind of originalism Bradley finds defensible rests securely in his acceptance of the Constitution of principle:

> The Constitution is not a collage of photographs of early national America. . . . The Constitution is comprised of principles whose practical import changes with time—as America changes—even as the principles remain the same. Indeed, many constitutional principles, historically recovered, are intrinsically dynamic. Others depend for their concrete application upon ever-changing circumstances.[66]

Indeed, it seems that thoughtful, conscientious originalists have little choice but to embrace this kind of Constitution. As Bradley points out, other versions of originalism are defective, in part because they render the Constitution unuseable for present purposes.

So it seems that nearly everyone today acknowledges that the Constitution *we* honor is a repository of concepts or principles—concepts or principles that are quite basic and general and, hence, in need of concrete content that can only be supplied by *us.* But this conclusion means that constitutional reason cannot be directed merely to *discovering* and then enforcing a meaning already in the Constitution. Reason necessarily assumes a less passive, more creative role.

Hardly anyone today denies this. Or rather, some critics like Bork may deny, but it seems that in practice they inevitably betray themselves. To be sure, almost without exception modern constitutional theorists still profess a kind of fidelity to the text. They typically insist (though their critics often remain unpersuaded[67]) that the requirement of a textual connection remains in force to constrain modern judges; an interpreter cannot justify just *any* result he might happen to like.[68] Still, the rights or principles or norms thought to be lurking in or emanating from the Constitution—equality, liberty, fundamental fairness, privacy—are sufficiently elastic that the textual constraints do not really chafe.

And though this situation may be worrisome from some perspectives—from the viewpoints, for example, of those who are concerned with things like majoritarian democracy, or "legitimacy," or rule-of-law predictability—the permissiveness of the open-textured Constitution is attractive insofar as it places few inhibitions on the free exercise of reason in constitutional discourse.

Remodeling Constitutional Reason

In sum, under decree of necessity the Constitution has been reconceived in a way that makes the exercise of reason possible while preserving at least the appearance of fidelity to the original text and project. But however necessary, this reconception has altered the meaning and the workings of reason in a fundamental way.

The alteration follows from the fact that although the open-textured Constitution does not significantly *inhibit* the workings of reason, it also does not to any significant degree *direct* the actual operations of reason: Insofar as the Constitution is open-textured it does not tell interpreters how to reason or what to conclude. So to the extent that modern constitutional discourse is to be an activity of reason, that reason must be supplied largely by the interpreters; it is not already consolidated in the text as it was supposed to be in the framers' scheme. As already noted, therefore, the reasoning that occurs in constitutional law merges to some degree with political and moral reasoning in general.

So far, so good. But at this point, the project of realizing reason in constitutional law must confront a subtle but potentially overwhelming obstacle: The viability of moral reasoning generally is currently under challenge. So if constitutional reasoning is a subset of political-moral reasoning, then the possibility of constitutional reasoning is likewise in jeopardy.

To put the point differently, if we have largely abandoned the framers' legalistic, "enumerated powers" constitutional strategy, we have also largely repudiated—or perhaps just lost touch with—the worldview that gave sense to their fundamental notions about "reason" itself.[69] And the obstacle that this more philosophical change poses to the project of governing human affairs in accordance with reason is more complicated, and more daunting, than the challenge of twisting a differently directed text to modern purposes. How constitutional discourse has tried to deal with that more fundamental obstacle is a subject that will be at the center of the discussion in the following chapters.

CHAPTER FIVE

After the Fall

Regulatory Reason

*B*y reconceiving the Constitution as an open-textured repository of principles and rights, modern theorizing has made room for the operation of a more free-standing reason that is loosely connected to but not inconveniently confined by a legalistic text devoted to a failed, "enumerated powers" strategy. The result, especially in academic discourse, is that to a significant degree constitutional reasoning becomes less a mode of thought peculiar to lawyers and more a subset of political-moral reasoning in general. The constitutional thinkers most committed to the governance of reason readily concede this fact, and indeed celebrate it. "The great constitutional clauses set out extremely abstract moral principles that must be interpreted before they can be applied," Ronald Dworkin maintains, "and any interpretation will commit the interpreter to answers to fundamental questions of political morality and philosophy."[1]

At this point, though, a different and more threatening difficulty arises. The merger of constitutional with moral reasoning occurs at a time when the possibility of moral reasoning has itself been placed in jeopardy by what I will call the collapse of Nature. This chapter begins by describing what that collapse entails and why it poses a challenge to the possibility of moral, and hence of constitutional, reasoning. The chapter then offers an exposition of the principal response of modern constitutional thought to this challenge; the response consists of what I will call "regulatory reasoning."

The Collapse of Nature

Recall from Chapter 1 that for the founding generation, reason was dependent on a particular understanding of Nature. As the product of a supremely wise Creator, Nature came with a built-in structure or design having both material and normative dimensions. And the human mind had been endowed by that same Creator with a faculty or capacity for discerning the design of Nature. This faculty or capacity was the positive component in what the founding generation called "reason." So moral statements, including statements about ethical or political principles or about rights, could be understood through reason by reference to this design.

Between the time of the founders and our own, however, the intellectual landscape has undergone a massive upheaval. In the intervening two centuries, the notion of Nature endowed with a built-in design and purpose has lost its plausibility, at least in academic discourse. Nature has come to seem more like raw material, not possessed of any inherent meaning, and upon which *we* must therefore impose an order or structure.

It is not necessary (fortunately, because it is also not possible) to explain here just when this change in worldviews occurred or what its causes may have been. Surely the transformation was both gradual and complicated. Perhaps the most obvious influence has been the rise of science, secularism, and atheism.[2] William Barrett observes that scientific materialism is "the pervasive current that flows around all modern philosophizing. That materialism need not be explicitly professed as a creed; it becomes the *de facto* philosophy of an era reaping great triumphs in the physical sciences and in technology. . . ."[3] As this scientific materialism or naturalism has come to seem axiomatic, thinking about the meaning of human life has necessarily changed. Bertrand Russell offered a characteristic if poignant expression:

> That man is the product of causes which had no prevision of the end they were achieving; that his origin, his growth, his hopes and fears, his loves and his beliefs, are but the outcome of accidental collocations of atoms; that no fire, no heroism, no intensity of thought and feeling, can preserve an individual life beyond the grave; that all the labors of the ages, all the devotion, all the inspiration, all the noonday brightness of human genius, are destined to extinction in the vast death of the solar system, and that the whole temple of man's achievement must inevitably be buried beneath the debris of a universe in ruins—all these things, if not quite beyond dispute, are yet so nearly certain that no philosophy which rejects them can hope to stand. Only within the scaffolding of these truths, only on the firm foundation of unyielding despair, can the soul's habitation henceforth be safely built.[4]

A different account of the collapse of Nature might focus on more ancient and in a sense opposite causes. A recent study by Louis Dupré suggests that the loss of the normative conception of Nature grows out of the nominalism of the Late Middle Ages. By emphasizing God's absolute power and freedom, philosophers like William of Ockham relieved divinity from the constraints of reason, and thereby dissolved the basis for believing that God and God's creation are commensurable with the operations of the human mind.[5] If Dupré's account is correct, then it took a very long time before the acid spill of medieval nominalism achieved its full corrosive consequences;[6] and by the time nominalism *did* achieve its effects hardly anyone realized that they were feeling the potent force of nominalism, or even remembered Ockham at all. But this is not to disparage Dupré's account: It seems that movements of human thought often *are* shamelessly erratic, tardy and undisciplined, not orderly or nicely linear.

What matters for present purposes is that a belief in normative Nature survived and prospered into the founding period—though omens of radical change were already evident[7]—but that by now such a belief has for the most part expired, at least for the time being and in influential sections of the culture. Just as the Jeffersonians took the cosmic design for granted and argued without embarrassment on the basis of this assumption, in modern legal and academic culture it is implicitly understood that such argumentation is out of bounds. So if a question about the continued existence of a species (say, the coelacanth) arises, no reputable scholar is likely to argue, as Jefferson cheerfully did with regard to the mammoth, that the creature *has to* exist because Nature would never allow any link in her work to be broken, and hence that empirical evidence on the question is superfluous.[8] Similarly, even the most ardent modern defenders of "rights," such as Ronald Dworkin, if asked for an account of how we got these rights and how we can know what they are, would not dream of responding as Jefferson did—that is, by asserting it to be "self-evident" that particular rights were conferred on us by "the Creator." This overall change in worldviews is fundamental; indeed, by one account the repudiation of normative Nature is the defining characteristic of modernity.[9]

So what does this change in the conception of nature and the cosmos do to "reason"? If reason is supposed to be a faculty for discerning the design in Nature, then when it turns out that there *is* no such design (or at least that we do not publicly acknowledge the existence of one), what is reason to do?[10] It is as if someone gave you a gadget designed to detect the presence of infra-red rays, or perhaps the universal ether, and then a scientist discovers that in reality such rays, or the ether, do not exist at all. Your gadget would be good for nothing. A like fate, it might seem, must have befallen our erstwhile faculty of "reason."

Reason in the Void

Some twentieth-century thinkers have drawn, even if they have sometimes then drawn back from, just this conclusion. A brief description of three such accounts,[11] different but converging on a common despair, may help to give a sense of the predicament in which the collapse of Nature has left moral reasoning.

Writing shortly after the close of World War II, Princeton philosopher W. T. Stace asserted that modernity is a product of a philosophical transformation that "though silent and almost unnoticed, was the greatest revolution in human history, far outweighing in importance any of the political revolutions whose thunder has reverberated through the world."[12] This revolution consisted of what I have here called "the collapse of Nature." The premodern world as Stace understood it was permeated by "the presupposition that there is a cosmic order or plan and that everything which exists could in the last analysis be explained in terms of its place in this cosmic plan, that is, in terms of its purpose." The cosmic plan and purposes, in turn, reflected "presumably the purposes of some overruling mind."[13] This worldview was shared by Plato and Aristotle, by the medieval Christian world, and indeed by other major religions as well, such as Hinduism and Islam.[14]

But modern science had overthrown this conception of Nature, not so much through particular discoveries or specific theories such as Darwinian evolution, but rather by providing "a new imaginative picture of the world. The world, according to this new picture, is purposeless, senseless, meaningless. Nature is nothing but matter in motion. The motions of matter are governed, not by any purpose, but by forces and laws." Faith in a cosmic plan, we now understand, was "the Great Illusion." To be sure, even in the wake of this revolution some people believed that "the world can go on just the same as before, as if nothing had happened." But this attitude was "shallow." In fact, the loss of faith in a cosmic plan signaled "the ruin of moral principles and indeed of all values."[15] Perhaps unconsciously echoing the Preacher of Ecclesiastes,[16] Stace opined that "[i]f the scheme of things is purposeless and meaningless, then the life of man is purposeless and meaningless too. Everything is futile, all effort is in the end worthless."[17]

True, there are occasional signs of a revival of religion, but religion cannot flourish in a purposeless universe.[18] The same verdict holds for the idealistic philosophies that have sometimes arisen to offer support for moral values. Such philosophies reflect "wishful thinking. They were born of the refusal of men to admit the cosmic darkness. They were comforting illusions within the warm glow of which the more tender-minded intellectuals sought to shelter themselves from the icy winds of the universe."[19]

There were also those who believed the crisis might be resolved by applying science to social problems, but Stace explained that this hope was "utterly naive."[20] At points Stace also seemed to imply that philosophy was powerless to address the crisis:

> No one any longer effectively believes in moral principles except as the private prejudices either of individual men or of nations or cultures. This is the inevitable consequence of the doctrine of ethical relativity, which in turn is the inevitable consequence of believing in a purposeless world.[21]

From deep within the abyss of despair, though, Stace somehow managed to pull back. On second thought, it was *possible* (though his discussion to that point would seem to have said otherwise) that "[p]hilosophers and intellectuals generally . . . [might] discover a genuine secular basis for morals. . . ." The general public probably would not understand this philosophy, if it ever developed; even so, the philosophically uninitiated just might be redeemed "through the techniques of mass education." In any event, the urgent imperative was to face reality: Man must learn to live without illusions and yet—though by Stace's own account this hope would seem to be as empty an illusion as any that he had debunked—"retain his ideals, striving for great ends and noble achievements. . . . If he can, all may yet be well."[22]

So in the end, Stace, a philosopher with perhaps a touch of the same tender-mindedness that he mocked in others, did not entirely give up on reason; he was able to imagine—albeit dimly and in spite of his own argument—a role for philosophy in redeeming morality after the fall of Nature. Arthur Leff, a legal scholar, was less sanguine. In an agonized essay arguing for both the necessity and the impossibility of natural law as a basis for legal and moral reasoning, Leff's core point was that normative or moral statements are always dependent upon an evaluator. "[A] good state of the world must be good *to someone*. One cannot escape from the fact that a normative statement is an evaluation merely by dispensing with any mention of who is making it."[23]

The observation may seem obvious enough—and tame enough—but for Leff it had "terrifying" consequences; it meant that "there cannot be any normative system ultimately based on anything except human will." After all, if normative or moral statements must always presuppose an evaluator, then who can perform that role? Leff thought there were two possible answers. The evaluator could be God; if so, then morality and moral reasoning might be redeemed. Modern thought is characterized, though, by "the presumed absence of God"; consequently, "the only available evaluators are people. . . ." But then if people disagree on a moral or political-moral question, there is no independent standard or criterion to appeal to, or to reason from. Much of Leff's essay addressed responses to this problem proposed by people from Nozick and Posner to Rawls and Unger, and tried to show that the responses were in vain. The sort of reasoning that once seemed meaningful within a theistic framework might persist out of custom or desperation, but it no longer made sense. "It is of the utmost importance to see why a God-grounded system has no analogues. Either God exists or He does not, but if He does not, nothing and no one else can take His place."[24]

This gloomy diagnosis, Leff conceded, was "so intellectually unsettling that one would expect to find a noticeable number of legal and ethical thinkers trying not to come to grips with it, if its avoidance were at all possible."[25] Alasdair MacIntyre's book *After Virtue* can be viewed as, in part, a more thorough survey of the modern avoidance strategies alluded to by Leff. In the premodern world, MacIntyre explains, moral reasoning was grounded in assumptions about a natural order—the Aristotelian belief in a "metaphysical biology" that endowed human beings with a *telos* or natural proper end, or the Stoic and Christian belief in a providentially backed cosmic order, or a Thomistic synthesis of classical and Christian views. Within these frameworks, "there is a fundamental contrast between man-as-he-happens-to-be and man-as-he-could-be-if-he-realized-his-essential-nature. Ethics is the science which is to enable men to understand how they make the transition from the former state to the latter."[26]

But with the collapse of belief in a normative natural order and consequently of a human *telos* or natural end, this understanding of morality ceased to make sense, and the kind of moral reasoning generated by it also lost its efficacy. What MacIntyre describes as "the Enlightenment project" attempted to fill the void by reestablishing morality on modern and secular foundations. MacIntyre analyzes the project's successive unsuccessful attempts to restore moral reasoning by replacing the discarded term in the moral equation—that is, the notion of an essential human nature or *telos*—with something else: first, with passions and desires (Hume and Diderot), then with formal reason (Kant), then with individual choice (Kierkegaard), then with intuition (G. E. Moore).

Each of these attempts was a response to the failure of the previous attempt. And the consequence of the cumulative failure was emotivism—the position that "all moral judgments are *nothing but* expressions of preference, expressions of attitude or feeling," that "moral judgments, being expressions of attitude or feeling, are neither true nor false," and that "agreement in moral judgment is not to be secured by any rational method, for there are none."[27]

Although he criticizes emotivism and emphatically denies it any universal validity, MacIntyre also concedes that emotivism is the characteristic position of *our* time. Indeed, given what he argues was the inevitable failure of the Enlightenment project, short of some revival of a viable conception of or replacement for Nature, we have no satisfactory alternative to emotivism. To be sure, our emotivism is often disguised in what on the surface look like rational moral arguments—often quite intricate ones. But these arguments are not grounded in any overall framework that we accept, and consequently when pressed our arguments come to nothing; they are "inherited incoherent fragments of a once coherent scheme of thought and action."[28] So MacIntyre offers the following diagnosis:

> Up to the present in everyday discourse the habit of speaking of moral judgments as true or false persists; but the question of what it is in virtue of which a particular moral judgment is true or false has come to lack any clear answer. . . . [M]oral judgments are linguistic survivals from the practices of classical theism which have lost the context provided by these practices. . . . Such sentences become available as forms of expression for an emotivist self which lacking the guidance of the context in which they were originally at home has lost its linguistic as well as its practical way in the world.[29]

How Is Constitutional Reason Possible?

Not everyone will be inclined to resist this conclusion, of course. Emotivism, under that or other names (such as "subjectivism" or "ethical noncognitivism"), is in fact popular among both philosophers and lay people. Philippa Foot observes that moral subjectivism "for the last sixty years or so, has dominated moral philosophy in England, America, and other countries in which analytic philosophy is taught."[30] And in everyday discussions people commonly say that morality is purely subjective and that there is no use arguing about moral questions since there is no way to convince anyone[31] (although it is also true that people often *do* argue about morality and talk in ways that presuppose that morality is more than merely subjective[32]). In short, emotivism as a philosophy might simply be true, so to speak—even though the philosophy deprives particular moral judgments of the capacity to be true or false.

But although both the philosopher and the lay person might be content to accept this conclusion, the constitutional lawyer or scholar cannot be so complacent. After all, emotivism holds that morality is something that it is impossible to reason about in any meaningful way. So insofar as the central issues in modern constitutional debates fall within a subset of morality, or "political morality," emotivism poses a serious threat to the view that constitutional law and constitutional discourse are an embodiment of reason.

One might expect, therefore, that the diagnoses offered by thinkers like Stace, Leff, MacIntyre, and others[33] (or, looming in the background, Nietzsche[34]) would induce a sense of desperation in constitutional lawyers and theorists. Leff himself concluded that in constitutional disputes "we really have no choice but to be arbitrary,"[35] and he discerned in contemporary legal and ethical thought a "discontent verging on despair."[36] And indeed, some scholars *have* worried about the problem Leff discerned.[37] But if constitutional lawyers are afflicted by Leff's despair, by-and-large they hide it well.[38] Indeed, it seems that when they consider the matter at all,[39] constitutional lawyers and scholars are likely to regard the loss of the normative conception of Nature not as spelling the doom of reason, but instead as emancipating reason. Making a blessing out of apparent adversity, modern thinkers may view the collapse of Nature as a liberating event that enables reason finally to claim its full dignity.

In this spirit, Martha Nussbaum argues that the supposition that moral reasoning depends on a transcendent ground is not merely false but degrading; the supposition "betrays a shame before the human." Ridding ourselves of that supposition will thus relieve our reasoning of an annoying encumbrance.

> [I]f we really think of the hope of a transcendent ground as uninteresting or irrelevant to human ethics, as we should, then the news of its collapse will not change the way we think and act. It will just let us get on with the business of reasoning in which we were already engaged.[40]

This position is understandable and even, in one sense, almost inevitable. In modern times, after all, a commitment to reason has always reflected an "aspiration for autonomy," as Ernest Gellner observes, or "an overwhelming desire for self-creation."[41] But as Leff noted at the beginning of his essay, a law given by nature would not merely provide a basis for moral reasoning; it would also *limit* our freedom.[42] From our perspective, therefore, the collapse of Nature has had the consequence of removing a major constraint on our autonomy.[43] If there is no design built into Nature, then we are free to design for ourselves. Lacking a preestablished providential plan, we can construct our own plan.[44] At long last we can proceed, first cognitively and then politically, to explore and execute the variety of "ways of world-making."[45] So the collapse of Nature makes for an immeasurable expansion in the jurisdiction of reason.

It is an intoxicating vision. But central questions remain unanswered. What does it mean in this liberated context to appeal to "reason"? If we have no choice except to construct a social order to our liking, then is there now any difference between "reason" and its antagonist from former days—a character or faculty often called "will"?[46] And if so, what exactly *is* the difference? In short, we must still address the pressing question: In the absence of Nature, what does it mean to "reason"?

This is a broad question that might lead us in a variety of directions. Fortunately, we need not consider all of the possible answers to this question. In fact, from among various alternatives, constitutional discourse has by-and-large adopted one kind of general response to the question; for attractive and understandable reasons it has embraced an approach that I will call "regulatory reason." In the discussion that follows, therefore, I will not pretend to address the whole of modern moral philosophy—any such effort on my part would be merely foolhardy—and will focus instead on this characteristic species of moral and legal reasoning.

The Modern Response—Regulatory Reason

What regulatory reason entails and why it is so attractive can best be understood by first considering how constitutional discourse has come to adopt this position.

The Constitution of Moral Conventions

Start by recalling MacIntyre's diagnosis of our current situation. The collapse of Nature, or of the classical worldview with its theistic and Aristotelian elements, left moral reasoning in the lurch, and the Enlightenment project has failed to reestablish moral reasoning on a sound secular basis; hence, emotivism is the characteristic position of our times. MacIntyre concedes the obvious—that "[u]p to the present in everyday discourse the habit of speaking of moral judgments as true or false persists"—but he argues that this habit is unsupported by any coherent framework that would give sense to moral talk.

This diagnosis confronts the ethical philosopher with a serious challenge—a challenge that philosophers have tried to meet (or perhaps, as Leff surmised, evade) in a variety of ways. For their part, judges and constitutional theorists usually have not attempted to meet the challenge directly and on its own terms. Instead, they have tried for the most part to exploit the cultural phenomenon that MacIntyre acknowledges—that is, the persistent "habit of speaking of moral judgments as true or false." It might turn out that this persistent habit, whether or not well grounded philosophically, is good enough for constitutional purposes.

MacIntyre concedes, in other words, that although moral philosophy and moral reasoning may be in a predicament, *moral beliefs* continue to flourish. Some moral beliefs are common within our society; we sometimes call these common beliefs, together with the social practices informed by them, moral "conventions." So leaving questions of truth or validity aside, perhaps those beliefs or conventions themselves provide all that the constitutional lawyer or theorist needs to work with.

The suggestion is attractive for several reasons. First, it seems compatible with much in our legal tradition. In interpreting the Constitution and especially in giving content to its more open-textured provisions, Supreme Court justices have often appealed, sometimes explicitly, to moral conventions—to the "traditions and collective conscience of our people"[47] or, somewhat more narrowly, to the "canons of decency and fairness which express the notions of justice of English-speaking peoples"[48] or, more narrowly still, to the "compelling traditions of the legal profession."[49] In addition, moral conventions are surely real, even if amorphous, and to some extent knowable; we learn about them sometimes from surveys and polls but most often from reading the newspaper, watching television, talking with friends and colleagues and neighbors. Filling in the content of the open-textured Constitution by looking to widely accepted moral conventions may also seem nicely democratic; it is after all "the people" who thereby supply the meaning of their supreme law. So it is not surprising that, as Sotirios Barber observes, the Supreme Court's "liberal defenders agree with its New Right enemies that constitutional words and phrases like *justice, equal protection,* and *due process* refer not to real things . . . but to subjective or conventional beliefs."[50] Sanford Levinson puts the point more generally: "'Truth' may continue to be a word within modernist culture, but only as a synonym for culturally shared conventions."[51]

Despite this across-the-board appeal, the resort to convention as the basis of constitutional reasoning generates serious and familiar objections, only two of which need be mentioned here.[52] The first objection is that conventionalism does not initially appear to provide much of a role within constitutional discourse for "reason"—or for any class of experts who profess to specialize in "reason." Ascertaining moral conventions appears rather to call more for simple observation, or perhaps for sociological research, than for philosophical reflection or scholarly argument. If the content of constitutional principles or rights is to be supplied by the moral conventions or beliefs of the people, in other words, then it seems that in difficult constitutional cases we would be better off consulting George Gallup—or, for that matter, Marge and Homer Simpson—than Laurence Tribe or Kathleen Sullivan or Ronald Dworkin. Indeed, we would be better off consulting *almost anyone* rather than the people whom we typically regard as our leading constitutional scholars. After all, how would academicians who spend their time hanging out in Ivy League lecture halls or hobnobbing at high-level scholarly conferences have any idea what "the people" think?[53]

A related objection points out that even if conventionalism leaves constitutional reason with some role, that role would seem to be a very passive or even reactionary one. Typically we have supposed that constitutional reason is somehow supposed to scrutinize and pass judgment on conventions, or on laws enacted in accordance with those conventions. But if the content of constitutional principles or rights is determined *by* conventions, then it seems that constitutional law would be limited to approving the status quo on the ground that it is in accord with convention or, worse yet, emulating the *Lochner* era Court by invalidating progressive measures on the ground that they deviate from convention. Do we have a convention of racial segregation? Well, then laws supporting a "separate but equal" regime would be in accord with the Constitution, while laws prohibiting racial discrimination might be invalid because they depart from convention-laden constitutional principles.[54]

These difficulties suggest that despite its initial appeal, the proposal to use moral conventions as the basis for reasoning about constitutional rights and principles at least needs to be refined. Somehow conventions need to be disciplined—subjected to "reason." The suggestion *sounds* sensible enough, and indeed familiar enough. After all, Enlightenment proponents of reason contemplated that a principal function of reason was to scrutinize and discipline traditions and conventions.

But the Enlightenment proponents knew, or thought they knew, what this meant: Reason would discern the design implicit in Nature and evaluate conventions by reference to that design. Today we can recite the same words—"Moral conventions and traditions cannot be accepted blindly; they must be tested by reason"—but, having lost Nature, we cannot mean the same thing. So what might we mean instead?

True Conventions?

One possible answer suggests that reason must scrutinize existing conventions to determine whether they are morally correct—or perhaps, though some will squirm at the word, "true"—by reference to some objective moral reality ascertainable by reason. In the last decade or so legal theorists like John Finnis, Michael Moore, and Michael Perry have begun to try to rehabilitate the position of natural law or moral realism toward which this suggestion gestures,[55] but their view is at this point very much a minority academic position. In judicial discourse "natural law" has been used more as an epithet to assail decisions a judge dislikes[56] than as a constructive or favored position, and the political controversy surrounding the charge that Supreme Court nominee Clarence Thomas had endorsed a natural law philosophy suggests that this attitude of hostility has not substantially softened. Lloyd Weinreb's assessment, though exaggerated, is nonetheless revealing:

> [T]he blunt truth is that . . . [natural law] is a curiosity outside the mainstream, regarded mostly as a side-show and not to be taken very seriously. Defending natural law as philosophy, one becomes accustomed to seeing a wry smile on the face of listeners, as if one were describing a private and somewhat peculiar hobby.[57]

Moreover, it seems highly unlikely that in practice the courts *could* adopt a natural law or moral realist approach to constitutional reasoning anytime soon simply because, as critics from John Ely to Jeremy Waldron have pointed out, modern natural lawyers have thus far been unable to supply any distinctive and useable natural law epistemology.[58] Thus, even if the justices wanted to reason like natural lawyers, it is not clear how they would go about doing that.[59]

For present purposes, these observations seem a sufficient response to the proposal that constitutional discourse should adopt a natural law or moral realist approach for examining moral conventions. Whether natural law theorists *could* develop a useable method of reasoning and, if so, whether judges and constitutional lawyers should then adopt that approach present complicated questions that need not be settled here. But there is, I think, reason to be skeptical. Though it seems unnecessary to rehearse the analysis in detail, Russell Hittenger has argued in essence that the modern natural law project is misguided to the extent that it tries to have a natural law without Nature.[60] I have elsewhere made a similar argument.[61] By this view, in other words, modern natural law talk is another instance of the phenomenon described by MacIntyre; it amounts to a fragmentary remnant of what was once a coherent form of moral discourse—but one that no longer makes sense given the collapse of Nature.

If this objection is correct, then it would follow that natural law is incapable of guiding constitutional discourse, at least within our current intellectual framework. But even if the objection is misconceived, the fact remains that natural law has not made much headway within constitutional discourse. Instead, constitutional lawyers and theorists have by-and-large adopted a different approach—one that seems more attractive and manageable—to the limitations of straightforward conventionalism.[62]

Disciplining Conventional Morality

In an early essay responding to a famous argument by the English judge Patrick Devlin, Ronald Dworkin succinctly outlined this characteristic function of modern moral reasoning. Questioning a proposal to decriminalize homosexual conduct between consenting adults, Lord Devlin had argued that a community may properly act to protect its deeply held moral beliefs and conventions.[63] And Devlin had innocently proposed that the way to discover what the people believe is to ask them. It did not matter that popular moral beliefs might arise more from inherited prejudices or gut feelings than from philosophical reflection; what was important, rather, was that the beliefs were widely and deeply held.[64]

Devlin's position provoked a barrage of criticism. Unlike some of Devlin's other critics, however, Ronald Dworkin did not adopt the libertarian position that the law should not regulate morality. "What is shocking and wrong," Dworkin argued instead, "is not [Devlin's] idea that the community's morality counts, but his idea of what counts as the community's morality."[65] Contrary to Devlin, who wanted to take conventional morality straight, so to speak, Dworkin would filter the people's raw beliefs and feelings through a philosophical mesh; and only the refined and purified product would qualify as "the community's morality."

Most fundamentally, a belief would count as part of a "moral position" only if a person could "produce some reasons for it."[66] And from this basic imperative Dworkin deduced additional criteria for assessing raw conventional attitudes or beliefs. Perhaps the most significant criterion was consistency. The reasons given in support of a belief would not initially need to reflect any consciously held general theory. But they *would* need to be consistent with a theory or principle that could be developed through examination and reflection; inconsistent moral beliefs could not qualify as a moral position.[67] In addition, the grounds given for a belief would not count as reasons—and thus would not elevate the belief to the status of a moral position—if they were based on "prejudice," or on "a personal emotional reaction," or on "rationalization," or if they merely reflected a "parroting" of the beliefs of others.[68]

In sum, while community morality was grounded in actual beliefs and conventions and did not presuppose any ostensible "moral reality," ascertaining the content of that morality was still largely a job for thinkers, not for pollsters or empirically minded social scientists (or for people who like to gab over the fence or at the local pub). "Reason" still had plenty of work to do in whipping the community's unruly moral sentiments into shape—in rendering the babbling mass of popular opinions orderly and intellectually respectable.

This approach suggests a method or style of moral reasoning that has come to pervade modern discourse, as the rigorous rule of Reason is modulated into a practice of "giving reasons"—and thence of talking about what is "reasonable" or about what opinions and views "reasonable" people would hold.[69] In this style of moral reasoning, the material that the thinker or advocate works with consists of the opinions, intuitions, judgments, and conventions that we ourselves hold, or that are familiar to us from the ordinary activities of life—from talking with neighbors and friends, reading newspapers, watching television. These familiar moral beliefs provide the basic stuff of the argument, and the advocate never tries to invoke some independent moral reality or transcendent standard by which some of the beliefs could be judged objectively wrong or false. So his style is utterly different from that of, say, the Bible-thumping fundamentalist preacher who might declare, "You all believe such-and-such, but the word of God says you're wrong!"

At the same time, the modern advocate *reasons*. Or, if this characterization begs a question at issue, we can at least say that he *argues*; he does not merely *report on* commonly held beliefs, in the manner of a Gallup poll, or complacently accept those conventions. His argument is internal to a given set of beliefs; it plays off one belief against others, seeking to reach what he may call a "reflective equilibrium."[70]

So the advocate tries to convince you that your belief A is inconsistent with your beliefs B and C, or with belief D (which you hold even more firmly than you hold A); and you should therefore relinquish belief A *in order to be consistent with your own beliefs*. In effect, the advocate argues, "You *think* you believe A, but if you will reflect upon your larger set of beliefs you will see that in reality you don't. You should stop thinking that you believe A, not because I can show you on independent grounds that A is false—I can't—but because, deep down, *you don't really believe A*." This kind of moral reasoning is, as Charles Taylor observes, a way of "increasing . . . self-clarity and self-understanding."[71]

As an example of this kind of argumentation, consider Judith Jarvis Thomson's famous and fascinating argument for a right to abortion.[72] The argument begins with a hypothetical dilemma; and Thomson's description of the situation is essential to the argument:

> You wake up in the morning and find yourself back to back in bed with an unconscious violinist. A famous unconscious violinist. He has been found to

have a fatal kidney ailment, and the Society of Music Lovers has canvassed all the available records and found that you alone have the right blood type to help. They have therefore kidnapped you, and last night the violinist's circulatory system was plugged into yours, so that your kidneys can be used to extract poisons from his blood as well as your own. The director of the hospital now tells you, "Look, we're sorry the Society of Music Lovers did this to you— we would never have permitted it if we had known. But still, they did it, and the violinist now is plugged into you. To unplug you would be to kill him. But never mind, it's only for nine months. By then he will have recovered from his ailment, and can safely be unplugged from you."[73]

After describing this hypothetical situation, Thomson then crucially assumes that "you will regard this as outrageous."[74] And your outrage in turn implies a belief, she supposes, that you may rightfully remove yourself from the violinist, even if this means he will die. With this judgment in place, Thomson proceeds to consider possible differences between this situation and that of a pregnant woman who finds herself attached to a fetus, and she tries to show that these differences do not persuasively distinguish the situations. Hence the right to abortion.

Thomson's argument has provoked considerable debate. What is important for our purposes, however, is not whether Thomson's conclusion is sound, but rather how her argument works. The basic raw material from which the argument proceeds consists of the reader's outraged reaction to the violinist scenario. Thomson presumes that reaction; she does not argue for it, or seek to explain it, or supply any metaphysical account of what the reaction means. She never alludes to any "moral reality" that might have inspired the reaction, or that the reaction might represent a judgment about. Rather, she takes the reaction or intuition as given, and thereafter treats it as a basic and reliable indicator of the reader's moral views. She then uses the criterion of *consistency* to try to assimilate the abortion problem to the violinist scenario.

If the argument succeeds, Thomson will have brought the readers' judgment into line with her own without ever invoking any notion of Nature or moral reality. Rather, she will in effect have persuaded readers that *their own beliefs* require them to affirm a right to abortion. Implicit in the overall approach is the assumption that if a reader had previously endorsed a different opinion, that opinion must have reflected a failure fully to think through the reader's own beliefs, as manifest in the presumed reaction to the unfortunate plugged-in musician.

Although Thomson's argument is unusually creative, the basic *method* of argument reflected in her essay is perfectly familiar, as one would expect it to be. If there is nothing *outside of* our beliefs to appeal to (such as God—or Nature, understood normatively), then we naturally reason from *within* our beliefs. The transition to this method of reasoning is easy enough—indeed, from one perspective it is not even a transition—because of course in one sense people have been reasoning from within their beliefs all along. What else could they have done?[75] The only difference—at once huge and yet from a certain point of view inconsequential—is that while older forms of moral reasoning featured some objective referent that moral beliefs were supposed to be *about*—man's *telos,* or God's will or, more generally, Nature—in the more modern version this referent recedes from view, so that the moral beliefs themselves are no longer indicators or representations of moral reality; rather, they *are* the primary material of morality. We can describe this kind of reasoning, which regards social beliefs and practices as the basic material for argument but as subject to the discipline of reasoned discourse, as a kind of reason-regulated conventionalism or subjectivism.[76] Or, for short, "regulatory reasoning."

Why Regulatory Reasoning Is Attractive— the General Answer

We can at the same time give a general description of regulatory reasoning and also appreciate its appeal by considering how it addresses the problem posed by the collapse of Nature. For the founding generation, as we have seen, "reason" contained two components. The ancient and more positive component consisted of a belief in a Nature endowed with inherent design or meaning accessible to the human mind. The more modern or negative component comprised a deep distrust of tradition, authority, and revelation—or of what the Enlightenment mind regarded as ignorance and superstition—in favor of "thinking for yourself."

The modern problem for this view, arising from what I have called the collapse of Nature, is that the positive component of Enlightenment reason is no longer available. Modern regulatory reason responds to this loss by, first, preserving the negative component—that is, the suspicion of authority and tradition, ignorance and superstition, "prejudice" and "parroting"—and, second, substituting the moral beliefs and conventions we retain for the Nature we have lost. The role of reason is thus to examine existing beliefs to see if they are in fact based on "reasons," rather than on ignorance, prejudice, and tradition.

In this way, at least on the surface, modern reason looks very much like its eighteenth-century predecessor—the main difference being that moral conventions have now replaced Nature. So regulatory reasoning is attractive because it preserves a certain continuity with the "reason" that the Enlightenment tradition has taught us to respect. In addition, regulatory reasoning allows us to maintain, at least outwardly, the *practices* associated with Enlightenment reason—that is, the give-and-take of "reasons," and the examination of beliefs for inconsistency and unreflective bias—without committing ourselves to any dubious or constraining notion of purposes or limits "built-in" to Nature itself. So it seems that regulatory reason permits us, as Martha Nussbaum says, to "get on with the business of reasoning in which we were already engaged."[77]

Why Regulatory Reason is Attractive— the Institutional Reason

If regulatory reasoning is familiar and attractive in moral discourse generally, it is especially congenial in constitutional discourse. That is because the regulatory approach assigns to judges and scholars a role for which they might plausibly claim some competence, and does not ask them to be theologians or philosophers in a grander sense. Judges and legal scholars might appear frankly ridiculous if they were to claim some special gift for discerning the ultimate content and contours of moral reality (assuming there is any such thing), as natural law prescriptions seem to require. In the regulatory version, happily, no such pretension is called for.

The job of judges, lawyers, and legal scholars, rather, is skillfully to examine and cross-examine the moral conventions of society insofar as those conventions manifest themselves in law. What could be more lawyer-like than to interrogate an ostensible moral position in order to detect latent inconsistencies or underlying biases and prejudices? Lawyers and judges would seem to be exercising the same skills, using moral conventions as the subject matter, that they routinely employ with respect to, say, expert witnesses. This function also fits nicely with a political vision—one clearly evident in different forms in the work of the young Alexander Bickel, Ronald Dworkin, Michael Perry, and others[78]—of legislators who act impulsively, often under irrational political pressures, but whose decisions can then be reviewed more deliberately and dispassionately by judges and scholars who will determine whether the legislative decisions are in accord with "reason."

Regulatory Reason and Constitutional Discourse

So it is understandable that regulatory reason might appeal to constitutional lawyers and scholars. But *is* reason-regulated conventionalism in fact the characteristic position in modern constitutional thought? Two different sorts of considerations might provoke doubt. First, constitutional lawyers and scholars typically do not explicitly declare any allegiance to moral conventionalism; indeed, they sometimes use language suggestive of moral realism. Second, at least on the surface constitutional discourse displays a seemingly riotous pluralism, encompassing a huge diversity of constitutional provisions, convoluted doctrines, and multipronged "tests." This pluralism might make it seem unlikely that *any* particular method of reasoning could be described as "characteristic." We will consider each of these doubts in turn.

Coy Conventionalists, Reticent Realists

It is true that most lawyers, judges, or scholars who argue on moral issues do not explicitly describe themselves as "conventionalists" engaged in regulatory reasoning. Their silence on this point is hardly surprising. After all, most people who argue about moral issues do not explicitly associate themselves with *any* particular metaethical position, or with any particular method of reasoning; they simply dive into the dispute at hand and argue away. Moreover, there are good reasons why lawyers and other people do not, and perhaps *cannot*, confidently claim any such attachment.

In the first place, it would often be imprudent on purely tactical grounds for someone advocating a view on a specific moral question—a pro-choice or a pro-life view of abortion, say—to hold herself out as a "moral realist" or a "moral conventionalist." Since such labeling is for most rhetorical purposes unnecessary, why would an advocate gratuitously alienate those who are suspicious of that position, or at least of the label? It seems wiser simply to make one's argument, not to classify it.

But even for those who might want to identify with a position, under current circumstances it is not so easy to be either a full-fledged moral realist or a dyed-in-the-wool conventionalist. For reasons discussed above, would-be realists labor under a disability: Absent some intuitively plausible account of what "moral reality" looks like, even the claim to be a moral realist might be no more than empty verbalism.[79] In this vein, Ronald Dworkin's criticism—that self-styled moral realists speak in "incomprehensible metaphors" by talking as if morality is "part of the furniture of the universe, that it is really 'out there' in some way"[80]—seems not only rhetorically effective but, at least in some instances, well deserved.

But conventionalists must endure a corresponding affliction. Realists like Michael Moore have convincingly argued that our moral vocabulary implicitly but demonstrably presupposes a realist position.[81] The statement, "Slavery is unjust," is by its terms *about* something other than the speaker's (or the culture's) attitudes and beliefs. Thus, the statement implies but is not synonymous with "I believe slavery is unjust," and it does not even logically imply "*This society* believes slavery is unjust." The statement might have been made by a radical antebellum abolitionist, for example, or by a libertarian contemporary of Aristotle—John Stuart Mill transported back two millennia—who knew perfectly well that his society as a whole did *not* believe slavery to be inherently unjust. Even if a conventionalist can explain away these realist overtones, perhaps by describing them as stubborn vestiges of an older, now-abandoned worldview in which moral discourse *was* self-consciously realist in character, the morally serious conventionalist is always at risk of falling into, or at least *seeming* to fall into, an embarrassing incoherence in which his arguments constantly presuppose something that he refuses to affirm.

There are at present serious obstacles, in other words, to being either a moral realist or a moral conventionalist. So it is not surprising that most people, including most lawyers and legal scholars, do not overtly commit themselves to either position. In discussions about primary moral questions, consequently, these metaethical divisions tend to disappear from view; most advocates end up arguing in much the same way. For example, the *kind of argumentation* used in John Garvey's book *What Are Freedoms For?*[82] is not all that different from the kind of argumentation evident in Ronald Dworkin's *Freedom's Law* and other books. Based on Garvey's other writings and commitments,[83] one would suspect that he and Dworkin diverge significantly in their views on the nature of morality. And indeed the two scholars reach very different conclusions on particular moral questions—reflecting, one would surmise, their different assumptions about the nature of morality. But in their *method of moral reasoning* Dworkin and Garvey are remarkably similar.

Without alluding to or defining any independent moral reality, both start with what they take to be familiar moral intuitions and conventions. Then they proceed to explore inconsistences, propose possible but previously unnoticed unifying accounts, and in this way deftly direct the reader toward their preferred conclusions.

In short, much modern moral argumentation might implicitly or at its roots be either a kind of unproclaimed realism or an unconfessing conventionalism. Why then have I characterized the sort of moral reasoning practiced in constitutional discourse as a kind of "reason-regulated conventionalism"? The warrant for this description is that as a matter of practice, contemporary moral discourse treats conventions as the basic stuff of morality and moral argument. In contrast to other bodies of moral discourse, such as the classical and Christian discourses described by MacIntyre, the typical moral discussion today studiously avoids describing or referring to any objective or independent moral reality. Some modern advocates—Garvey, perhaps—might in fact be realists, of course, but for the most part they tactfully keep their realist commitments to themselves. Conventionalism, in short, is the working philosophy of public moral discourse, including constitutional discourse.

In this respect, Ronald Dworkin is exemplary. Once in a while Dworkin *sounds* like a moral realist,[84] or even gingerly labels himself a realist,[85] and so he has occasionally been classified as such.[86] But most critics have regarded Dworkin as more of a conventionalist or antirealist,[87] and with good reason.

A recent essay illustrates the difficulty. In "Objectivity and Truth: You'd Better Believe It," Dworkin expressly states, "I regard my view of morality as a 'realist' one. . . ."[88] But what does this assertion mean? Within the essay Dworkin repeatedly distances himself from all metaphysical claims that are often thought to accompany realism, explicitly disavows any attempt to define "a distinct moral dimension,"[89] and mocks the view that morality somehow exists "out there" or as part of "the fabric of the universe."[90] So in what sense are moral properties or judgments "real"? In what is perhaps the closest thing in the essay to an explanation of morality's ontological status, Dworkin asserts: "Morality is a distinct, independent dimension of our experience, and it exercises its sovereignty. We cannot argue ourselves free of it except by its leave.. . ."[91] One might read this statement to mean that morality consists of especially intransigent or entrenched subjective judgments that we have a hard time shaking off. But this reading would be inconsistent with much in Dworkin's essay, which repeatedly insists, for example, that slavery and genocide would be morally wrong whether anyone thought so or not. In sum, Dworkin *says* that morality is real and not merely subjective; but it is not "out there," and it is not just "in here" either. The reader is left to wonder just where (and what) morality is, and what Dworkin can possibly mean when he says that his view is a "realist" one.[92]

Most important, Dworkin never pretends to give an account of any moral reality that is not reducible to conventional or subjective values. So whatever Dworkin may believe in his heart, he is for practical and public purposes a working conventionalist, and his method of argument is a reason-regulated conventionalism, or regulatory reason. And in this respect, Dworkin's method is typical of constitutional discourse generally.

The Monolithic Pluralism of
Constitutional Discourse

A different sort of objection to the claim that regulatory reasoning character-izes constitutional discourse calls attention to the apparent pluralism of that discourse—to its diversity of doctrines, tests, and techniques. This pluralism might suggest that it is misleading to describe *any* particular kind of reasoning as the "characteristic" mode of constitutional discourse.

On the surface, it is true, constitutional discourse displays significant di-versity, with a different multipart test, it seems, for virtually every provision in the Constitution. This diversity is both real and significant, and we will have cause to consider it again later. But the diversity is in another sense deceptive, because underneath the complexity the essential method of judicial review fol-lows a strikingly monotonous course. Robert Nagel remarks that "across a sur-prisingly wide array of subject areas, the Court strikes the same chord again and again: the government must justify its rules by articulating a sufficiently important purpose and by demonstrating that the rule in some degree will ac-tually achieve that purpose."[93] This instrumentalist approach is often de-scribed in terms of "means-end rationality" or of "balancing."[94]

And even these labels are deceptive. In fact, the judiciary does not realisti-cally have the competence to determine whether a particular legislatively cho-sen means is efficacious for accomplishing a particular end, nor have the courts ever devised any method of actually balancing competing interests.[95] Moreover, if the courts *were* actually attempting to perform these functions, they would be justly vulnerable to the familiar charge that they are usurping a legislative function.[96] But although generalizations will be imperfect in this context, it seems that the rhetoric of means-end rationality and of balancing is for the most part an oblique way of describing a different function. In good Dworkinian fashion, the courts examine proffered legislative objectives to de-termine whether these objectives actually constitute eligible reasons support-ing a law.

Consider first the cases in which courts say that a law is not an efficacious means of achieving some objective articulated by the state, and hence is in-valid under a "rational basis" test. Such statements might seem to mean that although legislators or other government officials *thought* the law would pro-mote some desirable objective, they were simply mistaken in this judgment; the law therefore would fail a requirement of instrumental or "means-end" ra-tionality. So understood, the decisions invite an obvious rejoinder: Why should judges, who after all are both unelected and largely insulated from the practi-cal problems at issue, substitute their judgment on *that* kind of pragmatic question for the judgment of elected officials or specialized agencies? But on closer inspection, this seems a misreading of the courts' "no rational relation" language. When courts say such things, they typically do not mean that other branches have in good faith erred in a debatable choice of means to achieve legitimate ends. Rather, they suggest that because there is *plainly* or obviously no efficacious connection between a law and some articulated objective, the natural inference is that the law was in fact adopted for some other motive—one that the state declines to acknowledge because it is grounded in something like "prejudice" and hence that cannot "count," as Dworkin would say, as a reason at all.[97]

For example, in *Romer v. Evans,* a recent decision invalidating a Colorado anti-gay rights initiative, the state had advanced two objectives for the law—protecting citizens' freedom of association, and "conserving resources to fight discrimination against other groups"—and the Supreme Court responded by declaring that the initiative would not serve these objectives.[98] But the point of the Court's declaration was not actually to disagree with a genuine state decision on the instrumental efficacy of the law. Instead, the Court denied the law's relation to the legitimate objectives mentioned by the state in order to argue that the state had not in fact acted to promote those objectives at all; the law must have been based on other, illicit motives.

So the Court asserted "the inevitable inference that the disadvantage imposed is born of animosity toward the class of persons affected"[99]—that is, gays and lesbians. In short, the real problem as the Court presented the case was not that the Colorado law flunked a test of "means-end" rationality, but rather that, in the Court's view, the law was in fact based on "animosity" or prejudice, and hence was not supported by anything that would "count" as a reason at all.

A similar analysis would fit the Court's other rare decisions striking down laws on "rational basis" grounds. In *City of Cleburne v. Cleburne Living Center,* for example, the Court considered and rejected various interests that the city asserted in defense of a zoning decision denying permission for a home for the mentally disabled to locate in a residential area. But the point of the Court's discussion was not that the city had in good faith erred as a matter of means-end rationality, but rather that the interests asserted by the city were not genuine; the city's decision was actually motivated, the Court thought, by "an irrational prejudice against the mentally retarded."[100] Similarly, in *United States Department of Agriculture v. Moreno,*[101] the Court struck down a federal regulation disqualifying certain nontraditional families from receiving food stamps because the law, which the Court evidently thought was aimed at "hippies," was based on "a bare . . . desire to harm a politically unpopular group."

In many other cases, the courts use the language of "balancing." For example, controversies involving free speech, free exercise of religion, race discrimination, gender discrimination, and a variety of "fundamental rights" have all given rise to doctrinal tests which, although variously formulated, appear to require courts to decide whether the rights or interests burdened by a law are outweighed by an "important" or "compelling" governmental interest. Such language might suggest that in striking down a law a court is saying that a legislature, agency, or government official undervalued a legitimate interest or somehow miscalculated the sum of interests favoring and opposing the law.

And in some instances the courts may indeed be making this sort of "second guess" judgment.[102] Again, though, if the courts are in fact purporting to make this kind of cost-benefit calculation, an obvious question arises: Why do courts have the authority or the competence to second guess legislatures or agencies on *these* kinds of practical or instrumentalist questions?[103]

Once again, however, this view of "balancing" decisions seems to misunderstand what is happening in the broad run of cases. Rather, as perceptive scholars have shown in area after area, "balancing" and "heightened scrutiny" can more plausibly be understood simply as techniques for determining whether a law is actually based on something that qualifies as a legitimate "reason" at all, or is instead grounded in prejudice or ignorance. Thus, John Ely has argued that the "familiar doctrine of 'suspect classifications,' though not generally so understood, turns out on analysis to function as a handmaiden of motivation analysis."[104] Ely explains that although legislative motivation is often hard to ascertain, the objective to which a law is most closely related is likely to be the one that in fact drove the legislative decision.[105] Consequently, "special scrutiny, in particular its demand for an essentially perfect fit, turns out to be a way of 'flushing out' unconstitutional motivation"[106]— of showing, that is, that a law was not actually based on legitimate reasons at all, but instead was inspired by something like racial prejudice.

In a similar vein, Cass Sunstein has argued that a whole variety of seemingly diverse constitutional doctrines and tests are oriented to achieving a single purpose—ensuring that laws are in fact based on some legitimate reason or "public value," rather than on "raw political power" or "naked preferences."[107] The Constitution was designed, in Sunstein's view, to promote government based on reason; hence, "[t]he role of the representative is to deliberate rather than to respond mechanically to constituent pressures."[108] Laws based on "naked preferences" fail this requirement of reasoned deliberation. So when courts apply a form of "heightened scrutiny" under any of a number of constitutional provisions, they are not really supervising or second-guessing substantive legislative calculations about how to achieve desirable objectives, but rather are simply making sure that laws are in fact based on legitimate reasons. If the legitimate reasons articulated by the state in support of a law are genuine, then the courts will not interfere; the point of judicial scrutiny is to ensure that articulated reasons *were* in fact the real reasons.[109]

Sunstein observes this function at work in decisions under provisions as diverse as the dormant commerce clause, the privileges and immunities clause, the equal protection clause, the due process clause, the impairment of contracts clause, and the eminent domain clause.[110] A similar quest for impermissible motives—motives grounded in prejudice or a mere desire to silence or harm—is discernible under the free speech clause[111] and the establishment and free exercise clauses.[112]

In short, in a variety of different areas it seems that under cover of the language of "means-end rationality" and "balancing," the courts are simply carrying out the regulatory or supervisory function of demanding that the state give reasons for its actions, and then scrutinizing the officially supplied reasons to see whether they are sincere or instead are really covers for emotion or prejudice or the "parroting" of tradition. Running through the diversity of doctrines and decisions, in other words, is a pervasive commitment to regulatory reason.

This commitment is understandable, perhaps inevitable. The open-textured nature of the modern Constitution means that for the most part reasoning must be supplied not by the document itself but by those who "interpret" that document; and the collapse of Nature means that regulatory reasoning is just about the only kind available to modern legal interpreters. So if this kind of reasoning has become ubiquitous in constitutional discourse, we have no cause for surprise.

But to understand why regulatory reasoning is an attractive response to the collapse of Nature is not to say that regulatory reason can actually achieve the constitutional aspiration to bring reason into governance in a way that will protect human affairs against the tyranny of force and fortuity. In fact, the regulatory approach is also deeply problematic. The next chapter considers some central difficulties that afflict regulatory reasoning.

CHAPTER SIX

Constitutional Reasoning, Constitutional Sophistry

*I*n the preceding chapter I argued that modern constitutional discourse is by-and-large committed to a version of reason that may be called "regulatory reason." Although regulatory practices and techniques may look very much like the sorts of practices and techniques that have always been associated with "reason," the essential point of the exercise has changed. In the modern approach, the function of reason is not to ascertain the design inherent in Nature, as it was for the Jeffersonians and for countless predecessors going back at least to Plato. Instead, reason supervises or regulates conventional moral beliefs and practices, demanding that they be supported by "reasons," and judging whether this demand has been met by asking whether statements offered in support of such conventions are inconsistent or are expressions of prejudice or emotion or parroting.

In the aftermath of the collapse of Nature, this version of reason is powerfully attractive. Indeed, it just might be the only form of moral reasoning left to us (although we can leave that question for moral philosophers to debate). In any event, as a sort of moral cross-examination, regulatory reasoning is a form of thinking that the training and intellectual skills of lawyers and judges render them especially competent to perform.

But regulatory reason also suffers from serious defects—defects which show their effects in constitutional discourse. This chapter examines those defects and their debilitating consequences.

The Deficiencies of Regulatory Reason

Regulatory reason provokes two central objections. Both objections criticize reason's claim to be the regulator of the community's conventions, but in different ways. The first objection challenges the regulator's *authority*. The second challenges the regulator's *integrity*. After examining these objections, the discussion will consider their consequences for constitutional discourse.

By What Authority?

Both objections can be illustrated by reference to Dworkin's response to Devlin. Dworkin argued, recall, that not all beliefs about moral issues actually held within a community can "count" as "the community's morality," or as a "moral position." Rather, beliefs must be supported by reasons; and grounds that are inconsistent or that are based on prejudice, emotion, rationalization, or parroting cannot qualify as eligible reasons.

These restrictions provoke an obvious question: "Why not?" or, more bluntly, "Who says so?" For example, what is Dworkin's warrant for declaring that a belief based on "a personal emotional reaction" cannot "count" as a moral position?

A natural lawyer or moral realist might be able to supply an answer to that question. Perhaps drawing on the concept of normative Nature that in different versions appealed to thinkers from Plato to Jefferson, she might be able to paint a picture of a moral reality that we can apprehend through dispassionate intellectual operations but not through emotion. So a belief based on emotion would be disqualified because, at least according to this kind of realist theory, emotion does not give us reliable access to the objective reality that our moral statements seek to represent. In a different kind of realist theory, of course, the heart might be a *better* instrument than the head for ascertaining moral reality; in that case, it might follow that a belief should count as a moral belief only if it *is* supported by emotion.[1]

But a sophisticated conventionalist like Dworkin is at best noncommittal about the existence of any moral reality.[2] Moral *beliefs* exist; and they may be significant because they exist, or because people in fact hold them. But the conventionalist does not suppose that there is any independent, objective reality backing up the beliefs, and against which the beliefs might be judged true or false. It would be nonsensical, therefore, for a conventionalist to assert that intellect, or emotion, or any other faculty is the best way of ascertaining objective moral truth. If beliefs matter *because people hold them,* then beliefs generated by emotion, if they are sincerely held, should count for just as much as beliefs generated by more dispassionate causes. So it seems that a conventionalist who decrees that beliefs based on emotion are somehow inadmissible is simply imposing what is on his own assumptions an arbitrary restriction. Perhaps *he* is irritated by beliefs based on emotion. But why should anyone else care?

The same question can be asked of regulatory reason's other disqualifying criteria, such as prejudice or parroting. For the founding generation, "reason" was a capacity for discerning the design inherent in Nature, and qualities like prejudice or parroting were objectionable because they suspended or impeded the operation of that capacity. So the negative component of reason—that is, the hostility to prejudice, tradition, and the like—complemented, and made sense by reference to, the positive component. Modern regulatory reason in effect tries to retain the negative component while abandoning the positive component. Standing alone, though, the negative component loses its excuse for being, and indeed turns against itself. Hostility to prejudice becomes itself just another prejudice. The suspicion of tradition has little basis except tradition—a sort of antitradition tradition.[3]

Indeed, the same analysis could be made even of what might intuitively seem to be the most compelling of the regulatory criteria—that is, the requirement of "consistency." Suppose we have a way of demonstrating that two moral beliefs held by a person are inconsistent:[4] So what? Again, the moral realist might have an answer to this question. If we assume that there is a moral reality that is itself orderly and coherent, then inconsistency in our beliefs would lead us to doubt that they accurately represent this reality; one or the other inconsistent belief (and perhaps both) must be false. In fact, the deeply entrenched notion that inconsistent statements somehow violate reason arises precisely from some such objectivist viewpoint. Thus, Aristotle's classic essay on the principle of noncontradiction expressly connects that principle to an objectivist ontology: The reason why contradictory statements are impermissible *as a matter of reasoning* is because *as a matter of reality*—of the reality that statements attempt to describe or represent—"it is impossible for the same thing to be and not to be at the same time."[5]

As noted, moral statements on their face appear to be describing or representing something beyond the speaker's own attitudes[6]—hence the impermissibility of contradiction.[7] Conversely, if we do not assume that the significance or value of moral beliefs depends upon their accurate representation of an independent moral reality, then why does it matter whether they are consistent or not?[8] Consider an analogy. We often suppose that matters of "taste" are purely subjective, and on this supposition it would seem silly or even meaningless to impose any requirement of consistency in that realm. If you say you like sweet-and-sour pork, for example, it would be fatuous for your dinner partner to reply that you can't really have that taste, or that the sensation you report can't really "count" as a taste, because "sweet" and "sour" are in fact inconsistent qualities. Or if a person says she wants pancakes for breakfast, it would seem preposterous if someone were to object, "You can't really want pancakes, because yesterday you said you *didn't* want waffles; and there is no culinarily relevant distinction either between pancakes and waffles or between yesterday and today." In the same way, if the important thing about moral beliefs is not that they represent an objective reality but simply that as a subjective matter we have them and care about them, as a conventionalist perspective suggests, then a requirement of consistency would seem similarly out-of-place in that sphere.[9]

Conventionalism All the Way Down?

Perhaps the regulatory conventionalist might respond by asserting that in fact we *do* have a deeply entrenched commitment to consistency, and that is all that matters. He might acknowledge, in other words, that there is no independent or "transcendent" *reason* for making consistency mandatory, but then go on to observe that as a matter of fact in our culture there happens to be a commitment to consistency. Would this merely traditional or conventional desire for consistency be enough to sustain the practice of regulatory reason?

The position has at least an initial appeal. After all, why *should* a conventionalist attempt to defend a belief in the value of consistency with anything other than a conventionalist justification? Having maintained that conventional *oughts* are all there is, why should he then allow the realist to maneuver him into trying to supply some transcendent or supra-conventional grounding for one of those *oughts*—that is, for the convention that we ought to be consistent?

Despite its initial plausibility, this thoroughly and internally conventionalist position seems untenable for at least two reasons. First, to say that in our culture there is a conventional commitment to consistency is at best to report only part of the truth. Purely as a descriptive matter, our conventions reflect only a weak and erratic commitment to consistency. To be sure, we *do* often say we value consistency, and we criticize people for perceived inconsistencies and try to make our own positions more consistent. (Of course, we might do this because we are still realists, or are unreflectively clinging to mental habits generated by former realist commitments.) But we also tolerate rampant inconsistencies—or even knowingly embrace them. "Do I contradict myself?", Walt Whitman asks—"Very well then I contradict myself."[10] Indeed, the very inconsistencies that the regulatory reasoner wants to eliminate—on the ground that they are inconsistent with our conventions—are themselves part of our conventions. And if we sometimes criticize such inconsistencies, we also sometimes shield them. If someone presses others too hard in exposing or objecting to inconsistent beliefs ("Ah, but you've contradicted yourself." "You've contradicted yourself again!"), we tend to regard that person as boorish and annoying; and the next time we don't invite him back.

So a question arises: Which of our practices should prevail—our practice of *criticizing* inconsistencies, or our practice of *maintaining* and sometimes even *protecting* inconsistencies? The moral realist might offer an answer to that question. But the conventionalist cannot appeal to anything outside of our conventions to resolve the conflict, and hence cannot insist that the convention of criticizing inconsistencies must prevail over the counterconvention. Or rather he *can* insist on consistency as a preeminent value; but in doing so he quietly departs from his own conventionalism.

A second and more fundamental objection to the "conventions all the way down" position points out that the position violates regulatory conventionalism's own regulatory criteria. After all, regulatory reason demands that a belief or convention be backed by a reason; it is that demand, once again, that distinguishes the so-called shallow conventionalism of Devlin from Dworkin's "deep conventionalism" which gives rise to regulatory reason. The very essence of the ongoing spirit of Enlightenment reason, as Robert Baird approvingly observes, is that "*no* idea, *no* proposition, *no* principle should be beyond critical assessment"—that for every one of our beliefs we should be able, if challenged, to give a reason.[11] But there is no apparent justification for dropping this demand for a supporting reason in the case of a conventional belief in the value of consistency—or for allowing, in the case of *that* belief, the normally inadmissible response: "Why do we believe in consistency? There's no *reason* for it; we just do." Merely to say that the aversion to inconsistency is deeply entrenched is not to *justify* that aversion any more than the observation of a deep-seated aversion to women's suffrage or interracial marriage justified those sentiments.

In the same vein, it seems likely that the widespread belief in the importance of consistency derives from a former, or perhaps present but tacit, commitment to some form of realism.[12] But the regulatory conventionalist cannot in good faith retain the specific belief while rejecting the more general position from which the specific belief is derived. To do that would be to reduce the conventional belief in consistency to an unreflective parroting of the opinions of others—of those, that is, whose commitment to consistency is or was reflectively grounded in some sort of realism. But parroting, like the holding of opinions unsupported by reasons, is a practice that regulatory reason condemns.

The point here, of course, is not to conclude that consistency either should or should not be a criterion for sound thinking, but merely to point out that a conventionalist framework does not support a requirement of consistency for beliefs held to be merely conventional. In short, regulatory conventionalism's proscription of inconsistent beliefs is no more justified, *on its own premises,* than is its proscription of beliefs grounded in emotion or tradition.

One can appreciate, of course, that the sort of regulatory criteria advanced by Dworkin and others would be appealing to a certain sort of person. In particular, it would not be surprising that people who gravitate to academic culture might often have a distaste for judgments inspired by emotion, or for parroting, or for what seem to them jumbled or uncouth beliefs.[13] This sort of proclivity might help to explain why an acute legal philosopher, Michael Moore, would disparage Devlin's "surface conventionalism"[14] and praise Dworkin's "deep conventionalism," even though Moore elsewhere inconsistently acknowledges that Dworkin's position is less coherent and less faithful *to conventionalism* than Devlin's.[15] But although a preference for beliefs that are tidy and not based on emotion is perhaps to be expected within academia, conventionalism offers no reason for imposing these preferences on the community generally. The imposition is not justified by reason; on the contrary, it seems frankly authoritarian.

The Question of Integrity

Suppose, however, that regulatory reason and the restrictive criteria that Dworkin associates with reason manage in some way to deflect this first objection and to establish their authority over raw convention in determining the community's morality. Do those criteria provide a method or approach capable of reliably adjudicating between beliefs that can be declared consistent with (properly regulated) community morality and other beliefs that do not deserve this certification?

Upon examination, it seems that Dworkin's approach depends on a set of distinctions that are at best delicate and highly manipulable, and at worst simply vacuous. As Dworkin explained in his response to Devlin, regulatory reason would require us to distinguish between beliefs based on unconscious or inarticulate principles (permissible) and beliefs based on "prejudices" (*not* permissible), between beliefs asserted to be "self-evident" (permissible) and beliefs for which no supporting reason is given (impermissible), between offering a reason that one has "been taught . . . by others" (permissible) and merely "parroting" the beliefs of others (impermissible), between holding a belief subject to "exceptions" (permissible) and holding a belief that is "inconsistent" with other beliefs (impermissible).[16] But it seems likely that any controversial belief will be susceptible to either classification, and thus will be eligible either to be counted as "moral" or to be refused such commendation.

What is the difference, after all, between acting on grounds that one has not reflected on and acting from "prejudice"?[17] Whether someone is acting from a "reason" or a "prejudice" is always a slippery question. It is hard enough to say, even in the abstract, just what distinguishes a prejudice from a reason—"one person's 'prejudice,'" Bruce Ackerman remarks, "is, notoriously, another's 'principle'"[18]—and it is next to impossible to determine on which side of the line a person's (or, in the case of an enacted law, a disparate group's) motivation falls. Thus, as Ackerman observes, we can "expect to find an abundance of stereotype-mongers and knee-jerks on all sides of every important issue—as well as many who have struggled their way to more considered judgments."[19]

Similarly, when a person can offer no independent reason for a belief she sincerely holds, wouldn't she always suppose that the belief can be known to be true on its own without independent supporting reasons? So what is the difference, other than perhaps artfulness of advocacy, between a person who says, lamely, "I'm convinced it's true but I'm afraid I can't think of a reason" and someone else who says, solemnly, "It's self-evident"? How would we ever be able confidently to assign a belief to one category rather than the other? Or how would we ever be able to say whether a belief that seems prima facie incompatible with a person's other beliefs is really and truly "inconsistent," or is merely an "exception" based on special considerations?

In short, the distinctions that Dworkin offers for sorting out moral judgments based on reasons from those that are not based on reasons are themselves resistant to "principled" application. Like Karl Llewellyn's "thrust and parry" list of canons of construction, which offers a canon to support either side of any issue of statutory interpretation,[20] Dworkin's approach provides a set of distinctions that can be invoked to show that almost any belief either is or is not in accord with "reason." Because the approach can be used either to approve or condemn almost any belief, it is not useful for distinguishing reason from the absence of reason; one might say that it lacks sufficient intellectual integrity for *that* purpose.

Conversely (and for the same reason), Dworkin's approach is a sumptuous source of arguments that lawyers or scholars might use to support their own positions and discredit those of their opponents. So what regulatory reason ultimately provides, it seems, is a sort of all-purpose rhetoric. More bluntly, regulatory reason provides the resources for sophistry. Dworkin's own recent discussion of the abortion controversy can serve as a helpful illustration.

A Case Study: Reasoning About Life

Dworkin begins his analysis by framing the problem.[21] Abortion, he observes, presents the most incendiary issue currently facing us. In view of this divisiveness, it may seem urgent that a compromise position be found; and indeed some authors and scholars have proposed compromises. But so long as the debate is framed in the familiar way, these compromises are unlikely to prove attractive. In particular, Dworkin is concerned that "no proposal that does respect [a right to abortion] could possibly be accepted by people who believe that abortion is murder, that it violates the most fundamental rights and interests of unborn children."[22] And in fact, he notes, that is just what millions of people, as well as institutions such as the Catholic Church, *say* they do believe.[23]

So in order to clear the path for a compromise, a major task is somehow to dislodge the view that "abortion is murder," or that "it violates the most fundamental rights and interests of unborn children." But how is this task to be carried out? The most direct approach, it seems, would be to demonstrate, somehow, that the position is simply false. Although millions of people may believe that abortion is murder, perhaps it could be persuasively shown that their belief is incorrect.

But this approach poses difficulties for a sophisticated conventionalist like Dworkin. What exactly would it even mean for the belief in question to be "false"? What sort of moral reality is available against which a moral assertion of this kind *could be* true or false? Rather than attempting to show that the commonly expressed pro-life view is false, therefore, Dworkin adopts what is at once a more modest and more audacious approach, and one more consistent with the regulatory version of reason: Primarily using the criterion of consistency, he sets out to show that most of the people who claim that abortion is murder or that a fetus is what Dworkin sometimes calls "a full moral person"[24]—that is, an entity or person with interests and rights of its own—do not actually believe their own claims. So individuals who oppose abortion, pro-life groups, and institutions like the Catholic Church have been systematically (albeit perhaps innocently) misunderstanding and misrepresenting their own views. They may *say* they think that abortion is murder, and they may even thoughtlessly suppose they do think that; but in reality these people and groups do *not* think that abortion is murder.

Do Pro-Lifers Know What They Believe?

But how could an outsider like Dworkin ever be in a position to tell pro-life individuals and groups that they do not really believe what they say they believe, and what by Dworkin's admission they may unreflectively think they believe?

Dworkin offers two claims in support of this daring argument. One claim is set forth only in summary form in the Preface to a later edition of the book:

> [P]eople cannot have the thought that a fetus has interests of its own from the moment of conception, because *there is no such thought to be had.* If people were to carry placards announcing a belief in square circles, we would not do well to understand them as thinking that circles could be square. We would search for some coherent thought to attribute to them, a different thought they meant to express by saying what they did. The idea that a fetus can have interests of its own before it can have any kind of mental life is not so obviously a self-contradiction as the claim that a circle can be square. But, if my arguments are right, it makes no more sense. So we cannot claim to *understand* people if we attribute that "idea" to them: attributing incoherence is rather a confession of failure to understand. We must do better, and that is what I try to do.[25]

What we might call Dworkin's strong claim thus suggests not only that no one *does* believe the fetus is a moral person and abortion is murder, but that no one *could* actually believe such things because they are self-contradictory and unintelligible, like the "idea" of a square circle. But why or how are these pro-life notions self-contradictory? Dworkin admits in the Preface that the belief that a fetus is a moral person does not initially *appear* to be self-contradictory or incoherent; and he refers the reader to the arguments in the body of the book.

But this reference amounts to an invitation to a party that never takes place. In fact, in the book itself Dworkin does not even argue, much less demonstrate, that it is *self-contradictory* to suppose that the fetus is a moral person, and hence that "there is no such thought to be had." Instead, he maintains that "*very few people*—even those who belong to the most vehemently anti-abortion groups, actually believe that, whatever they say."[26] The contenton that "very few" people hold the belief in question implies that a few people *do* hold that belief, and hence that it is at least a thought that can "be had." And indeed, in other writings Dworkin appears to concede that the notion that the fetus is a person is a perfectly coherent idea that can "be had" (although this notion does not necessarily negate a right to abortion).[27] So it appears that Dworkin's strong claim for the view that pro-life rhetoric misrepresents the real beliefs of pro-lifers amounts to a misrepresentation of his own argument.

Most of Dworkin's analytical effort goes to the defense of a more modest (but still quite daring) claim. This more limited claim can be presented in four propositions. (1) Many pro-life individuals *say* they believe that the fetus is a moral person and that abortion is murder. (2) But most of these same individuals also allow for a right to abortion under limited circumstances, such as rape or incest. (3) These exceptions are inconsistent with the contention that the fetus is a moral person and that abortion is murder. (4) Therefore, pro-life individuals who allow for these exceptions must not really believe that the fetus is a moral person and that abortion is murder.

Dworkin's more limited argument represents a splendid example of regulatory conventionalist reasoning. The argument does not invoke any transcendent standard or "moral reality" against which moral beliefs might be measured; it attempts to work *within* the system of moral beliefs held by Dworkin's readers, using conventional moral beliefs as its raw material but subjecting those beliefs to intense cross-examination. In the course of this cross-examination, Dworkin plays off some of the moral beliefs he supposes his readers to hold against other beliefs that some of them profess to hold. In this way, he tries to show not that the beliefs he criticizes are false in any objective sense, but rather that these readers are guilty of inconsistencies, and hence that they do not really hold the beliefs in question at all—even if they have previously said and thought that they did hold these beliefs.

If it succeeds, the argument is a nice illustration of how reasoning can occur without Nature, or without any presupposed objective moral reality.[28] Conversely, if the argument does *not* succeed, its failure would lend support to a hypothesis proposed earlier—that regulatory reasoning amounts to a kind of at-your-service rhetoric, or sophistry. And in fact, upon examination Dworkin's argument seems vulnerable to the objections discussed previously.

Resisting Regulation

Consider possible responses that a pro-lifer might make to Dworkin's regulatory argument. One possibility, of course, is that a person might be convinced. "You're right, Professor Dworkin. I *thought* I believed that the fetus is a 'moral person,' as you say. But upon reflection, I guess I really *don't* believe that." Dworkin indicates in his Preface that although he never expected to convince all of his opponents, he does hope that thoughtful pro-life individuals will react in this way.[29]

But of course there are other possible responses. One reaction might be simply to shrug off the inconsistency Dworkin describes. "You say my belief equating abortion with murder is inconsistent with allowing abortion in cases of rape and incest. I don't know—maybe it is. So what? I'm not a logician; lots of my beliefs are probably inconsistent. That doesn't mean they're not my beliefs."

This response may seem a bit brazen, but is the response unacceptable? It depends. As noted earlier, a moral realist might plausibly argue in this situation that if two beliefs are logically inconsistent, then they cannot both accurately describe a unitary moral reality. So at least one of the inconsistent beliefs must be *false*. But a conventionalist cannot in good faith say this, so Dworkin argues instead that if a person's professed beliefs are inconsistent, then the person does not actually hold one of the inconsistent beliefs. But *this* claim is simply a non sequitur; there is no law of logic or, more to the point, of psychology that precludes a person from sincerely holding inconsistent beliefs.[30]

Indeed, it seems that Dworkin's revised, strong claim that the pro-life premise is self-contradictory or incoherent is offered precisely in an attempt to patch up this crucial fissure in his argument. And if Dworkin could in fact support the summary assertion made in his Preface—that is, if he could show that the idea of the fetus as a moral person is unintelligible in the same way that the idea of a square circle is—then perhaps he would have shown that no one can in fact believe the fetus is a moral person because "there is no such thought to be had." As noted, however, in his book Dworkin does not demonstrate, or even argue, that the "fetus as a moral person" idea is in itself incoherent or self-contradictory. He contends, rather, that this idea is inconsistent with *other* beliefs typically held by pro-lifers. But that weaker argument, even if correct, does nothing to show that pro-lifers do not actually hold the beliefs they profess to hold.[31]

A different response to Dworkin's argument might accept both his contention that typical pro-life views are inconsistent and his assumption that, for whatever reason, inconsistencies in belief are intolerable or impossible; but it might then eliminate the conflict by retaining the beliefs Dworkin wants to dislodge while discarding the beliefs that he wants to preserve. In other words, a pro-lifer might say, "I firmly believe that the fetus is a moral person and that abortion is murder. I had also *supposed* that abortion is permissible in cases of incest and rape. But you've convinced me, Professor Dworkin, that these ideas are inconsistent, and that I cannot or should not hold inconsistent beliefs. So I guess the prohibition on abortion must be absolute: Consistency forbids any exceptions—even for rape or incest."

In short, Dworkin projects that pro-lifers will resolve the ostensible inconsistency in their professed views by abandoning the belief that abortion is murder. But nothing in his argument prevents them from resolving the inconsistency (if they are persuaded that there is an inconsistency that needs resolving) by embracing the opposite conclusion. And indeed, proponents of more severe restrictions on abortion often frame their arguments in just this way, calling attention to the same ostensible inconsistencies relied on by Dworkin but resolving those inconsistencies by advocating more unqualified prohibitions.

Finally, a pro-lifer might deny that the beliefs Dworkin discusses are in fact inconsistent. Why need it offend against logic for a person to maintain (a) that a fetus is a "moral person" and (b) that there should nonetheless be a legal right to abortion in certain limited circumstances? Dworkin's contention turns on a controversial and somewhat idiosyncratic view of what it means to say that someone has a "right." More specifically, he appears to assume that if someone has a "right" then (a) the right must be absolute, so that no countervailing concerns can overcome or qualify it, and (b) government has a legal duty to protect the right.[32] If these assumptions are valid, then it *does* seem inconsistent to hold both that the fetus has a "right" to life and that government should allow a woman to override that right in some circumstances such as rape or incest.

Again, a certain kind of moral realist conceivably might argue that "rights" are objectively real things that *do* have these properties. And Dworkin's assumptions admittedly exploit what Mary Ann Glendon has described as "[t]he exaggerated absoluteness of our American rights rhetoric."[33] Still, for a conventionalist, "rights" must ultimately be grounded in conventions just as other moral qualities or judgments are. And in the conventions of our own legal culture, neither of Dworkin's assumptions about rights is widely accepted. On the contrary, lawyers and legal scholars routinely say that someone has a "right" without supposing that the right is somehow absolute, or that it cannot be overcome by other rights or concerns.[34] Indeed, in other writings where he is not making this particular argument, Dworkin himself candidly acknowledges that even if the fetus were a "person" for constitutional purposes, the state could nonetheless authorize abortions when supported by "compelling interests," including in rape and incest cases.[35]

In addition, we also often talk about "moral rights" as distinguished from "legal rights." The distinction implies that something may in some sense be a "right" but that government will not and perhaps should not enforce it by law. I am not defending these usages here, of course, but merely observing that they are perfectly conventional. And if "rights" are understood in this familiar way, then there is no inconsistency in holding that a fetus has a "right" to life but that government might allow a woman to override this "right" in some circumstances, such as rape or incest.[36]

In the end, then, it is hardly surprising if Dworkin's argument has not convinced many pro-life individuals or groups. On the contrary, there is no apparent reason why anyone *should* change opinions because of Dworkin's argument. Dworkin has not even tried to show that the pro-life premise is false in any objective sense. Instead, he has claimed in essence that he knows the minds of pro-lifers better than they do themselves. Indeed, he goes so far as to suggest that he understands Catholic doctrine better than the popes of the last century have understood it; properly interpreted, he argues, Catholic belief does *not* hold that the fetus is a moral person or that abortion is tantamount to murder—a century of papal declarations to the contrary notwithstanding.[37] These are heroic claims, to put the point charitably.[38] But Dworkin's arguments for the claims are wholly inadequate; they leave pro-life individuals with a variety of ways of explaining that they do in fact believe what they have repeatedly said they believe.

The Futility of Regulatory Reason

It will be helpful at this juncture to reflect on the point of the preceding discussion—to understand both what the point *is* and what the point *is not*. One conclusion that someone might naturally draw is that Dworkin's argument fails in the sense that it is not likely to persuade many pro-lifers to change their views—a failure that is hardly surprising, one might add, given the notorious difficulty of the abortion question and the passion with which many people maintain their opinions on that particular question. But this conclusion, although perhaps correct in itself, also misses the point of the preceding discussion.

The problem with Dworkin's argument is not that it fails to convince people. In fact, it is possible that some people *have been* convinced, and in any event it seems that people are occasionally convinced by similar argumentation on other issues. But the deeper problem is that there is no reason why the argument *should* convince anyone, or why someone who holds to his former view is acting contrary to "reason." And in this respect Dworkin's argument merely illustrates the deficiencies of regulatory reason generally—deficiencies that are not unique to the abortion controversy, but rather affect *any* moral issue.

More specifically, a regulatory argument on any moral question is susceptible to the same four responses that a pro-lifer might make to Dworkin's argument about abortion. We can consider the responses in reverse order. First, a person can virtually always respond to a regulatory argument based on alleged inconsistencies by denying that her beliefs are actually inconsistent. Most issues are sufficiently complicated that it is not difficult to characterize beliefs in a way that will make them appear either consistent or inconsistent.[39] Thus, liberals often accuse Moral Majority types of inconsistency in claiming to value life—that is, the life of the fetus—in the abortion context, while devaluing life by supporting capital punishment. The Moral Majoritarians can easily respond that they *do* adhere to a consistent principle—that *innocent* life should never be deliberately extinguished. They defend the right to life of both fetuses and adults, but not of either fetuses or adults who have been convicted of premeditated homicide.

With regard to affirmative action, likewise, nearly everyone believes, in some sense, in rewarding individual "merit," meeting institutional and societal needs, and remedying past injustices. Each of these concerns is susceptible of very different formulations, however, so it is not difficult for both supporters and opponents of affirmative action to describe the factors in a way that makes their adversaries appear guilty of inconsistencies while avoiding the charge that they themselves are being inconsistent.

As a second response to a regulatory argument, one can always resolve a perceived inconsistency by retaining the beliefs that the regulator seeks to eliminate while jettisoning the beliefs that the regulator wants to preserve. Within a realist framework this alternative is more constrained. The point is not to achieve consistency for its own sake, but rather to adopt moral judgments that correspond to moral reality, or that are *true*. So a perceived inconsistency may lead to a further question: Which of the inconsistent beliefs is true? But on nonrealist assumptions this question is empty; consequently, anyone is perfectly free, if she is so inclined, to achieve consistency by abandoning either or any of her inconsistent beliefs.

Third, within a conventionalist or subjectivist framework one can always simply shrug off the fact of inconsistency—or of emotion, or parroting. One always has the entirely cogent rejoinder: "So what?" As discussed earlier, a conventionalist position offers no good justification for disallowing beliefs merely because they are inconsistent, or are based on an emotional reaction, or have been inherited from others. Of course, the would-be regulator can always insist, "I (or, more likely, 'we') find this kind of belief really obnoxious." But a perfectly adequate response is always available: "*I* don't."

There is of course a fourth possibility: Someone might be convinced by the regulatory argument. More accurately, some people might be induced to change their opinions. But even if this happens, it is misleading to say that the regulatory argument has "succeeded" in any very important sense. The problem is that within a conventionalist framework one cannot say that the person who changes her opinion now holds a truer or sounder view than the person whose opinion remains unchanged. There is no way to say, in other words, that the person who adopts one of the first three alternatives—denying the inconsistency, admitting the inconsistency but resolving it by retaining the challenged beliefs and discarding others, or simply shrugging off the inconsistency with a "So what?"—has reached an *incorrect or false conclusion,* or has committed an *error in reasoning.* She has simply chosen a different option.

Regulatory Reason as Sophistry

Indeed, the existence of these diverse alternatives raises an interesting question: How do we account for the fact that people sometimes *are* induced to change their opinions even though they are not compelled by reason to do so? Two descriptions of this change offer themselves for consideration. One possibility is that the person whose opinion changes has discovered in the course of the argument that a different opinion just suits her better; it is somehow more attractive or more comfortable. In this depiction, the regulatory reasoner is much like a clothing salesperson. ("Let's just set that opinion you've been wearing over here for a moment and have you try this one on. . . . Now, that's really *you!*") Or the reasoner is like a waiter tempting diners with the dessert tray. ("I'd recommend the personal autonomy a la mode. It's been getting rave reviews.") Moral "reasoning," in this view, amounts to a method of flattering the listener's ego or of enticing the listener's appetite for moral opinions.

A different description would assert that the person whose opinions change has simply been tricked, or "taken in." Perhaps he was unaware of the available options. He may not have been clever enough to describe his beliefs in a way that deflected the regulator's charge of inconsistency. Or maybe he had a lingering sense that inconsistent or emotion-inspired beliefs are somehow out-of-bounds—Who knows why?—and the regulatory reasoner took advantage of his innocence on this point. (Of course, the regulatory reasoner might not be guilty of *consciously* exploiting anyone's gullibility; very likely the regulator himself has a lingering sense that inconsistent or emotion-inspired beliefs are—Who knows why?—somehow out-of-bounds.)

So by one description, the regulator induces a change of opinion by *flattering the ego or the appetites* of the listener. By the other description, the regulator uses the rhetorical resources that the regulatory approach offers by *tricking* the listener (and perhaps himself as well). Both images—the advocate as flatterer, the advocate as trickster—were in fact used by Plato to depict a kind of advocacy that he deplored.[40] And as it turns out, Plato's analysis of sophistry is illuminating with respect to contemporary moral reasoning as manifest in constitutional discussions.

Conventionalism and Sophistry

Sophistry is the art associated with a group of expert rhetoricians who practiced their craft in Greece at the time of Socrates and Plato. The sophists were
not all of a piece. Judgments about them were divided at the time of Plato and
have been divided ever since. In Plato's depiction, however, two facts stand
out. First, the sophists were associated with a conventionalist view of truth.
Second, their conventionalism precluded the sophists from inquiring into or
caring about objective truth, and hence left them little choice but to persuade
by appealing to the beliefs and desires and conceits of their audience, and
then manipulating those beliefs and desires and conceits through the clever
use of words.

Greek thought of Plato's time was in turmoil over the familiar (to us) issue
of nature versus convention (or *physis* versus *nomos*).[41] Were beliefs, including
ethical beliefs, grounded in some kind of objective reality, or were they merely
subjective or conventional? Plato had derived from Socrates a commitment to
realism, or nature.[42] Conversely, Plato's dialogues repeatedly associate his opponents, and especially the sophists, with the conventionalist position.[43]

In *Theatetus*, for example, Plato ascribes to the revered sophist Protagoras
the subjectivist or conventionalist slogan "Man is the measure of all things,"
and then mercilessly attacks that position. In the *Republic*, Plato explains the
connection between conventionalism and sophistry:

> Each of these private teachers who work for pay, whom the politicians call
> Sophists and regard as their rivals, inculcates nothing else than these opin-
> ions of the multitude which they opine when they are assembled and calls
> this knowledge wisdom. It is as if a man were acquiring the knowledge of the
> humors and desires of a great strong beast which he had in his keeping, how
> it is to be approached and touched, and when and by what things it is made
> most savage or gentle, yes, and the several sounds it is wont to utter on the
> occasion of each, and again what sounds uttered by another make it tame or
> fierce, and after mastering this knowledge by living with the creature and by
> lapse of time should call it wisdom, and should construct thereof a system
> and art and turn to the teaching of it, knowing nothing in reality about which
> of these opinions and desires is honorable or base, good or evil, just or unjust,
> but should apply all these terms to the judgments of the great beast, calling
> the things that pleased it good, and the things that vexed it bad, having no
> other account to render of them. . . .[44]

In short, the sophists know nothing of *truth*; instead, their conventionalism
leads them to advocate and exemplify the art of verbal flattery and persuasion
by manipulating "the opinions of the multitude."

Plato treats this art, and its practitioners, with ardent contempt. The
sophists are "flatterers,"[45] "wizards," "the chief pundits of the deceiver's art,"[46]
"supreme imitators and tricksters."[47] A sophist "does not like honestly to confess that he is talking nonsense," and so "shuffles up and down to conceal the
difficulty" or "deck[s] himself out with vain words."[48] Sophists specialize in
"the forced and artificial chiming of word and phrase," and in "all the sub-

tleties and cavils that lead to nought but opinion and strife."[49] Their art consists of "playing with words but revealing nothing."[50]

But Plato's criticism does not simply assert that the sophists happen to be especially depraved men. Though his opinion of their character is surely not a commendatory one, he includes even men widely regarded as honorable, such as Pericles, in his general indictment.[51] Plato's more basic contention is not that sophists happen to be unscrupulous, but that conventionalism inevitably leads to sophistry.

Reason, after all, is concerned with discovering what is objectively true and good.[52] If you do not believe in the objectively true and good, therefore, you cannot truly make use of reason. The only thing left is to appeal to, or "flatter," beliefs people already have, and to use words in clever fashion in order to manipulate people's beliefs toward the conclusions you want them to reach. And that is just what the sophists do—and what, for pay, they teach others to do. In sum, Plato suggests that conventionalism cannot support the exercise of reason; it can only promote sophistry.

The Senility of Sophistry

Sophistry compensated and honored its practitioners—at least its eminent ones—handsomely. But sophistry also had, and has, its limitations, even on its own terms. In particular, if sophistry becomes widely recognized for what it is then it also becomes transparent, and thereby loses its rhetorical efficacy. Once we realize that Gorgias can make a persuasive sounding argument for any position,[53] we become automatically suspicious of every argument he makes.

But in that event, what is the sophist to do? Once the sophist's craft loses its power, it seems, the natural tendency is for the sophist to berate or insult his opponent—to assert, perhaps subtly, perhaps loudly and forcefully, that the person who remains unpersuaded is just being obtuse or stubborn or unreasonable. So when Thrasymachus cannot confute Socrates in argument, he resorts to name-calling. Socrates is a "buffoon," a "pettifogger," a "shyster."[54] He is "simple-minded."[55] Since he is too dense to grasp Thrasymachus's point, there is really nothing left but to "take the argument and ram it into [Socrates'] head."[56] A frustrated Polus adopts a different version of the same tactic; he laughs at Socrates, and suggests that Socrates' views are so manifestly ludicrous that actual refutation is superfluous.[57] Callicles calls Socrates "a true mob orator" who engages in "driveling."[58]

A parallel deterioration is apparent in contemporary constitutional discourse. For example, Ronald Dworkin reacts to criticisms of his abortion argument by making a fierce ad hominem attack on his opponents; he suggests that pro-lifers who find his argument unconvincing are simply impervious to reason, and he compares them to people who murder abortion doctors:

> Some were puzzled by what they took to be my political expectations. They thought I believed that the book would convince all anti-abortion campaign-

ers to lay down their placards and join the pro-choice party instead, and critics pointed out, correctly, that the motives that drive many enemies of freedom of choice are too deep—too unexamined, unreasoned, and visceral—to respond to argument at all. I did not mean to deny this: people who are willing to shoot doctors in front of abortion clinics are unlikely to read a book like this one, or to be persuaded by it if they did.[59]

The passage is an vivid instance of contemporary sophistry in conspicuous decline. The advocacy advances under the banner of "reason." Unfortunately, within a conventionalist framework reason has little to work with. On its own conventionalist assumptions it cannot argue that the moral views it opposes are simply wrong or false in any objective sense. Consequently, regulatory reason is limited to attempting to show that the regulator's opponents hold inconsistent beliefs—a charge which, even if true, loses its sting within a conventionalist framework—or else that they are speaking from thoughtlessness or prejudice, and hence do not really even believe what they say they believe. And when this attempt is unpersuasive, as it very likely will be—after all, how could a distant academician seriously expect to understand the beliefs of millions of people whom he has never met, and for whom he obviously has little sympathy, better than they do themselves?—the regulator is reduced to making ad hominem attacks on those who persist in maintaining that they know their own minds. The would-be thinker ends up lavishly bestowing epithets like "unreasoned," "unexamined," "visceral" (or, to recall Dworkin's response to the sort of community morality defended by Lord Devlin, "shocking," "prejudiced," and "parroting") on the positions he opposes. The aspiration to "reason" first slides smoothly into an elegant sophistry, and then degenerates into an unseemly exercise in bullying.[60]

For quite a different manifestation of late-stage sophistry, consider John Rawls's resolution of the abortion controversy:

Suppose further that we consider the question in terms of these three important political values: the due respect for human life, the ordered reproduction of political society over time, including the family in some form, and finally the equality of women as equal citizens. (There are, of course, other important political values besides these.) Now I believe any reasonable balance of these three values will give a woman a duly qualified right to decide whether or not to end her pregnancy during the first trimester. The reason for this is that at this early stage of pregnancy the political value of the equality of women is overriding, and this right is required to give it substance and force. Other political values, if tallied in, would not, I think affect this conclusion. . . . [A]ny comprehensive doctrine that leads to a balance of political values excluding that duly qualified right in the first trimester is to that extent unreasonable. . . .[61]

By contrast to Dworkin's intricate display of rhetorical virtuosity and his spirited ad hominem reply to those who disagree, Rawls's peremptory declaration is at once more bland and more bluntly authoritarian; his pronouncement amounts to thinly veiled *ipse dixitism*—a sort of reasoning by fiat—hardly worthy of the label "sophistry." Rawls's brief discussion of abortion is part of a chapter explaining (and is evidently intended to be a concrete illustration of) what he calls "public reason." But is there anything in Rawls's pronouncement that entitles it to that honorific label?

In form, to be sure, Rawls's statement purports to explain his conclusion that a woman's right to choose an abortion should prevail during the first trimester. The ostensible explanation, or "reason," however, amounts to nothing more than a restatement of his conclusion in different words ("The reason for this is that at this early stage of pregnancy the political value of the equality of women is overriding. . . ."), supplemented by the equally conclusory declaration that if some people believe differently, their views are "to that extent unreasonable."[62] But *why* are those views unreasonable? And how does Rawls know that they are unreasonable? How has the "balance" of competing interests Rawls alludes to been performed? Or is the "balance" merely a metaphor—and if so, for what?

With respect to these central questions, Rawls simply has nothing to say. The invocation of "reasonableness" signifies what it so often does in modern discourse;[63] the assertion that a particular position is "reasonable" (or "unreasonable") means, ironically, that actual *reasons* cannot or will not be offered.[64] We are called upon to conform to the author's view because if we do not we are declared to be "unreasonable." One is reminded of the familiar junior high school understanding of why you should dress in a particular way or listen to a certain kind of music—because it's what "everybody" does (or at least everybody who "counts"). The adolescent fashion is powerfully sustained by a sort of overlapping consensus. In the same way, Rawls's pronouncement on abortion amounts to a bald assertion of personal or cultural authority.[65] Thus, within a single paragraph[66] the pretension to "reason" dissolves into reason's old antithesis—authority.[67]

The Degeneration of Constitutional Discourse

Plato describes the degeneration of sophistry into name-calling and verbal violence. A similar turn is evident in the writings of constitutional scholars like Dworkin, as we have seen. But Dworkin is hardly unique in this respect. Constitutional discourse generally reflects a practice of sophistry in a state of exuberant degeneration.

If we survey the scene of modern constitutional law and thought, the spectacle may seem bewildering. Our gaze falls upon dozens of doctrines— a three- or four-part formula or test, it seems, for every significant clause in the Constitution, and for some (like the free speech clause) an assortment of overlapping formulas. We encounter a host of terms and techniques deployed by courts across the constitutional board in seemingly willy-nilly fashion: means-end analysis, "balancing" (in a variety of ad hoc and "definitional" versions), multiple tiers and tracks and presumptions, motive analysis and impact analysis.

These formulas, tests, and techniques may create the appearance of discursive precision, but the appearance is illusory; if anything, the plethora of techniques and the multiple layers of loose doctrine free the courts to reach and justify a variety of different results. Robert Nagel explains:

> Despite their superficial precision, neither the content nor the shape of modern formulae communicates clarity and constraint. The formulae are demands—multiple, repetitive, shifting, and sometimes inconsistent. The style reflects intellectual embarrassment about the existence of judicial discretion, but is designed to assure plentiful opportunities for its exercise. In combination with the mechanical tone of formulaic opinions, the palpable range of choice inherent in the formulae communicates, not objectivity, but power without responsibility. Rather than binding, the formulaic style frees the Court, like some lumbering bully, to disrupt social norms and practices at its pleasure.[68]

In a similar vein, Judge Posner endorses Holmes's comment that after all was said and done a law was constitutional "unless it made him want to puke," and Posner goes on to suggest that in the end constitutionality is determined by something like a "puke test." He quickly adds that neither he nor Holmes should be understood literally. "The point is only that our deepest values—Holmes's 'can't helps'—live below thought and provide warrants for action even when we cannot give those values a compelling or perhaps any rational justification. This holds even for judicial action."[69]

Nagel's and Posner's observations focus on the eclectic rhetoric and illusory rationality of *judicial* discourse. If we leave the writings of judges and roam a little farther into the academic literature, the complications—and hence the rhetorical possibilities—multiply exponentially. Now economists and sociologists and philosophers, some old and some new, some familiar and some foreign—Derrida and Durkheim, Hayek and Habermas, Locke and Lacan, Mill and Merleau-Ponty, Rawls and Rorty—appear as players in the game.

This seething sea of doctrines and techniques and theories and authorities provides the rhetorical resources that lawyers, judges, and scholars may use to argue, *as a matter of constitutional law,* for virtually any position that the climate of political opinion might view as colorable in the first place.[70] Should government guarantee a minimum income, along with shelter, food, and clothing, to all citizens?[71] Should individuals, or legislators, be free to consult their religious beliefs in deciding which candidates or which bills to vote for?[72] Should there be some sort of legal remedy for the "state of servitude" inherent in the role of wife and mother?[73] Should government regulate the production and sale of pornography?[74] Are affirmative action programs appropriate and desirable?[75] With respect to each of these questions, it seems, either an affirmative or negative answer can now be shown to be not merely prudent (or imprudent) but, given the current state of constitutional discourse, actually *required* (and *prohibited*) by the Constitution.

In this situation, Mark Tushnet argues that "[t]he limits of craft . . . are so broad that in any interesting case any reasonably skilled lawyer can reach whatever result he or she wants."[76] Sanford Levinson sees the Constitution as "a linguistic system" or a "uniquely American form of political rhetoric," and he maintains that "[t]here is nothing that is unsayable in the language of the

Constitution. . . ."[77] Levinson's comment sounds much like that of Laurence Tribe and Michael Dorf, who in criticizing Ronald Dworkin's theory of interpretation acknowledge "the possibility of making noises in the Constitution's language that *sound* like an argument for just about anything."[78] Paul Kahn qualifies the indeterminacy argument slightly while leaving the relevant conclusion intact; the law is not wholly indeterminate, but it is indeterminate enough that plausible arguments can be given for contrary outcomes in any given case. "True, not everything can be said, but usually enough can be said to support as objective, within the bounded professional community, either of two possible outcomes of a controversy."[79] Corroborating Kahn's observation, Robin West points out that on her "progressive" understanding, the Constitution requires numerous measures that on a "conservative" understanding are constitutionally forbidden, and she concedes that both approaches can claim considerable support in the language and history of the Constitution.[80]

A protean rhetoric that has become notoriously competent to support almost any position is in danger of losing its efficacy. Similarly, once it is understood that a particular text can plausibly mean anything and everything, the text may come to mean nothing: It becomes not a meaningful text, but more a kind of political Rorschach blot. Hence, the prodigality of constitutional rhetoric threatens to rob it of persuasive force. In the course of a passionate call for retrenchment, Laurence Tribe of all people now notes with alarm that "the text of the Constitution can be read to justify just about any decision—and so can safely be ignored."[81] Other prominent constitutional scholars wonder whether under current conditions it is any longer possible to distinguish parodies of constitutional argument from serious arguments.[82]

But as Plato's depiction of the sophists illustrates, when actual argumentation and reasoning lose their power to persuade, what remains is the ugly discourse—or, if "discourse" overdignifies, the practice—of demonizing and name-calling. Such a development is discernible in constitutional law. Citing "a substantial number of Supreme Court decisions, involving a range of legal subjects, that condemn public enactments as being expressions of prejudice or irrationality or invidiousness," Robert Nagel has persuasively shown that "to a remarkable extent our courts have become places where the name-calling and exaggeration that mark the lower depths of our political debate are given a more acceptable, authoritative form."[83] And after the name-calling and pejorative labeling, of course, there is the bottom line of authority or force. Thus, the one sentence in a judicial decision that really "persuades" is typically the same: "It is so ordered." As H. Jefferson Powell comments, "[c]ontemporary American judges do not impose the rule of reason on Caesar, they *are* Caesar."[84]

In short, one who comes to modern constitutional discussions hoping to encounter the clean discursive rigor that "reason" connotes will instead be drawn into a sort of labyrinthine emptiness. Whether one considers the drearily stylized, solemnly insipid droning that so often emanates from the courts or the unmoored expositions of wearisome ideologies characteristic of the more ambitious academic literature, there simply is very little in the discourse that merits the label of "reason." By all indications, rather, modern constitutional discourse is a veritable Babel.

The allusion deserves further elaboration, and we will return to it. First, though, we need to notice a paradox. The preceding discussion has suggested that constitutional discourse is in a degenerate condition. Though strongly worded, perhaps, this indictment is not especially daring; in one area of constitutional law after another, legal scholars and sometimes Supreme Court justices call attention to the chaotic condition of the doctrine and the decisions, and of constitutional interpretation generally.[85] And yet, strangely, legal scholars and judges do not typically conclude that constitutional discourse itself has been in any important sense discredited by these observations, or that the time has come to consider abandoning this discourse. On the contrary, they doggedly persist in the discourse with almost puritanical earnestness. Why do they do this? The next chapter reflects on this puzzle.

CHAPTER SEVEN

Rationalizing the Constitution

*T*he conclusion of the preceding chapter might seem to have brought our inquiry to its natural end. The constitutional enterprise was, and is, a project of freeing human affairs from the powers of force and fortuity and bringing them under the governance of reason. But the aspiration to establish reason resulted, first, in the failure of the framers' legalistic strategy for embodying the enduring conclusions of reason in a written text and, more recently, in a discourse that pays constant lip service to "reason" but in fact amounts to a degraded practice characterized by obfuscation, sophistry, name-calling, and the exercise of cultural authority and political power. The aspiration to reason, it seems, has traveled full circle; it has deteriorated into something that is the opposite of reason.[1]

Still, there is something unnatural about ending the inquiry and the story here. The problem is not that the conclusion is too extreme or wild, but rather that for all its severity it is at the same time so thoroughly commonplace and yet so apparently impotent. In fact, the judgments expressed in the preceding chapter are harsh but hardly unprecedented. Consider the similar judgments expressed by scholars from a variety of points on the political and jurisprudential spectrum. Robert Bork's sweepingly critical evaluations of the bulk of modern constitutional law and theory are well known. Richard Epstein's similar judgments are only slightly less familiar. Robert Nagel's assessments, compared to which my own may seem quite bland, have been noted earlier. George Carey discerns a "constitutional crisis" in which the Supreme Court dispenses "legal mumbo jumbo" in behalf of decisions like *Roe v. Wade* that are in reality "morally and constitutionally monstrous."[2] Michael Paulsen finds Supreme Court opinions to be "pseudo-sophisticated legalese," "arid, technical, unhelpful, boring, . . . unintelligible," "formulaic gobbledygook." And Paulsen is not being especially severe on people who wear robes; legal scholarship, he thinks, is even worse—"incomprehensible, pretentious, pompous, turgid, revolting, jargonistic gibberish."[3]

From the other end of the continuum, Morton Horwitz describes in more elegant but no less astringent terms a "crisis of legitimacy in constitutional thought in which the generally accepted paradigms and modes of thought are no longer felt capable of yielding convincing solutions to constitutional questions."[4] Duncan Kennedy believes that in purporting to interpret the Constitution "the justices are constantly engaged in naive manipulation"; and constitutional decisions reflect "the bizarre impact of self-delusion on the implementation of the political agenda by the judge. . . ."[5] Sanford Levinson muses that "the 'death of constitutionalism' may be the central event of our time."[6]

Nor do these ominous judgments issue only from those situated toward the left and right borders of legal thought. Paul Kahn completes a thoughtful review of attempts to explain the legitimacy of the Constitution by concluding that the attempts have failed and that the enterprise can go no further; thus, "constitutional theory has reached an end."[7] Alexander Aleinikoff's study of modern constitutional decisions leaves him with "the eerie sense that constitutional law as a distinct form of discourse is slipping away." Aleinikoff reports that the dominant form of constitutional discourse—balancing—"has lost its ability to persuade." Referring to an opinion by Justice Potter Stewart that Aleinikoff takes to be exemplary of modern constitutional decisions, he explains: "Although Stewart's opinion uses all the right words, in the end they are simply that: just words. No conviction, no belief in the justness of the result informs the opinion."[8] Observing "increasing signs of intellectual incoherence" in constitutional decisions, Jefferson Powell maintains that the discourse is caught in "a conceptual and moral quagmire from which it does not appear to have the resources to escape." Consequently, the courts' decisions are less an expression of reason than a manifestation of "violence [that] is increasingly wayward, increasingly brutal." The truth is that "constitutionalism is one of the most seductive masks worn by state violence."[9]

Somewhat more cautiously, Dan Farber suggests that Supreme Court opinions are "increasingly arid, formalistic, and lacking in intellectual value"; they display "the labored exploration of material that, in the end, turns out to lead nowhere." Farber worries that "[f]requently, opinions today almost seem designed to wear the reader into submission as much as actually to persuade."[10] Leslie Gielow Jacobs discerns a "widening chasm between what [the Supreme Court] claims it is doing in interpreting the Constitution and what it realistically can be doing. . . ."; and this "contradictory and potentially self-destructive" behavior has generated a "crisis of legitimacy."[11]

And yet there is something odd about these seemingly apocalyptic judgments. Though one would exaggerate only slightly to say that there appears to be a virtual consensus among scholars that constitutional law is in the throes of a "crisis of legitimacy," those same scholars seem as a rule remarkably nonchalant about the ostensible crisis. Confronted with Levinson's claim about the "death of constitutionalism," the typical scholar is likely to react neither with alarm nor denial, but rather with an affirming nod and a yawn—and she will then return to work on her latest article recommending an adjustment in the third prong of the four-part test for commercial speech or explaining why the

Court's decision invalidating Colorado's anti-gay rights initiative was clearly a correct interpretation of the Constitution even though Justice Kennedy's opinion for the majority makes no sense at all. Every year the law reviews turn out hundreds and thousands of pages of these articles, which may contain short sections explaining how the existing decisions and doctrines are in utter disarray, but then go on to reach a blandly buoyant conclusion. In short, never was a body of thought and discourse so sanguine in the face of its widely proclaimed, imminent demise.

How should we account for this curious blend of the eschatological and the cheerily complacent? The answer to that question is no doubt complex. A detached observer might view contemporary constitutional discourse as expressing a fascinating mixture of the hope that springs eternal (The doctrine of this or that clause is in abominable shape, yes; but surely with a little fine-tuning it can be made serviceable), denial in the face of the intolerable (How can we own up to a situation so bleak?), self-serving deception and self-deception (A legal career, particularly a professorial career, still offers substantial benefits, especially considering the alternatives, so . . .), and quiet desperation (What else are we supposed to do?). In this chapter, however, I want to explore only one facet of the phenomenon—one that reflects and bears most directly on the constitutional aspiration to achieve governance by reason, and that can thus bring to a conclusion our inquiry into the commitment to the "life of reason" manifested in the constitutional project.

Reasons and Rationalizations

It will be helpful at this point to set aside the line of analysis developed over the last several chapters, at least temporarily, so as to come at the problem from a different angle. We can begin by taking note of a familiar distinction. In everyday life, we commonly distinguish between "reasons" and what we often call "rationalizations." You say you did something for such-and-such reasons. Someone critical of what you did may argue that your reasons were bad or misconceived. Or she might make a different kind of criticism; she might say, "You're just rationalizing." This criticism *might* be taken to imply that the reasons you have advanced were bad ones, but it need not be understood in that way. Primarily the criticism makes a different point: It suggests that what you now present as "reasons" were in fact invented *after* you had already acted. You are now trying to justify an action actually performed because of some other, probably less admirable motive.

Reasons, in this usage, are grounds that we are conscious of *before* acting, and that in fact motivate our actions. *Rationalizations* are excuses that we manufacture *after* the fact to justify actions that were in reality performed for different reasons or because of other motives. Reasons are ex ante; rationalizations are post hoc.

Still, one might wonder why the term "rationalization" generally carries pejorative connotations, or why the assertion "You're just rationalizing," if convincing, is typically regarded as a cogent or even decisive criticism.[12] Shouldn't the only question be whether the rationalization is persuasive? If it *is* persuasive, then doesn't it follow that the person offering the rationalization acted properly, even if the rationalization does not describe the person's actual ex ante motive? Suppose, in other words, that something offered as a reason *is* really a rationalization—so what?

One plausible answer to this question might distinguish between the desirability or moral quality of the *action* and the wisdom or moral quality of the *actor*. Even if a rationalization can persuasively show that *your action* was for the best, in other words, *you* still do not deserve commendation if you acted for other, baser motives. Suppose, for example, that you act selfishly in an effort solely to promote your own interests, but you badly miscalculate the consequences of your action and thus end up primarily benefiting someone else instead. The benefit you inadvertently confer earns you no praise; selfishness is not rendered laudable by being joined with incompetence.

These reflections do not exhaust the matter, of course, but they are enough to show that it *is* cogent to assert that a proffered reason is merely a rationalization, whether or not the rationalization itself is persuasive. And our everyday discourse reveals that we understand this. Accused of rationalizing, we may confess or we may deny, but we do not typically respond with "Sure, I'm rationalizing. So what?"

Given our usual condemnation of rationalizing, it is noteworthy that in constitutional discourse a different set of assumptions seems to obtain. Lawyers, judges, and legal scholars—especially legal scholars—routinely and unapologetically engage in a practice that has all the symptoms of rationalization, and that they may even describe as rationalization. It is worth reflecting on the meaning and significance of this pervasive practice.[13]

The Rationalizing Enterprise

Constitutional discourse exhibits rationalization at several levels. The first level involves the kind of thinking and argumentation practiced by lawyers and judges. Though forced to argue in the terms of the formulaic three- and four-part doctrinal tests that have come to dominate most areas of constitutional law, lawyers may understand that these tests are highly malleable, and hence can be used to justify a variety of results. Consequently, an argument in these terms is not likely to determine how a case is actually decided.[14] So lawyers understand that the truly persuasive factors, or what we might think of as the "real reasons," must somehow be packed into arguments and briefs around the more overtly doctrinal arguments—perhaps, as appellate litigators sometimes emphasize, in the statement of the facts.[15]

Likewise, since the days of the Legal Realists it has become almost a hackneyed point that the factors or reasons that lead a judge to favor a particular decision are often quite different than the reasons or arguments supplied in the opinion to justify the decision. Judge Joseph Hutcheson offered one well-known (if somewhat idiosyncratic) version of what often happens. Hutcheson distinguished between the "the judgment or decision, the solution itself" and "the apologia for that decision" or "the rationalization." The process by which a judge reaches a decision consists of "feeling or 'hunching out,'" while the postdecision process amounts to "the logomachy, the effusion of the judge by which that decree is explained or excused."[16]

This phenomenon has generated a familiar distinction between two different phases of a judicial decision: In the first or "discovery" phase, the judge reaches a tentative decision on what may be nonlegal grounds, and in the second or "justification" phase, the judge explains or supports the decision using the language and doctrines of law—or in the (perhaps merely hypothetical) case in which no such explanation can be devised, starts over again. Although the distinction between discovery and justification of legal decisions has been criticized,[17] by and large the legal culture seems quite untroubled by the two-phase account.[18]

Nonetheless, at the level of lawyerly advocacy and judging, the phenomenon of rationalization remains somewhat controversial, and therefore somewhat veiled. But rationalization comes fully out of the closet, proudly and without embarrassment, in scholarly criticism and analysis. To be sure, legal scholars often discuss the reasons explicitly given in judicial opinions. But scholars also commonly suppose that the sorts of doctrinal reasons given by judges are at best a surface account or starting point,[19] and that the job of the scholar is to go behind or beneath the official explanations to examine the real reasons that justify (or fail to justify) a decision. Indeed, the sort of legal article that limits itself to reviewing and assessing the doctrinal reasoning actually presented in a judicial opinion is typically thought worthy of a modest student note or comment, but not of serious professional legal scholarship.

So the fact that the reasons given for a decision in a judicial opinion may be conclusory or superficial or simply wrong—and from a scholarly perspective, judicial opinions nearly always exhibit at least one of these deficiencies—provides no sufficient basis for condemning the decision. On the contrary, authors of law review articles often seem to take it for granted that the reasons given in an opinion will be incomplete or suggestive at best, and that noting this incompleteness is merely a sort of mandatory preliminary gesture before the serious work of proposing and examining the more weighty potential justifications for the decision can begin. It would be only a slight overstatement to say that the analysis contained in the hundreds of volumes of law review literature published each year takes this to be its primary task—that is, penetrating the official accounts offered in judicial opinions in order to reveal or devise the real reasons that may support the courts' decisions, and then subjecting those real reasons to scholarly examination.

In this way, legal scholarship—especially constitutional scholarship—is at its core an enterprise of rationalization.[20] Indeed, by the time the scholarly analysis can be supplied, a case will typically already have been argued and decided, and in fact will be a year (or perhaps several decades) old. So any scholarly justification offered for the decision will necessarily be post hoc. Though made with reference to several particular scholars, Judge Posner's observation might easily be generalized:

> Notice . . . the *belatedness* of the type of constitutional theorizing illustrated by Strauss and Amar-Widavsky, and in the case of abortion by Dworkin as well. Constitutional issues percolate in the lower courts for years before they reach the Supreme Court. Yet scholarly interest in the issues rarely perks up until the issue has not only reached the Supreme Court but been decided by it. So mesmerized are constitutional scholars by the Supreme Court . . . that often they delay too long in writing to have a chance of having an impact on constitutional law. By the time they reach the battlefield, the battle is over.[21]

If the scholarly analysis will be post hoc, it will also, not necessarily but in all likelihood, be a justification that would not have occurred to the judges themselves. Of course, whether from modesty or strategy, a scholar may sometimes ascribe a theory or justification to the judges, rather than claiming personal credit for having invented it. Thus, in commending a controversial affirmative action decision, Ronald Dworkin suggests that the majority opinion by Justice Brennan "contains two different arguments"—an "explicit" and, unfortunately, demonstrably defective argument, but also a "much more successful" argument that was not explicitly made and hence "must be reconstructed from independent remarks."[22] More typically, however, the legal scholar does not even pretend that the judge was conscious of or actually motivated by the sort of reasoning that the scholar may offer in justification of a decision. And one suspects that judges might sometimes be less than comfortable with the academic rationalizations offered in behalf of their decisions.[23]

The rationalizing enterprise is perhaps most conspicuous with respect to decisions of the Warren Court that were (and sometimes remain) controversial in the general population but that are popular within legal culture—decisions like *Griswold v. Connecticut* or, in the aftermath but still in the spirit of the Warren Court, *Roe v. Wade*. Of course, *Brown v. Board of Education* is the leading example. Few legal scholars, it seems, have been satisfied with the reasoning of the Court's opinion in *Brown*. The opinion limits itself to discussing the school setting. So its argument seems too narrow—and probably also disingenuous, when in retrospect we know that the Court would shortly repudiate the "separate but equal" principle across-the-board, and without further explanation.[24] *Brown*'s reliance on questionable social science studies has also seemed objectionable.[25]

At the same time, virtually all legal scholars agree that *Brown* reached the correct result. Indeed, Mark Tushnet has observed that "[f]or a generation, one criterion for an acceptable constitutional theory has been whether that theory explains why [*Brown*] . . . was correct."[26] Consequently, for forty years legal scholars (including myself[27]) have been inventing new and better justifications for the *Brown* decision.

Of course, scholarly rationalizations vary in zeal and scope. A good deal of law review literature focuses on particular decisions, or on small clusters of decisions, without proposing any general theory of constitutional law. We might think of this category of scholarship as ad hoc post hoc rationalization. In this vein, Mark Tushnet describes the "cottage industry of constitutional law scholars who write revised opinions for controversial decisions."[28]

At a different level, more ambitious scholarship seeks to rationalize entire areas of constitutional law, or even the whole of constitutional law. A prominent example of grand rationalistic scholarship is Bruce Ackerman's project entitled *We the People.*[29] Ackerman ranges over the whole of constitutional law, offering innovative interpretations of constitutional cases and events ranging from the Reconstruction amendments to the *Lochner* era to the New Deal, and including his own justifications for controversial modern cases like *Brown* and *Griswold.* At the heart of Ackerman's revisionist history is the novel idea that the Constitution can be amended in ways other than through the procedure described in Article V. Thus, Ackerman considers the reelection of Franklin D. Roosevelt in 1936 to have signified or crystalized a major—indeed, a transforming—constitutional amendment. Though never written out in the way that most other amendments have been (mainly because it was never presented to the people or described *as* a constitutional amendment), the content of the New Deal Amendment is something like "the activist state is hereby approved."

Ackerman's revisionist constitutional history is palpably rationalistic in all of the relevant respects. Plainly, it is offered *after*—decades after—the cases and events it discusses. Moreover, it turns out that the major modern cases, although their reasoning was often obscure or deficient, were still rightly decided because they correctly extracted the meaning of a constitutional amendment; and they succeeded in reaching the correct constitutional conclusions even though the justices responsible for these decisions did not even realize that they were interpreting an amendment and even though the people who adopted that amendment were not conscious of putting that meaning into the amendment, or indeed of having adopted an amendment at all.

Ackerman's grand rationalization—or, in his more dignified term, "retrospective synthesis"[30]— is interesting, bold, and imaginative precisely because no one before Ackerman had suspected the existence of the "activist state" amendment. And indeed, although Ackerman has now proclaimed the discovery of this amendment, even scholars and judges of considerable imagination or ingenuity still find the discovery "startling" and "incredible,"[31] or "bizarre."[32] It is as if Haley's Comet had somehow gotten stuck in earth's gravitational field and had been circling near the planet for decades, but no one had realized this until some kids looked up and noticed the comet at last week's Cub Scout campfire. In any event, in Ackerman's rationalized constitutional history, decisions like *Brown, Griswold,* and others enlarging the powers of the national government or creating new rights were justified, although the justices who decided those cases did not really understand why, because they correctly interpreted a provision of the Constitution that no one knew existed.

Ackerman is only among the more recent and ambitious of the grand rationalizers, of course. He is preceded by, among others, the principal authors of *The Federalist Papers.* At the Philadelphia convention, recall, James Madison, Alexander Hamilton, and their allies opposed many of the central measures that were ultimately incorporated into the Constitution—especially the compromise concerning representation of the states in Congress—on the grounds that these measures were unjust and contrary to principle. Yet in the ratifying debates these delegates generally found themselves forced to present these central features not as lamentable compromises—that would have been an unappealing defense—but rather as the culmination of the best available political science. "Unrepentant they simply lost the vote," Robert Wiebe remarks, "and in the process they became federalists in spite of themselves."[33] Hence, *The Federalists Papers* arguably constitute the first, and probably the most magnificent, instance of grand constitutional rationalization.[34]

Is Rationalization Reasonable?

Of course, a rationalization offered by one judge or scholar may be criticized by other judges or scholars. Perhaps the most common form of criticism takes a straightforward approach; it tries to show that the particular rationalization is unpersuasive on its own terms. Thus, judges and scholars routinely criticize a rationalization by trying to show that it is somehow flawed on the merits. For example, Ackerman's grand rationalization of constitutional law has been attacked on the grounds that it does violence to the constitutional text, or distorts American history, or misunderstands and misdescribes the cases it relies upon.[35]

In a given instance, these kinds of criticisms on the merits may or may not be persuasive, of course. My interest here is in a different kind of criticism that, perhaps surprisingly, is rarely if ever made. Even if a particular rationalization is utterly convincing, isn't it still objectionable simply by virtue of being *a rationalization*? In ordinary life, as noted earlier, the assertion "That's just a rationalization" has clout, even if the rationalization supplies what could have been good reasons for an action or decision. Why isn't the same true in legal and constitutional discourse?

Doubts about Rationalization

Suppose, for example, that the official reasoning given in the opinion in *Brown v. Board of Education* is demonstrably flawed, but that later scholars—Alexander Bickel, Bruce Ackerman, Robert Bork, Laurence Tribe, and others—have provided compelling alternative justifications for the decision. The alternative justifications show that Earl Warren and his brethren got the right result—albeit not for reasons that they themselves understood or articulated. We should be thankful, presumably, that they got it right. But important questions remain.

For example, how should the later appearance of a persuasive rationalization affect our evaluation of Earl Warren and the Court on which he served? Should we conclude that they were just lucky? Or perhaps that they were blessed with some sort of special intuitive faculty, or juristic sixth sense, that pointed them to correct results despite the palpable inadequacy of their explicit reasoning? Neither supposition seems especially reassuring, but what is the alternative? Perhaps they *did* understand the true justification but for some reason declined to express it. But this seems unlikely: If there was a better legal justification than the one they gave, and if the *Brown* justices were actually aware of the better justification, why would they hide it? And why would years or decades have to pass before the most astute legal scholars managed to hit upon the true justification that the Court knew all along but inexplicably concealed?

These specific questions about the *Brown* Court lead to a more general question: What does the pervasive and typically unapologetic practice of rationalization say about the sort of enterprise jurists and constitutional scholars are engaged in? We have seen that from the beginning, but especially in modern times, constitutional discourse has been depicted as an exercise of *reason*—indeed, as the principal place where reason exerts itself on the governance of the polity. But this depiction fits badly with an enterprise in which it seems that the true reasons for the most important decisions are frequently unknown to the people making the decisions—in this case, the judges—but instead have to be supplied years or even decades later, and usually by a different group of people—that is, legal scholars.

This doubt is reinforced, I think, by one plausible response to the previous questions about the *Brown* Court. Earlier I asked how we should assess the *Brown* justices if we believe, as most scholars do, that the explicit reasoning offered by the Court was deficient. Were the justices just lucky, or were they endowed with some special faculty for reaching right results even though they could not articulate *why* those results were right? One is tempted to respond, I think, that these questions overlook the obvious. *We know* that racial segregation is deeply wrong. So did the justices in *Brown*. Who knows?—it is even possible that at some level the justices in *Plessy v. Ferguson* realized this as well, although they managed to conceal this knowledge from the nation, and perhaps even from themselves.

Just how to explain the wrongness of racial segregation in a rigorous way may present a problem; after all, as we have seen, modern moral theory is in considerable disarray. But this difficulty does not change the fact that "we" *know* segregation is wrong. So the *Brown* justices did not need either luck or any special faculty; they only needed the courage or integrity to do what they knew—and what we all know, if we are honest—to be right. To be sure, development of an adequate legal rationalization for that decision may have awaited future thought and work. But after all, the important thing is not getting the proper legal rationalization—Is it?—but rather getting the proper result; and that is what the Warren Court was good at.[36]

This is a tempting assessment, I think, and it may even be right in some sense, at least with respect to *Brown*. But it also leaves huge questions. Suppose it is true that we all somehow "know" that racial segregation is wrong: Still, *how* do we know that, and what exactly do we even mean when we say that segregation is wrong? And should we so easily gloss over the vexed question of the relationship between law and morality?

Most important for present purposes, the assessment I have just given jeopardizes the long-standing claim of constitutional law to be an enterprise

governed by "reason." The assessment suggests, rather, that some more mysterious and elemental force (or perhaps Holmes's "felt necessities of the time"[37])
guides our convictions and decisions, leading us to "know" certain things although we cannot articulate convincing reasons for them, and thus relegating
"reason" to a post hoc, epiphenomenal role. "The wind bloweth where it list-
eth, and thou hearest the sound thereof but canst not tell whence it cometh
and whither it goeth: so is everyone that is born of the Spirit."[38] This diagnosis
might in the end be right, but it entails relinquishing the claim that constitutional law is *directed by* reason.

　　In sum, the pervasive fact of rationalization in constitutional discourse en-
dangers the claim of constitutional discourse to be an enterprise governed by
reason. So we may ask: What is the role of reason in constitutional law after
all? Let us consider three responses to the challenge posed by rationalization.

Rationalization as the Method of Reason?

The first response attempts to minimize the tension between reasons and rationalizations by observing that an enterprise may genuinely be directed by
reason even though the reasons are produced post hoc. Imagine a situation in
which we cannot reliably determine until *after* a decision is made whether the
decision is justified, or whether it is in accord with reason. We might in this
situation make a decision based on a hunch or best guess, or even a coin flip,
and *then* examine the decision to see whether it was justified. If it was, we
would respect the decision, build on it, continue in the direction it pointed. If
it was *not* justified, then we would revoke or revise the decision and move in a
different direction. This process might not be as linear, or as reassuring, as
one in which we could know in advance whether a decision is justified. It is
more halting, more hit-and-miss. But the process might still be regarded as an
enterprise governed by reason.

　　Scholarly defenses of the two-phase, discovery/justification model of judicial decision-making already advocate something like this view of how reason
works. By this account, a judge initially comes to favor a particular result not
on the basis of "the law," but rather because of other nonlegal and perhaps
nonrational factors. But this admission does not subvert the legality or rationality of judicial decisions because the judge still must not actually make and
announce the decision he is inclined to favor unless his predisposition or intuition or "hunch" can be rationalized in legal terms. Law disciplines the judge
post hoc, in a sense, but the discipline is no less real for coming after the
judge "discovers" the result on other grounds.[39] Reason might operate in the
same way.

　　As the example of judicial decision-making suggests, this depiction of ra-
tionalization-as-directing reason may be plausible—but only under certain
conditions. First, post hoc rationalization seems most likely to be an actual directing force when the rationalization is provided at least roughly contempora-
neously with the decision, and by the same people or institutions that are
making the decision. Conversely, if the rationalization is provided well after

the decision and by people other than and without authority over the actual decision-makers, its power to correct or redirect decisions diminishes. Second, in order to serve as a meaningful disciplining or governing force, the method of post hoc rationalization would need to be relatively determinate; it must be able to show convincingly that some decisions within a relatively contained sphere are correct and others are not. On the other hand, if the language of justification is sufficiently loose that it can rationalize a wide range of decisions, then it seems that the after-the-fact rationalization is more likely performing the function we attribute to it in everyday life—that of apologist or excuse-maker or spin doctor—than the function of director or governor.

So can the rationalizing enterprise in constitutional law meet these requirements? The first of these conditions is arguably satisfied *for judicial decision-making*. In this process, discovery and justification are performed almost simultaneously and by the same person; the judge must check to see whether there is a persuasive rationalization before her decision even becomes final and is announced to the public.

But the first condition is not satisfied with respect to the rationalizing enterprise of legal scholarship. As discussed earlier, legal scholars may take years in devising and evaluating possible justifications for important judicial decisions. With respect to landmark decisions such as *Brown* or *Roe*, many scholars have criticized the reasoning offered in those opinions, but whether adequate justifications can be devised (and if so, what the plausible justifications are) remain controversial issues even today.[40] Meanwhile, of course, the decisions become entrenched; and the question of initial justification may become displaced, as has happened with *Roe*, by the inertia of stare decisis.[41] And even if scholars move rapidly, they have no authority over judges; it is questionable how much attention, if any, judges even pay to academic writing. In this context, it is far-fetched to suppose that the scholarly debates represent exercises in reason that actually direct the judges' decisions in post hoc fashion.[42]

The second requirement—the requirement, that is, of relative determinacy—does not seem to be met in constitutional law either at the stage of judicial decision-making or at the stage of legal scholarship. On the contrary, the discourse of constitutional rationalization is sufficiently loose that it does not operate as a serious practical constraint on most constitutional decisions. The question of legal determinacy has been hotly debated, of course, and there is probably no across-the-board answer to that question. It makes sense to suppose that some areas of law are more determinate than others. But as preceding chapters have suggested, constitutional law surely does not rank high on the scale of determinacy or precision. In area after area, scholars demonstrate the ease with which nebulous doctrinal tests composed largely of general or conclusory "prongs" can be used to rationalize a range of different results. Religion clause doctrine may be unusually incoherent, to be sure, but one leading scholar's appraisal of that doctrine—that it is "so elastic in its application that it means everything and nothing"[43]—would need to be toned down only slightly for many other areas of constitutional law.[44]

Of course, the inadequacy of legal doctrine to explain and justify results is one reason why legal scholars typically feel compelled to go beyond the grounds given in judicial opinions in search of the real reasons that do or do not justify a decision. And scholarly explorations may indeed bring to light different and, perhaps, more cogent reasons for or objections to decisions. But however one appraises the virtues of legal scholarship, it would be implausible to suggest that scholarship makes the law *more determinate*. On the contrary, legal scholarship has the effect of multiplying the number of approaches and perspectives, and of greatly extending the spectrum of arguments and reasons, that can be used to justify or criticize a decision. Thus, legal scholarship expands rather than restricts the scope of possible rationalizations.

In sum, although it is imaginable in the abstract that an enterprise might actually be governed or directed by reason even though the reasoning occurs post hoc, that possibility simply does not seem to fit the facts of rationalization in constitutional law. So if we are to salvage the claim that constitutional law is an expression of reason as against the fact of pervasive post hoc rationalization, we need some other account of how reason directs the enterprise.

The Cunning of Constitutional Reason

It may be helpful at this point to step back and take a more panoramic view of the problem we are considering. The specific question that provokes our discussion is how the fact of pervasive rationalization should affect our judgment both of particular cases and courts, such as the *Brown* decision and the Warren Court, and of the general claim of constitutional law to be an expression of reason. But consider for a moment the broad historical backdrop for that question.

If we reflect on the development of our constitutional system, it may seem remarkable how often actions or decisions that seemed casual or trivial at the time, and that may have been taken almost without thought, come to have tremendous and sometimes beneficial significance in our political development.[45] Take the Bill of Rights.[45] Contrary to his earlier position, and in order to satisfy a campaign promise, Madison introduces a list of rights in the First Congress. His list reflects a studied effort to avoid "everything of a controvertible nature."[46] Impatiently, and almost without thought or discussion, Congress and then the states approve most of these rights, with many legislators regarding them as "a few milk and water amendments," "trash," or "nonsense." And for decades this judgment seems to be vindicated; the rights lie dormant in the constitutional text.[47] Then, a century-and-a-half after their adoption, they emerge as major bulwarks in the protection of liberties—and, of course, as a source of authoritative answers to the most deep-seated political and social controversies, which now are resolved by the invocation of what "the Constitution requires."

Sometimes these rights function in what most would regard as a salutary way—but one quite opposite from what those who casually adopted the rights expected. Nearly all scholars agree, for example, that the establishment clause was intended at least in part to *protect* state-established religion from federal intervention.[48] But 150 years later (and as a result of an "incorporation" decision that was at best dimly understood by those who made it, if indeed they were conscious of having made such a decision at all), that clause is found to authorize federal intervention to *eliminate* offensive state religious practices.

Take another example: A justice inserts an obscure footnote in a mundane opinion upholding a prohibition on the interstate shipment of "filled milk."[49] The footnote asserts nothing, but instead raises several questions; as the justice's law clerk later explains, its "modest hope" is to stimulate discussion within the legal profession.[50] And even this timid ambition seems to be quickly frustrated: A world war breaks out, causing lawyers and commentators to turn their attention elsewhere. Later, though, the footnote is rediscovered, and now is treated as having settled the questions it meant to raise.[51] Gradually achieving the status of "the most celebrated footnote in constitutional law,"[52] a few sentences intended as a starting point for discussion become the foundation for numerous decisions attempting to protect minorities from majoritarian oppression (not to mention for volumes of learned legal analysis[53]).

Of course, even with the benefit of hindsight, not everyone lauds these developments. And even those who do would not depict *all* of our constitutional history in triumphalist terms; we cannot forget *Dred Scott* and *Lochner,* which after all were also justified by reference to constitutional provisions probably not designed to secure those particular results. On the whole, though, it is remarkable how often provisions or actions whose wisdom and reason were not appreciated at the time have come to constitute the foundation for the legal edifice that *our* reason celebrates.

So how do we account for the transformation of the trivial and thoughtless into something momentous and worthy of reason's approval? This question may be simply a grander version of the question asked earlier about the significance of rationalization. But looking at the problem in a more sweeping fashion may suggest a second overall account of the role of rationalization in an enterprise dedicated to governance by reason. It almost seems that "reason" is not merely a faculty confined to finite human intellects. Instead, Reason— and here we should probably use the upper case—almost seems to be a sort of benevolent foreign power working through the often uncomprehending agents of judges and politicians. Reason, it seems, is a sort of Muse that speaks through its chosen poets who often know not what they say—like the divinity that prompted the rhapsode Ion in Plato's dialogue to utter inspired things about Homer although Ion himself could not even understand or account for his utterances.[54]

If we were to adopt this view, we would of course not be the first to do so. In Hegel's philosophy of history, for example, Reason is not merely a mundane human faculty for analyzing propositions and sifting arguments, or for deducing conclusions from given premises.[55] On the contrary, Reason—which Hegel also describes as the "World Spirit," or sometimes as "God"—appears as an immanent force operating upon and through history to bring about its own fulfillment.

But Reason realizes itself not through the conscious exercise of mundane human reason. "The first glance at history," Hegel observed, "convinces us that the actions of men spring from their needs, their passions, their interests, their characters, and their talents. Indeed, it appears as if in this drama of activities these needs, passions, and interests are the sole springs of actions and the main efficient cause."[56] Like the delegates to the Philadelphia convention, Hegel held that "[p]assions, private aims, and the satisfaction of selfish desires are . . . closer to the core of human nature than the artificial and troublesome discipline that tends toward order, self-restraint, law, and morality." Consequently, history *appears to be* an affair of "violence," "unreason," "evil," "vice," and "ruin." The unfolding of temporal events seems not to be the work of reason at all, but rather of that old nemesis of reason—human "will."[57]

These appearances are misleading, though, because in reality Reason is subtly operating through its human agents, who unknowingly work to further Reason's designs.

> These vast congeries of volitions, interests, and activities constitute the tools and means of the World Spirit for attaining its purpose, bringing it to consciousness, and realizing it. . . . [T]hose manifestations of vitality on the part of individuals and peoples in which they seek and satisfy their own purposes are, at the same time, the means and tools of a higher and broader purpose of which they know nothing, which they realize unconsciously.[58]

Reason's surreptitious way of enlisting individuals who are unknowingly conscripted to serve its purposes is what Hegel called "the cunning of Reason."[59] But Reason in its hidden wisdom does not make equal use of all individuals. In particular, there are certain "historical men," or "world-historical individuals," or "heroes"—men like Alexander, Caesar, and Napoleon—who have a special role in Reason's plan.[60]

> Such individuals have no consciousness of the Idea as such. They are practical and political men. But at the same time they are thinkers with insight into what is needed and timely. They see the very truth of their age and their world, the next genus, so to speak, which is already formed in the womb of time. . . . The world-historical persons, the heroes of their age, must therefore be recognized as its seers—their words and deeds are the best of the age.[61]

A Hegelian conception of Reason might at first glance seem nicely crafted to preserve the claims of constitutional reason even in the face of pervasive rationalization. By this view, courts like the *Brown* Court and decisions like *Brown, Griswold,* and *Roe* might be seen as having been directed by Reason, even though the actors and recorders who moved under Reason's dictate did not fully grasp, and thus gave only inadequate accounts of, the justifications for what they did. It will only be with the benefit of hindsight, if at all, that we will come to understand the real justifications for actions performed and decisions made under the mysterious urgings of Reason; but the delay in no way negates the fact of such influence. When Reason speaks, it is not always ours to reason why.

In addition, the Hegelian notion that Reason works especially through certain heroes, or world-historical individuals, seems nicely compatible with much modern constitutional theorizing. The important developments in our constitutional history, by this view, are closely associated with certain larger-than-life figures who stand out for the role they have played—Thomas Jefferson, James Madison, John Marshall, Abraham Lincoln, *perhaps* Oliver Wendell Holmes (although his place on the list currently seems more doubtful than it once might have), Franklin D. Roosevelt, Earl Warren . . . perhaps even the odd herculean constitutional scholar.

It is not that these figures have always clearly *understood* the significance or the comprehensive wisdom of their actions and decisions. Indeed, their deficiencies in articulation, like the Court's in *Brown,* sometimes strongly suggest that they did *not* fully grasp the meaning of or justification for what they did. For the most part they were, after all, "practical and political men," like Hegel's heroes. But also like Hegel's great men, they somehow possessed "insight into what [was] needed and timely." And for their age they "must therefore be recognized as its seers—their words and deeds are the best of the age." In this spirit, Earl Warren can be explicitly designated a "hero" by someone like John Ely,[62] not because Warren fully understood or articulated the wisdom that drove him—if he had, Ely's book devoted to that task would have been superfluous—but because, as Hegel put it, Warren somehow saw "the very truth of [his] age and [his] world." In short, the Hegelian conception serves nicely to provide a rationalization for the work of the constitutional rationalizers.

Rejecting Hegelian Reason

Nonetheless, it seems that constitutional lawyers and scholars have not been eager to call upon Hegel for assistance. And upon reflection, there is good reason for their reticence. It is not just that Hegel's philosophy of history seems unfashionably elitist in exalting its heroic "historical men," or that his talk of trampling flowers and crushing to pieces anything in Reason's path[63] betrays a joyous irreverence toward cherished norms of justice and morality. Nor is the problem just that few if any modern constitutional scholars—or anyone else—can actually believe in Reason as a World Spirit mysteriously immanent in history. We could no doubt bring ourselves to believe in that force if it were convenient to do so.

But it is *not* convenient. The deeper problem is that the Hegelian approach, though it would preserve the *word* Reason, would sacrifice the substance of "reason" as understood in the Cartesian tradition and embraced in constitutional thinking. The whole point of the commitment to "reason," after all, has been to seize control of our own fate. Reason, as Ernest Gellner has observed, has been the catchword for describing an "aspiration for autonomy" and an "overwhelming desire for a kind of self-creation."[64] And the Hegelian Reason-as-World Spirit appears not to satisfy this desire, but rather to frustrate it. "Reason" becomes just another term for "God," as Hegel acknowledges[65] (although the relationship between this "God" and the traditional God of the Bible is murky at best[66]). And arguing for the rule of Reason in history seems an oblique way of saying that God uses us in spite of ourselves to achieve his purposes in history.

This is no way to achieve autonomy; indeed, it seems the opposite of autonomy. Thus, not taken in by the terminology, Gellner appropriately discusses Hegel's notions under the heading of "Enemies of Reason."[67] So it seems that the Hegelian approach is not in the end a promising way of rescuing the claim that constitutional law is an enterprise directed by reason.

So it seems that two initially promising ways of reconciling rationalization with reason turn out to be fruitless. But if the pervasive fact of rationalization cannot be accommodated either as a post hoc method of exercising human reason or as a belated recognition of imminent historical Reason, then where are we left?

The Pretense of Reason

There is third possibility—one more obvious and commonsensical but perhaps more painful to contemplate. Constitutional discourse might be largely garden variety rationalization, serving approximately the same purpose that rationalization serves in everyday experience: Its function is to create the appearance that we have acted on the basis of certain reasons—or, more grandly, of "reason"—when in fact we have not.

From the beginning, as we have seen, our constitutional system was grounded in an aspiration to be governed by reason. All earlier states and governments had been directed largely by authority and tradition, force and fortuity. *Our* aspiration was to free ourselves from servitude to these blind or tyrannical masters. For the first time in history, we would have a government designed and directed by reason.

But we have found no way to satisfy that aspiration. The original plan to consolidate the conclusions of reason by embodying them in a legal document—a written Constitution—has proven inadequate to the task. Subsequent efforts to establish a practice of regulatory reason have likewise failed. This is not to deny that what we might call "reasoning"—reading and writing, asserting and responding, talking and thinking and arguing—is a prominent part of our political process. There is plenty of such "reasoning" in our system—just as there was plenty of "reasoning" in the Athens that executed Socrates, and in the papacy-prince struggles of the Middle Ages, and in the English Parliament against which we revolted, and in the common law system which we hoped to transcend. Our aspiration was to establish a government based on reason in some purer, more exalted sense. It is that more heroic aspiration that we have found no way to realize.

So what to do? We might simply admit that our aspirations were too grandiose, or that reason seems condemned to playing a merely marginal role in human affairs, or that the notion of reason as something independent of tradition and authority may have been misconceived from the beginning. But making these admissions might require a strength of character that we do not possess.

At the very least, the admissions would deprive us of a kind of rhetorical wellspring that many of us—lawyers, judges, and especially legal scholars—are wont to dip into on an almost constant basis. But the consequences of the admission might be even more severe: The admission might amount to a kind of professional and cultural suicide. *I* can admit that I am not a good pianist because I never claimed to be one. Being a good pianist is not at all important to my concept of myself. It might not be so easy for Van Cliburn to make a similar admission: For him, the admission might negate something central to his very identity. In the same way, if we have from the beginning conceived of our Republic as, in Henry Steele Commager's phrase, "The Empire of Reason," then it may not be so easy to admit that reason has not played, and probably cannot play, the directive and redemptive role that we have assigned to it.

I should quickly admit that this diagnosis is not one that I offer with much confidence. Indeed, it seems unlikely that the diagnosis would be troubling to American culture generally. While there have been those whose deepest faith and commitment have been directed to the Republic of Reason, many Americans have no doubt been attached to different visions—to a "Christian nation," or to a pluralistic melting pot symbolized by the Statue of Liberty, or to a nation "conceived in liberty and dedicated to the proposition that all men are created equal." Reason might after all be only one theme—and not the dominant theme at that—in a fantastically complex cultural pastiche.

But reason *has* been the dominant theme in our legal culture—and especially in the constitutional culture that has developed around the practice of judicial review. It is, once again, the association of constitutional law with "reason" that has seemed to support the claim by constitutional lawyers, scholars, and judges of a power to overrule the decisions of the people and their officials made through the mundane and often messy processes of democratic politics.

Rationalization as the Culmination of Reason

So admitting the inefficacy of independent reason might be especially painful for the residents of that cultural neighborhood—only one of many in the American political community—that is called "law." And thus arises the urgent need for an enterprise of rationalization: If we cannot actually realize the aspirations of reason, then perhaps we must settle for creating the *appearance* of governance by reason. Hence the hundreds and thousands of pages of constitutional rationalization that fill volumes of judicial reports and law reviews each year.

This relegation of the aspiration to be governed by reason to the realm of appearance may be disappointing in one sense, but it is also liberating. Within that realm, after all, the hard practical realities that in the outside world seem to frustrate and mock reason at every turn can, to some extent, be ignored or imagined away, leaving reason more ample scope for uninhibited self-realization. So it should not be surprising that in recent decades, as judges and constitutional scholars have proliferated and scholarship has grown more imaginative and ambitious, the law itself has swollen in its scope and complexity. It covers more spheres of life. Its rationalizations become more aggressive, more ambitious in force and scope, more intimidating in their intricacy. The Constitution's majestic generalities ("Congress shall make no law . . . abridging the freedom of speech. . . .") develop into a plethora of techniques and distinctions and three- and four-prong tests.

Despite their jealously defended insularity, of course, courts are still forced to reckon in some respects with vulgar political realities. The legal academy, by contrast, is largely spared such unpleasant encounters; in that realm the aspiration to realize reason in the Constitution—in the historic Constitution of rare but heroic judicial decisions like *Brown,* and in the more reliably heroic Constitution of the law reviews—goes virtually unchecked. So legal scholars discover new constitutional rights and invent new constitutional remedies. For example, we learn from one prominent scholar that the Constitution "guarantees the material support necessary to a productive and unalienated work life, to a healthy private home and community life, and to meaningful participation in the public sphere of democratic decision making."[68] It turns out that the Constitution is a nobler document than we ever dared to imagine.

To be sure, it may yet happen that in looking out upon the world, as scholars sometimes do, a leading constitutional thinker may be profoundly puzzled to observe concrete injustices that will not be whisked away simply by judicial enforcement of "the Constitution." The phenomenon "begs for explanation."[69] But the necessary explanation is quickly forthcoming: As in more standard theodicies, some evil must be allowed to persist in deference to the value of freedom. Democratic freedom, that is, requires that although the Constitution fully embodies justice, not all aspects of the Constitution should be *judicially* enforceable. Some aspects of justice must be left to be realized by the people themselves through the more democratic institutions of government. So the perfection of the Constitution itself[70]—of the Constitution of academic reason, that is—remains unimpaired.

In the ethereal world of the constitutional scholar, it seems, the best of all possible constitutions has finally become what in the innocent infancy of the Age of Reason Jefferson predicted it would be: an unprecedented engine of reason "competent to render our fellow-citizens the happiest and the securest on whom the sun has ever shone."[71] Reason, free at last from the traditional constraints that had for so long confined it, is finally receiving its due. The honor is conferred—most impressively, and again and again—in the pages of the *Harvard Law Review* and the *Yale Law Journal.* It is just a small irony of history, perhaps, that these most prestigious publications are the modern legal voices of institutions founded a century-and-a-half before the Constitution by Calvinists (those most un-Jeffersonian partisans of an irresistible, ultimately inscrutable God); and those most prestigious institutions are still situated by the same sea which brought the Calvinist predecessors of the prophets of reason to these shores—and which, incidentally, still rolls on as it rolled five thousand years ago.

Epilogue
The Constitution of Babel

We began, chapters and generations ago, with a project to free human governance from the tyranny of force and fortuity, and in their place to put something called "reason." And we have seen how that aspiration led first to the construction of a legalistic Constitution designed to embody the political *conclusions* of reason, and later to the open-textured Constitution of principle designed to promote a *discourse* of reason. Upon inspection, however, the reigning discourse has scant claim to the title. On the contrary, contemporary constitutional debates, whether carried on by justices or scholars, present a spectacle of confusion and futility—of overt rationalization and escapist self-deception, or of sophistry so transparent that, having lost its power to beguile, it degenerates into name-calling and authoritarian bullying.

The spectacle irresistibly calls up the image of "Babel." In modern usage, "Babel" connotes confusion or unintelligibility. But the allusion also taps into a more searching myth that has fascinated humans almost from the beginning. Michael Oakeshott, who wrote two different essays entitled "The Tower of Babel,"[1] observed that some version of the myth "is to be found among the stories of the Chinese, the Caldeans and the ancient Hebrews, and among the Arab and Slav peoples, and the Aztecs of Peru. It has been told in the Greek, the Latin, the Celtic, and the Teutonic languages and in the tongues of those who for millennia have moved about the islands of the Pacific ocean."[2] The story's universal fascination derives from its central theme, which makes it both important to consider but also difficult (for us) to grasp and talk about: "It is concerned with earth and heaven; with men and Gods and how they stand to one another."[3]

The Tower of Babel

Probably the best known version of the story, in this country at least, is in the biblical book of Genesis.[4] But for a slightly more elaborate telling, we can consult Josephus:

143

[After the great flood] God bade [Noah's descendants] to send out colonies, that they might not quarrel with each other but cultivate much of the earth and enjoy an abundance of its fruits; but in their blindness they did not hearken to Him, and in consequence were plunged into calamities. . . . For when they had a flourishing youthful population, God again counselled them to colonize; but they, never thinking that they owed their blessings to His benevolence and regarding their own might as the cause of their felicity, refused to obey. Nay, to this disobedience to God's will they even added the suspicion that God was plotting against them in urging them to emigrate, in order that, being divided, they might be more open to attack.

They were incited to this insolent contempt of God by Nebrodes, grandson of Ham the son of Noah, an audacious man of doughty vigour. He persuaded them to attribute their prosperity not to God but to their own valour. . . . He threatened to have his revenge on God if He wished to inundate the earth again; for he would build a tower higher than the water could reach and avenge the destruction of their forefathers.

The people were eager to follow this advice of Nebrodes, deeming it slavery to submit to God; so they set out to build the tower with indefatigable ardour and no slackening in the task; and it rose with a speed beyond all expectation. . . . Seeing their mad enterprise, God was not minded to exterminate them utterly, because even the destruction of the first victims had not taught their descendants wisdom; but He created discord among them by making them speak different languages, through the variety of which they could not understand one another. The place where they built the tower is now called Babylon from the confusion of the primitive speech once intelligible to all, for the Hebrews call confusion "Babel."[5]

Modern allusions to "Babel" typically mean to incorporate the conclusion or outcome of the mythical story—that is, confusion. But the story itself also explores the cause of that confusion. And it seems that the ultimate cause of the debacle, simply put, was human pride—pride not merely in the conventional sense of inordinate self-esteem but in the classic or Augustinian sense,[6] in which pride denotes an attitude of revolt against providential governance with the aim of establishing human self-rule in its place. In more current terminology, the cause of confusion—of "Babel"—was an overweening determination to realize human autonomy.

The Constitution as Babel?

Might the comparison of constitutional law to Babel fit the story in this more complete sense? We should acknowledge at the outset that in the modern legal academy, perhaps partly as a consequence of developments discussed in earlier chapters, the question itself seems alien, and we probably do not have the discursive resources even to consider it in a straightforward way. Still, it is possible cautiously to explore some parallels.

The most crucial parallel concerns the central role of pride. In considering the constitutional project, of course, we have talked not about pride, but rather about "reason." But as should by now be apparent, the qualities tend to converge. "Reason" has meant different things, as we have seen, but over the last few centuries, as Ernest Gellner observes, "[o]ne of the central themes, perhaps indeed the central obsession, of Cartesian rationalism is the aspiration for autonomy. There is the overwhelming desire for a kind of self-creation. . . . Man uses Reason to make himself."[7] Reason, in other words, is less an epistemological position than an attitude, or an aspiration of the human spirit.[8]

Gellner's study, offered as a vindication of reason, recounts how Descartes's views about knowledge and how to acquire it were debunked by philosophers like Hume and Kant; Kant's notions were in turn shown to be naive by sociologists like Durkheim; Durkheim's position came to be seen as inadequate because . . . —the story goes on and on. Yet all of these thinkers were committed to "reason." So "reason," as this history makes clear, does not denote any particular epistemology or method, nor does it describe any constant or agreed-upon way of conceiving of the world and of our ways of knowing it. Instead, the consistent commitment that unites these thinkers, and that defines a central element in the modern mind and temperament, is the "Promethean aspiration to autarchy and self-creation."[9] Though Gellner invokes the Greek myth, not the Hebrew story, the aspiration and attitude he describes seem precisely the ones that drove the builders of the Tower in the tale told by Josephus. In short, modern Reason is ancient Pride.

And indeed, a current of pride runs through the constitutional project from the outset. In the beginning, the founding generation manifested a buoyant but still constrained pride. Reason did not rebel against the providential framework of Nature, but at most rejected the received ways of understanding that framework—tradition, authority, revelation, scripture—in favor of trusting in human intellect. So even the most fervently "enlightened" Americans exhibited a sort of epistemological pride—nothing more. Later, "reason" came to describe a more aggressive aspiration, repudiating the cosmic framework or design and demanding the right to create the world for itself.

To be sure, in constitutional discourse, with its stodgy, stylized vocabulary of precedent and text and doctrine, pride is typically disguised. Still, manifestations of pride, at least in its more ordinary sense of conceit or presumption, are readily discernible. For those immersed in constitutional culture these manifestations may be so familiar as to seem unremarkable. But consider some instances that happen to have appeared in the preceding discussion. Examples began to accumulate in the very first paragraph, as Thomas Jefferson and James Wilson boasted that the Constitution was "unquestionably the wisest ever yet presented to men" and "the best form of government that has ever been offered to the world."[10] Later we observed Ronald Dworkin describing judges as the "princes" of "law's empire," and in even more exalted fashion designating philosophers—"if they are willing," as at least one of them apparently is—as the empire's "seers and prophets."[11]

Or recall Dworkin explaining to a century of popes that they have misunderstood and misrepresented Catholic doctrines. Or John Rawls decreeing, apparently without sense of obligation to explain or qualify, that any reasonable balance of competing interests will support a right to abortion in the first trimester and that any view inconsistent with this position is simply "to that extent unreasonable."[12]

The issue of abortion in particular, it seems, has in recent years elicited outpourings of presumption, not only by scholars like Dworkin and Rawls but also by judges. Remember the *Casey* decision, with its celebrated Joint Opinion.[13] Abortion is of course an issue that has been debated endlessly by lawyers, politicians, philosophers, theologians, columnists, teachers, students, and citizens generally.[14] Yet in *Casey*, three justices—all of whom had been placed on the Court, as it happens, during a period in which relative anonymity, so to speak, was a leading prerequisite for successful appointment[15]—saw it as their right and duty to "call[] the contending sides of a national controversy to end their national division by accepting a common mandate rooted in the Constitution."[16] It turned out, according to the plurality itself, that the decision was not so much "rooted in *the Constitution*" as in the doctrine of precedent and—ironies begin to pile up at this point—in the justices' perception that a contrary decision would undermine the Court's legitimacy by making it appear to be an institution influenced by politics.[17] Nonetheless, the plurality gravely declared that "the character of a Nation of people who aspire to live according to the rule of law" is ultimately to be measured by the people's willingness to put aside their deeply held views and accept the justices' pronouncements on this and other divisive questions.[18]

For many, statements like these amount to "an extravagant expression of hubris."[19] Mary Ann Glendon suggests that the *Casey* opinion will be "remembered less for its result than for its grandiose portrayal of the role of the Supreme Court in American society."[20] Conversely, from a more detached or perhaps more cynical perspective, the justices' pronouncements might be merely a source of amusement, as when the family's four-year-old peremptorily declares that "I've decided we're all going to Disneyland today," and that the way to pay for the trip is to "just write a check." ("Isn't that *cute,*" the parents joke, as they go about their business.) But whether one finds the justices' self-important declarations exasperating or merely comical, the statements surely exude a presumption that would be remarkable coming from *any* source, and that is all the more remarkable given the character of these authors.[21]

Still, the *Casey* opinion—like the statements by Wilson and Jefferson, Dworkin and Rawls—are most obviously manifestations of pride in the conventional sense. Do these pronouncements also reflect pride in the more classical sense as depicted in the Tower of Babel myth? More generally, the critical question is whether the constitutional project follows the same course and ends up at the same place as the Babel story. And the answer to that question, it seems, is ambiguous.

If the Babel analogy holds true, the final outcome of pride—and thus of the presumption that for us goes under the names of "reason," or "constitutional law"—would be confusion. As the preceding chapters suggest, there is ample evidence of confusion in current constitutional debates. So in this respect the parallel remains intact.

In other respects, though, the analogy may seem to break down. After all, the Tower story ends in disaster. No one can understand anyone else. The Tower is abandoned. The people are dispersed. The builders are punished for their pride.

The constitutional project, by contrast, seems so far to be at least a qualified success story. To be sure, if we concentrate on constitutional *discourse* from a purely academic perspective, examining that discourse for its cogency or intellectual coherence, there may be cause for disappointment, even despair. But if we consider the overall political system that constitutional law has established and helped to govern, our assessment may change. Political problems and injustices abound, to be sure. But the American political system *does* seem to have achieved a measure of freedom and economic prosperity unprecedented in human history. As two constitutional scholars report,

> Our Eighteenth-Century federalist Constitution has survived the totalitarian menaces of Naziism and communism and has fostered the creation of the freest and wealthiest nation in human history. The extended commercial republic of which Publius wrote in *The Federalist Papers* now reaches from sea to shining sea and supports a population eighty times larger than during the Founding era. Areas that were wilderness in Publius's time now teem with cities, factories, universities, churches, highways, airports, and other indicia of advanced civilization.[22]

So the commitment to reason may seem to have paid off after all, and the analogy to the Babel project appears inapt.

The Fruits of Reason?

Is this dismissive conclusion sound? Suppose, in other words, that our political system *does* enjoy an unprecedented level of freedom and prosperity. How should we account for this success? More specifically, do our successes vindicate the faith we have placed in "reason"? Do they show that the more apt mythical analogue for our constitutional project is the one Gellner cites—that is, the Promethean story, where with a little help men stole fire from the gods and got away with it—not Babel?

At this point it may be worth considering the analysis of Reinhold Niebuhr, who more than once invoked the Tower of Babel myth as a metaphor for understanding American politics and history.[23] The application of the myth was hardly limited, in Niebuhr's view, to this country; on the contrary, "man is constantly tempted to forget the finiteness of his cultures and civilization and to pretend a finality for them which they do not have. Every civilization and culture is thus a Tower of Babel."[24] But the story has special force for us, he suggested, with our pretensions to reason. "[M]odern man is a rationalist," Niebuhr observed, "who builds Towers of Babel without knowing it. The primitive sense of guilt expressed in this myth is the fruit of an insight too profound for modernity's superficial intelligence."[25] And he warned:

> If either moral pride or the spirit of rationalism tries to draw every element in
> an historic situation into rational coherence, and persuades us to establish a
> direct congruity between our good fortune and our virtue or our skill, we will
> inevitably claim more for our contribution to our prosperity than the facts
> warrant. This has remained a source of moral confusion in American life.[26]

As this quotation indicates, however, Niebuhr did not deny the tremendous political and technological achievements of American civilization. How then was the comparison to Babel cogent? Part of Niebuhr's answer was that our achievements, real though they are, are neither as important nor as enduring as we like to suppose. And the very significance of our accomplishments may lead us to overvalue or overestimate them. "Human pride is greatest when it is based upon solid achievements; but the achievements are never great enough to justify its pretensions."[27]

This observation has a certain timely plausibility. We sometimes wonder whether our prosperity, though real enough (for some people), may have been purchased through injustice and oppression, like the elegant opulence of (some classes of) the antebellum South. Or from a more discerning perspective the material prosperity and freedom we celebrate might be merely vulgar and licentious—enticing but ultimately demeaning to the human spirit.[28] Moreover, we are sometimes afflicted with a sense of impending crisis, lending force to Niebuhr's observation that "[o]ne of the most pathetic aspects of human history is that every civilization expresses itself most pretentiously, compounds its partial and universal values most convincingly, and claims immortality for its finite existence at the very moment when the decay which leads to death has already begun."[29] It is hard to read Niebuhr's statement without remembering Sanford Levinson's speculation that "the 'death of constitutionalism' may be the central event of our time."[30]

But these disquieting reminders, even if apt, are also in a sense not sufficient to fully vindicate the Babel analogy. The Babel building project, after all, was an exercise in complete futility; it never did and never could attain, even in part, its objective of reaching and challenging heaven. By contrast, our achievements in freedom and prosperity seem both valuable and real, even if we may sometimes exaggerate them, and even though they may not endure to the end of time. If reason is responsible for these achievements, then it seems unduly severe to dwell on their finitude. Reason may not deserve infinite praise, but it should receive the honor due it.

But *does* reason deserve the credit for the liberty and prosperity this country has enjoyed? Niebuhr considered alternative explanations. One possibility was that the beneficial conditions that have prevailed in this country are largely attributable not to human effort and the exercise of human reason, but rather to providence. Though this explanation may seem inadmissible today, it would not have seemed so, Niebuhr observed, to the colonizing and founding generations. "Both the Puritans and the Jeffersonians attributed the prosperity [of the country] primarily to a divine providence which, as Jefferson observed, 'led our forefathers, as Israel of old, out of their native land and planted them in a country flowing with all the necessaries and comforts of life.'"[31] And of course, neither Jefferson nor the Puritans were being innovative in attributing beneficial historical developments to the designs of providence. As usual, they were anticipated by, among others, Plato.[32]

In the contemporary climate of academic opinion, however, an account of the country's successes that rests on the notion of "America as the darling of divine providence"[33] is not likely to gain many converts. For us, though not for the founders, "providence" amounts to the antithesis of the "reason" which, as Gellner observes, defines us.[34] Niebuhr understood this. "Modern man's confidence in his power over historical destiny prompted the rejection of every older conception of an overruling providence in history."[35] But Niebuhr had another suggestion: To the extent that we cannot admit *providence* as an explanation, perhaps we can accept something else: *fortuity*. So he emphasized "the degree [to which] the wealth of our natural resources and the fortuitous circumstance that we conquered a continent just when the advancement of technics made it possible to organize that continent into a single political and economic unit, lay at the foundation of our prosperity."[36]

This suggestion might evoke a slightly more congenial response. It converges nicely with accounts of the political and economic successes of this country given by other, more secular historians, as in the famous thesis of Frederick Jackson Turner that the country's democratic character resulted from the challenge of meeting frontier conditions.[37] Moreover, an appeal to fortuity resonates with much in the spirit of our time, such as "chaos theory"[38] or, in law, the Critical emphasis on contingent or nonrational factors in history and legal development.[39]

Still, fortuity as a controlling force is at least as threatening as providence is to the project of governance in accordance with reason. "Providence" suggests that our affairs are in reality guided by something *above* or greater than human reason, while "fortuity" implies that the controlling agent is something *beneath* or less than reason; but either view undermines the notion that we are directing our own affairs through the exercise of our own reason. Indeed, in the founding period, as we have seen, fortuity or fate was (along with force) one of the enemies that reason was supposed to overcome. So from the standpoint of the constitutional project, the providence and fortuity accounts offer little to choose between.

The two accounts may also converge in a more fundamental sense. Even if there is a providential design in history, it hardly follows that finite human beings would have the ability to discern that design. Not comprehending the overall plan, we would perceive historical happenings as random, disconnected, contingent. So perhaps fortuity is simply the face that providence wears when addressing *us*. And recognizing our inability to comprehend providence's cosmic plan, or even to know whether there is one, we should perhaps not try to see farther than we can.[40] Indeed, the attempt to penetrate the face of fortuity would itself be a manifestation of unwarranted arrogance. So Niebuhr advised: "If it is not possible for modern man to hold by faith that there is a larger meaning in the intricate patterns of history than those which his own virtues or skills supply, he would do well to emphasize fortune and caprice in his calculations."[41]

A Moral of the Story?

So what do these reflections add up to? What is the moral of the story? Was the common opinion reported by Machiavelli correct after all?—"[W]orldly events are so governed by fortune and by God, that men cannot by their prudence change them, . . . and for this they may judge it to be useless to toil much about them, but let things be ruled by chance."[42] Should we renounce the effort to live by reason and tend to our gardens, thereby abandoning our future to providence or chance?

In different ways, it seems, this prescription both follows from but is also incompatible with the preceding discussion. Start with the sense in which the prescription is incompatible. If history *is* governed by a providential plan, then presumably the very aspiration to live in accordance with reason, vain though the aspiration may ultimately be, is part of that plan. For those generations that have lived in the day or at least the sunset of the Enlightenment, in other words, our role in the cosmic comedy seemingly calls upon us to act out the unenviable part of a self-important jester who has deluded himself into thinking he is king. The part is comically presumptuous, to be sure; but it would be equally presumptuous to suppose that we can defy the providential scheme that has assigned us this embarrassing role. And we can perhaps console ourselves—I do—by reflecting that for all we know, a self-deceived and high-sounding fool may be as essential to the overall plot as a sagacious hero.

Or perhaps there is no overall design, so that blind fortuity rules. In that case, it seems that fortuity has blindly formed us in such a way that a commitment to "reason" is a part of our very identity and constitution. "Rationalism is our destiny. It is not our option," Gellner observes with a sort of defiant resignation. "We are a race of failed Prometheuses."[43] In the fatalistic view, in short, we are what we are, and we will do what we will do; and for us, it seems, this means living—or trying to live, or at least pretending to live—by reason.

But this conclusion has a tendency to dissolve itself. What we are, once again, is a species that attempts to live in accordance with what reason teaches. So if it turns out that reason teaches the futility of trying to live in accordance with reason, then it may be that we *will* abandon the life of reason after all. And if we *do* follow this course, then it also seems we cannot be defying any providential plan. On the contrary, the providential plan, if there is one, apparently will have ordained just this course for us. The plot will be the old, paradoxical one—a variation on the Socratic story, really—in which the fool finally becomes wise by renouncing his pretensions to wisdom.

So we end in a conundrum—one of many that we have encountered in trying to follow the trail of reason. And if there is any admonition that flows from this confounding conclusion—and it is hardly self-evident that there is one—perhaps the admonition is that whatever we do, we should do it with humility. That at least was Niebuhr's conclusion. Without denying the fact of human agency and responsibility not only for our personal but for our collective fate, he insisted on calling attention to

> the possibility and necessity of living in a dimension of meaning in which the urgencies of the struggle are subordinated to a sense of awe before the vastness of the historical drama in which we are jointly involved; to a sense of modesty about the virtue, wisdom and power available to us for the resolution of its perplexities; to a sense of contrition about the common human frailties and foibles which lie at the foundation of . . . our vanities; and to a sense of gratitude for the divine mercies which are promised to those who humble themselves.[44]

▣ Notes

Introduction

    1. The quotation from Jefferson is from Michael Kammen, A Machine that Would Go of Itself 44 (1986). The quotation from Wilson is from Alpheus Thomas Mason & Gordon E. Baker, Free Government in the Making 237 (4th ed. 1985). Hamilton's exclamation was in Federalist No. 36, in The Federalist Papers 224 (Clinton Rossiter ed. 1961).

    2. Federalist No. 1 (Hamilton), in The Federalist Papers, *supra* note 1 at 33 (emphasis added).

    3. Federalist No. 9 (Hamilton), in The Federalist Papers, *supra* note 1 at 72.

    4. Quoted in Henry Steele Commager, The Empire of Reason 189 (1977).

    5. Paul W. Kahn, Legitimacy and History 216 (1992).

    6. Commager, *supra* note 4 at 40.

    7. *See* H. Jefferson Powell, The Moral Tradition of American Constitutionalism 263–64 (1993):

> Both in its historical origins and in its contemporary self-description, the constitutional tradition has as its purpose the creation of a sphere in which reason guides the social and political relationships of human beings. . . .

    8. Ronald Dworkin, Taking Rights Seriously 149 (1977).

    9. Bruce A. Ackerman, Private Property and the Constitution 39 & *passim* (1977). "[Constitutional] Policymaking," Ackerman explains, "will be strengthened by philosophical efforts to provide convincing foundations for abstract talk criticizing established social practices." *Id.* at 182.

    10. Robert H. Bork, The Tempting of America 252–59 (1990).

    11. Robert H. Bork, Neutral Principles and Some First Amendment Problems, 47 Ind. L.J. 1, 1, 2–19 (1971).

    12. Suzanna Sherry, The Sleep of Reason, 84 Georgetown L.J. 453, 466 (1996).

    13. Christopher L. Eisgruber, Madison's Wager: Religious Liberty in the Constitutional Order, 89 Nw. U.L. Rev. 347, 349 (1995).

    14. Kahn, *supra* note 5 at 16.

    15. Cass R. Sunstein, The Partial Constitution 24 (1993). *See also* Walter Berns,

Taking the Constitution Seriously 20 (1987) ("America was the first new nation, the first nation to embody the principles of the new or improved science of politics, and the first to be built on the foundation of the rights of man.").

16. Robert F. Nagel, Judicial Power and American Character 98 (1994).

17. Planned Parenthood v. Casey, 505 U.S. 833, 849 (1992).

18. John Rawls, Political Liberalism 216 (1993).

19. Nagel, *supra* note 16 at 43.

20. *See, e.g.,* Thomas C. Grey, The Constitution as Scripture, 37 Stan. L. Rev. 1, 23–25 (1984) (proposing modest, essentially pragmatic justification for judicial review); Thomas W. Merrill, Bork v. Burke, 19 Harv. J.L. & Pub. Pol'y 509 (1996) (advocating Burkean or "conventionalist" approach to constitutional law).

21. Thomas Paine, Age of Reason, in The Theological Works of Thomas Paine (1882).

22. *See* 1 Adolph Thiers, The History of the French Revolution 411–12 (G.T. Fisher tr. 1850):

> The first festival of Reason was celebrated with much pomp on the 20th of Brumaire, (10th November): all the sections repaired to it with the constituted authorities. A young woman represented the Goddess Reason: this was the wife of the printer Momoro, one of the friends of Vincent, Ronsin, Chaumette, Hebert, and the like. She was clothed in white drapery; a mantle of sky blue floated from her shoulders; her dishevelled hair was covered with the cap of liberty. She was seated in an antique chair surrounded with ivy, and borne by four citizens. Young girls dressed in white and crowned with roses preceded and followed the goddess. Then came the busts of Lepelletier and Marat, musicians, troops, and all the armed sections. Discourses were pronounced, and hymns sung in the Temple of Reason; they then went to the convention, and Chaumette addressed them in these words:
>
> "Legislators! Fanaticism has given place to reason. Her dim eyes have not been able to support the burst of light. To day an immense crowd of people have gone to those gothic arches, which for the first time have served as an echo to truth. There the French have celebrated the only true worship, that of liberty, that of reason. There we have uttered our wishes for the success of the arms of the republic. There we have abandoned inanimate idols for reason, for that animate image, the master-work of the nation." As he uttered these words, Chaumette pointed to the living Goddess of Reason. The young and beautiful woman who personated her, descended from her seat and approached the president, who gave her a fraternal kiss amidst universal bravoes and shouts of "Long live the republic. Long live reason. Down with fanaticism." The convention which had not yet taken part in these solemnities was carried away, and followed the procession which returned a second time to the Temple of Reason, and there sung a patriotic hymn.

23. *See* Emerson's essays "Nature," "Divinity School Address," and "Self-Reliance" in Selected Writings of Ralph Waldo Emerson 186, 198; 241, 246; 257, 272 (1965).

24. Alasdair MacIntyre, Whose Justice? Which Rationality? (1988).

25. Niccolo Machiavelli, The Prince 91, in The Prince and The Discourses (Modern Library ed. 1950).

26. "[I]t may be true that fortune is the ruler of half our actions," he conceded, but "she allows the other half or thereabouts to be governed by us." *Id.*

27. The Discourses 383, in Machiavelli, *supra* note 25.

28. Quoted in John Patrick Diggins, The Promise of Pragmatism 112 (1994). Dig-

gins describes the conclusion reached by Adams after his years of historical research and reflection: "History was unreasonable because it remained indifferent to human intelligence and defied any sequential pattern or logic of development. . . . [H]istory itself could even be irrational in that there is no logical connection between the course of historical actions and the leaders' motives for performing them." *Id.* at 78.

29. *See* Walter Lippmann, Drift and Mastery 19 (1961) (first published 1914) ("This book . . . begins with the obvious drift of our time and gropes for the conditions of mastery.").

30. For a helpful discussion of the deliberately "democracy-restraining" dimension of the Constitution, see Henry Paul Monaghan, We the People[s], Original Understanding, and Constitutional Amendment, 96 Colum. L. Rev. 121, 169–77 (1996).

31. Plato, Gorgias 466b–472d, 466d (Edith Hamilton & Huntington Cairns 1961). Throughout this book, citations to Plato's dialogues are to the Hamilton and Cairns collection. *Cf.* Susan Wolf, Freedom within Reason 67–68 (1990):

> We might also point out that if one lacks the ability to act in accordance with Reason, one cannot be responsible even if one is autonomous. For dogs and psychopaths might conceivably be autonomous in the sense that they might be ultimate sources of their own actions, able to act on no basis. But because they lack the ability to act on a basis—in particular, the basis of Reason—they are not responsible in the sense that would allow them to be deserving of deep praise and blame.

32. St. Augustine, City of God 5 (Bk. I. preface) (Henry Bettenson tr., Penguin 1984).

33. Sunstein, *supra* note 15 at 24 (emphasis added).

34. *See* Gerald J. Postema, Bentham and the Common Law Tradition 30–38 (1986).

35. Commager, *supra* note 4 at 71.

36. Sherry, *supra* note 12 at 466.

37. *See* Richard Rorty, Consequences of Pragmatism xiv (1982) (asserting that "'philosophy' can mean simply what Sellars calls 'an attempt to see how things, in the broadest possible sense of the term, hang together, in the broadest possible sense of the term.'").

38. James Boyd White, Justice as Translation 8–9 (1990).

39. The best example I know of this sort of work, at least in recent legal scholarship, is Joseph Vining, From Newton's Sleep (1994).

Part I

1. James Q. Whitman, Reason or Hermeticism? 5 S. Cal. Inter. L.J. 193, 195, 197, 198–99 (1997). Professor Whitman's intriguing essay depicts a side of eighteenth century reason that seemingly had more in common with magic and alchemy than with secular rationalism and science.

Chapter One

1. Gen. 1:1, 27.

2. Plato scholars have differed over the extent to which the character Socrates in different dialogues accurately reflects the historical Socrates, but that question is not important to the present discussion.

3. Phaedo 96a.

4. *See* Jonathan Barnes, Early Greek Philosophy 36–42 (1987).

5. Phaedo 96d.

6. *Id.* at 97c (emphasis added).

7. *Id.* at 98c.

8. *Id.* at 99b.

9. For a critical discussion of modern naturalism by a legal scholar, see Phillip E. Johnson, Reason in the Balance (1995).

10. Plato, The Laws 891c.

11. *Id.* at 889c.

12. *Id.* at 891b, 890a.

13. *Id.* at 892a–c.

14. *See* Barnes, *supra* note 4 at 47.

15. William Barrett, Death of the Soul 7 (1986). Barrett also describes the continuing influence of this viewpoint:

> [S]cientific materialism was to become *de facto* the dominant mentality of the West in the three and a half centuries that followed [the achievements of Kepler, Galileo, and Newton]. It ruled not so much as an explicit and articulate philosophy, but more potently as an unspoken attitude, habit, and prejudice of mind. And in this unspoken form, it is still regnant today. The bulk of our research money is still channeled along the paths that accord with this materialism.

Id.

16. *See* Henry Chadwick, The Early Church 76 (rev. ed. 1993).

17. *See* Henry Chadwick, Augustine 17–24 (1986).

18. Arthur O. Lovejoy, The Great Chain of Being 43–48 (1936).

19. *Id.* at 144–82.

20. *Id.* at 50–52.

21. Phaedo 97c.

22. *Id.* at 97e–98b.

23. Lovejoy, *supra* note 18 at 99–143, 227–41.

24. *Id.* at 121–22.

25. *Id.* at 140 (quoting Kant).

26. *Id.* at 328.

27. *Id.* at 102, 201.

28. Like any other major philosopher, Aquinas has of course provoked divergent interpretations. But for one legal scholar's summary of Aquinas's natural law position, see Lloyd L. Weinreb, Natural Law and Justice 53–63 (1987).

29. Lovejoy, *supra* note 18 at 183.

30. *See, e.g.,* Bernard Bailyn, The Ideological Origins of the American Revolution 24 (1967) (observing that "Jefferson, who actually read [Plato's] *Dialogues*, discovered in them only the 'sophisms, futilities, and incomprehensibilities' of a 'foggy mind'—an idea concurred in with relief by John Adams. . . .").

31. *See, e.g.,* Ralph Ketcham, Framed for Posterity: The Enduring Philosophy of the Constitution 19–25 (1993) (arguing that the Constitution was a culminating achievement of Enlightenment thought); Andrew J. Reck, The Enlightenment in America II: The Constitution, 44 Rev. Metaphysics 729, 747 (1991) (Constitution "exemplifies the best principles of Enlightenment thought and style as adapted to the peculiar situation of the United States of America").

32. *See generally* Ellis Sandoz, A Government of Laws: Political Theory, Religion, and the American Founding (1990).

33. Henry May has identified four different strands or phases of the Enlightenment, which he calls the Moderate, Revolutionary, Skeptical, and Didactic Enlightenments. *See generally* Henry F. May, The Enlightenment in America (1976).

34. *See* J. C. D. Clark, The Language of Liberty 1660–1832 at p. 14 (1994): "No-one in the English-speaking world then referred to 'the Enlightenment' or supposed that such a thing was shared on both sides of the Atlantic. . . . The Enlightenment is an explanatory device of historians . . ." (citations omitted).

35. Daniel J. Boorstin, The Lost World of Thomas Jefferson viii, 34–35 (1948 1993 ed). *See also id.* at 49:

> [T]he Jeffersonian was . . . impressed with the unique necessity of *every* animal and vegetable species to the large plan of nature. . . . He viewed himself as but a link, though the highest, in the great chain of beings, all the parts of which had been closely connected by the hand of the divine Maker.

36. *See id.* at 29:

> In the familiar passage in the Declaration of Independence, the Being who endowed men with their unalienable rights is described as 'their Creator,' and throughout Jeffersonian thought recurs this vision of God as the Supreme Maker. . . . The Jeffersonian God was not the Omnipotent Sovereign of the Puritans nor the Omniscient Essence of the Transcendentalists, but was essentially Architect and Builder.

37. *Id.* at 30.

38. May, *supra* note 33 at 295.

39. *Id.* at 49, 280.

40. Boorstin, *supra* note 35 at 239 ("The God invoked by the Jeffersonians was necessarily an intelligible being. . . .").

41. *Id.* at 3–11, 237.

42. *Id.* at 106, 54.

43. *Id.* at 54. *See also* May, *supra* note 33 at 296 ("For the problem of evil, cosmic or human, the Jeffersonian faith has no answers.").

44. Boorstin, *supra* note 35 at 149, 139.

45. *Id.* at 45 (quoting Seybert).

46. *Id.* at 51–53.

47. *Id.* at 174.

48. May, *supra* note 33 at 264.

49. May, *supra* note 33 at 215. May adds:

> This view was more important to the deists, whose God depended solely on the evidence of nature, than it was to the liberal Christians, for whom nature merely corroborated revelation. As for the Bible, those more inclined to deism left it alone in their scientific utterances, while those more specifically Christian, from Rittenhouse to Samuel Smith, insisted that true science and Scripture could never be in disagreement.

50. Boorstin, *supra* note 35 at 30.

51. *Id.* at 31 (quoting Jefferson).

52. Thomas Jefferson, Notes on Virginia, in The Life and Selected Writings of Thomas Jefferson 187, 208 (Adrienne Koch & William Peden eds. 1944).

53. *Id.* at 208–09 ("To add to this, the traditional testimony of the Indians, that this animal still exists in the northern and western parts of America, would be adding the light of a taper to that of the meridian sun.").

54. *See* Lovejoy, *supra* note 18 at 153–54, 242–43.

55. Boorstin, *supra* note 35 at 155, 140–41.

56. *Id.* at 171–72.

57. *Id.* at 190–91.

58. May, *supra* note 33 at 302.

59. Boorstin, *supra* note 35 at 194. *See also id.* at 196 (observing that in the Jeffersonian scheme "no claim [of rights] could be validated except by the Creator's plan. . . .").

60. *See, e.g.,* Mary Ann Glendon, Rights Talk (1991).

61. Boorstin, *supra* note 35 at 196.

62. May, *supra* note 33 at 96–101, 312, 337.

63. *Id.* at 3–101.

64. *See* James Q. Whitman, Reason or Hermeticism, 5 S. Cal. Inter. L.J. 193 (1997).

65. Eccles. 1:10.

66. *See* Carl L. Becker, The Heavenly City of the Eighteenth Century Philosophers (1932).

67. My claim is not that the founders adopted Descartes's specific positions on philosophical questions such as "innate ideas," or that they imbibed the spirit of Cartesian rationalism directly from Descartes. A century-and-a-half separated Descartes's *Meditations* from the Philadelphia convention, and Descartes's thought was mediated, challenged, and revised by thinkers like Locke and Hume. A good deal of scholarship in recent decades has discussed the route through which rationalist and other ideas reached the American founders. Were the Americans more influenced by Locke, for example, or by the thinkers of the Scottish Enlightenment? These specific genealogical questions are not crucial to the present discussion, however, and I will take no position on them.

68. Rene Descartes, Discourse on Method, in Discourse on Method and Meditations 8 (Laurence J. LaFleur tr. 1960).

69. Phaedo 89d–90c.

70. Alasdair MacIntyre, After Virtue (rev. ed. 1984).

71. Robert H. Bork, The Tempting of America 255 (1990).

72. Descartes, Meditations, in Descartes, *supra* note 68 at 76–77.

73. Descartes, Discourse on Method, in Descartes, *supra* note 68 at 24–30.

74. *Id.* at 12, 9, 15.

75. If we follow the method outlined, he predicted, then "there cannot be any propositions so abstruse that we cannot prove them, or so recondite that we cannot discover them." *Id.* at 16.

76. *Id.* at 17. For a careful discussion of the different ways in which Descartes did and did not prescribe universal doubt, see Nicholas Wolterstorff, John Locke and the Ethics of Belief 191–96 (1996).

77. Charles Taylor, Philosophical Arguments viii (1993).

78. Ernest Gellner, Reason and Culture 157 (1992).

79. *Id.* at 158.

80. This aspiration *defines* us, even though it cannot be fulfilled. We are what we are, precisely because this strange aspiration is so deeply inherent in our thought. We may never fulfil its demands fully, but we are what we are because our intellectual ancestors tried so hard, and the effort has entered our souls and pervaded our cognitive custom. We are a race of failed Prometheuses. Rationalism is our destiny. It is not our option, and still less our disease. We are not free of culture, or Custom and Example: but it is of the essence of *our* culture that is rooted in the rationalist aspirations.

Id. at 159.

81. *See id.* at 57–62. For a recent study assigning Locke much of the responsibility often ascribed to Descartes for the modern orientation toward reason and tradition, see Wolterstorff, *supra* note 76.

82. For an admiring description of how Aquinas blended reason, revelation, and philosophical authority, together with a more mournful account of how later movements like nominalism and the *moderna devotio* came to view the Thomistic synthesis as too rationalist, see Etienne Gilson, Reason and Revelation in the Middle Ages 70–89 (1938).

83. *See* James Davison Hunter, Culture Wars 119–25 (1991).

84. Gellner, *supra* note 78 at 58–59.

85. "'Have courage to use your own reason!'—that is the motto of enlightenment." Immanuel Kant, Metaphysics of Morals and What is Enlightenment? 83 (Lewis White Beck tr. 2d ed. 1990).

86. *See generally* Morton White, Philosophy, *The Federalist,* and the Constitution (1987).

87. *Cf.* Suzanna Sherry, The Sleep of Reason, 84 Georgetown L.J. 455 (1996) ("In some ways, it is easier to describe what reason is by explaining what it is not.").

88. Jefferson, *supra* note 52 at 729.

89. Sherry, *supra* note 87 at 456 (citations omitted).

90. Henry Steele Commager, The Empire of Reason 1 (1977).

91. *Id.* at 45–47. *Cf.* Sandoz, *supra* note 32.

92. Commager, *supra* note 90 at 71, 72.

93. *Id.* at 41.

94. Jefferson, *supra* note 52 at 430–33.

95. Thomas Paine, Age of Reason 6, in The Theological Works of Thomas Paine (1882) (emphasis added).

96. Gail Heriot, Songs of Experience, 81 Va. L. Rev. 1721, 1739 (1993).

97. 1 Sources of Chinese Tradition 17 (Wm. Theodore de Bary, Wing-tsit Chan, & Burton Watson compilers 1960).

98. For a contemporary celebratory essay, see Sherry, *supra* note 87.

99. *See* Bailyn, *supra* note 30 at 230–32, 318–19.

100. Commager, *supra* note 90 at 3.

Chapter Two

1. Cass Sunstein, The Partial Constitution 24 (1993).

2. William Van Alstyne remarks that "read today, from beginning to end, our Constitution actually looks quite undistinguished as a complete and ordered political document." William W. Van Alstyne, The Idea of the Constitution as Hard Law, 37 J. Legal Ed. 174, 179 (1987).

3. *See* Plato, The Laws.

4. Andrew Reck observes that the Constitution "appeals to a conception of higher law, particularly natural law, which provides the Constitution with goals, imbues its form with content, and at the same time invokes a transcendent order of norms by which the achievements of the People may be measured." Andrew J. Reck, The Enlightenment in America II: The Constitution, 44 Rev. Metaphysics 729, 748 (1991).

5. Notes of Debates in the Federal Convention of 1787 reported by James Madison (int. by Adrienne Koch 1966) [hereinafter "Madison's Notes"] at p. 371.

6. *Id.* at 411.

7. *Cf.* Morton White, Philosophy, *The Federalist* and the Constitution 26 (1987)

(arguing that the philosophy of natural rights was "familiar enough to make it unnecessary for the authors [of *The Federalist*] to become entangled in efforts to define natural rights or to state the grounds for believing that men have them").

8. Madison's Notes, *supra* note 5 at 208.

9. White, *supra* note 7 at 211–12.

10. *Id.* at 206.

11. Bruce Ackerman, We the People: Foundations 20 (1991). *See also* Harold J. Berman, The Impact of the Enlightenment on American Constitutional Law, 4 Yale J. L. & Human. 311, 329 (1992) (noting that radically innovative aspects of the Constitution include its system of federalism, a government of delegated powers, and judicial review).

12. *See* M. E. Bradford, Original Intentions 3 (1993).

13. Madison's Notes, *supra* note 5 at 564.

14. *Id.* at 28–33.

15. *Id.* at 29.

16. Lance Banning describes the effect of the proposal of the Virginia Plan:

> And before the hesitant could catch their breath, they found that the agenda for the meeting had been radically transformed. The Virginia Plan not only sketched a radical solution to the problems of the Union. It also drew the delegates inexorably into a reconsideration of the fundamental nature of republics. . . .

Lance Banning, The Sacred Fire of Liberty: James Madison and the Founding of the Federal Republic 114 (1995).

17. Madison's Notes, *supra* note 5 at 223.

18. *Id.* at 156.

19. *See, e.g., id.* at 203, 222–23, 228.

20. *Id.* at 204, 293, 296.

21. *Id.* at 56–57, 77, 82, 447.

22. *Id.* at 85, 449, 182–83, 362.

23. James R. Stoner, Jr., Common Law and Liberal Theory: Coke, Hobbes, and the Origins of American Constitutionalism 216–17 (1992). However, this assertion may not mean all that it might seem to if, as Craig Klafter has argued, Americans in the post-Revolutionary and early National periods were committed to a "scientific perception of law" that led them to rework the common law both in its substance and in its method. Craig Evan Klafter, Reason over Precedents: Origins of American Legal Thought 128 (1993). Klafter maintains that American lawyers developed a unique approach to the common law that involved "using arguments based on standards of reason rather than precedent to persuade judges to resolve disputes by modifying or replacing the law in question." *Id.* at 100.

24. William James, Pragmatism, in Pragmatism and Other Essays 109 (1963).

25. O. W. Holmes, Collected Legal Papers 211 (1920).

26. *Cf.* Reck, *supra* note 4 at 745 (asserting that the framers made use of "the light from both the candle of reason and the lamp of experience").

27. Madison's Notes, *supra* note 5 at 161.

28. *See* Henry Steele Commager, The Empire of Reason 175 (1977) ("[The Republic's] institutions were fashioned not by the vicissitudes of history, but by the laws of Reason and the dictates of Common Sense."). *Cf.* Ackerman, *supra* note 11 at 180 ("Publius does not suppose he can adapt a blueprint that has succeeded elsewhere. There is no effort to recapture a golden age; no notion that somebody else has built a better mousetrap.").

29. William Van Alstyne notes that most constitutions written since ours have much more complete enumerations of rights, often including "rights to minimum subsistence, work, education, and essential health care"). Van Alstyne, *supra* note 2 at 178.

30. William E. Nelson, The Fourteenth Amendment 9 (1987).

31. Robert H. Wiebe, The Opening of American Society 8 (1984). Madison's question appears in Federalist No. 51, in The Federalist Papers 320, 322 (Clinton Rossiter ed. 1961).

32. *See* John Patrick Diggins, The Promise of Pragmatism 432 (1994): "At the time of the Constitutional Convention the framers saw power as springing from the alienated (i.e. 'fallen') human condition, and thus, like 'passion,' it was impossible to restrain by appeals to moral and political authority." *Cf.* Daniel W. Howe, The Political Psychology of *The Federalist,* 44 Wm. & Mary Q. 485, 491–92 (1987) (arguing that in the faculty psychology of *The Federalist* the rightful order of human motives was reason, then prudence, then passion, but in the actual human condition this order was reversed so that "passion was the strongest and reason the weakest").

33. Madison's Notes, *supra* note 5 at 131, 266, 288.

34. *Id.* at 235.

35. *See* Charles A. Beard, An Economic Interpretation of the Constitution of the United States (1913). *Cf.* Wiebe, *supra* note 31 at 20 (asserting that the new Republic was the product of "a full array of selfish, parochial, and mercenary motives. There was not a saint in the lot of these gentlemen.").

36. *See* Lance Banning, *supra* note 16 at 208–09 (arguing that the hope for improvement in the quality of representation was clearly a secondary consideration for Madison).

37. Madison's Notes, *supra* note 5 at 576–78. Andrew Reck explains that the Electoral College was intended "to assure that the election of the two highest officials to the federal government would be determined by persons of wisdom and virtue who would be most capable of selecting the best candidates available without succumbing to the wiles of demagogues or transient political passion." Reck, *supra* note 4 at 750.

38. Madison's Notes, *supra* note 5 at 194–95. *See also id.* at 233.

39. *Id.* at 452.

40. *See, e.g., id.* at 194 (Madison), 443 (Mason).

41. *Id.* at 126. *See also id.* at 464.

42. *Id.* at 323. *See also id.* at 525.

43. *Id.* at 338.

44. *Id.* at 615. *See also id.* at 64 (George Mason fears "a more dangerous monarchy, an elective one").

45. *Id.* at 464.

46. *Id.* at 615, 649.

47. *See* Federalist No. 9 (Hamilton), in The Federalist Papers, *supra* note 31 at 72:

The science of politics, however, like most other sciences, has received great improvement. The efficacy of various principles is now well understood, which were either not known at all, or imperfectly known to the ancients. The regular distribution of power into distinct departments; the introduction of legislative balances and checks; the institution of courts composed of judges holding their offices during good behavior; the representation of the people in the legislature by deputies of their own election: these are wholly new discoveries, or have made their principal progress towards perfection in modern times.

48. Madison's Notes, *supra* note 5 at 233, 175.

For Madison's retrospective and to some extent apologetic reflections on this problem, see Federalist No. 37, in The Federalist papers, *supra* note 31 at 224, 230–31.

49. In a letter, Marci Hamilton suggests that the framers' view of human nature was not as bleak as my portrayal indicates. "The very choice of a representative system indicates [the framers'] innate optimism about the possibility of human goodness in the service of others." *See also* Marci A. Hamilton, Power, Responsibility, and Republican Democracy (Review Essay), 93 Mich. L. Rev. 1539, 1545 (1995) (arguing that "[a]cknowledging that humans have the capacity to act honorably in the best interests of others is absolutely essential to a theory of representation. . . ."). Perhaps, but I don't think the inference is a necessary one. The framers might have chosen a representational constitutional system not from optimism about the virtue of future representatives but simply because they had to choose *some* form of government, and a representative system seemed the least evil alternative. Or they might have viewed representatives simply as self-serving proxies for the interests of self-serving constituents. Indeed, Hamilton acknowledges that most modern theorists *have* understood representation in just this way, though she herself criticizes this position. *See, e.g.,* Marci A. Hamilton, Discussion and Decisions: A Proposal to Replace the Myth of Self-Rule with an Attorneyship Model of Representation, 69 NYU L. Rev. 477 (1994). Still, in the final analysis I don't think my understanding of the framers' view of human nature is seriously inconsistent with Hamilton's; the difference lies mostly in the emphasis. Thus, I fully concur with Hamilton's assertion that "[t]he U.S. Constitution's plan for representative democracy can be summarized by this aphorism: hope for the best, but expect—and plan for—the worst." 93 Mich. L. Rev. at 1539. The difference is that Hamilton properly calls attention to the hoping for the best, while my portrayal emphasizes (also properly, I hope) the expecting and planning for the worst.

50. *See* Beard, *supra* note 35 at 73–151.

51. Madison's Notes, *supra* note 5 at 233, 240, 421.

52. *See, e.g., id.* at 240, 262, 278.

53. *Id.* at 240.

54. *Id.* at 418.

55. *Id.* at 421.

56. *Id.* at 215.

57. *Id.* at 229. Bedford elaborated:

Look at Georgia. Though a small State at present, she is actuated by the prospect of soon being a great one. S. Carolina is actuated both by present interest & future prospects. She hopes too to see the other States cut down to her own dimensions. N. Carolina has the same motives of present & future interest. Virga follows. Maryd is not on that side of the Question. Pena has a direct and future interest. Massts has a decided and palpable interest in the part she takes. Can it be expected the small States will act from pure disinterestedness.

58. *Id.* at 230.

59. *Id.* at 231.

60. *Id.* at 242.

61. *Cf.* Paul W. Kahn, Legitimacy and History 12 (1992) (arguing that in the view of *The Federalist Papers*, "[s]cience and legitimacy could achieve a marriage by seizing the unique historical opportunity presented in the postrevolutionary period").

62. *See, e.g.,* Edward C. Banfield, Was the Founding an Accident?, in Saving the Revolution: *The Federalist Papers* and the American Founding 265, 268 (Charles R. Kesler ed. 1987):

Providence favored the efforts of the people of the United States to form a more perfect union by, among other things, favoring the Convention that gathered in Philadelphia to—as it turned out—draft a constitution. The number of delegates was neither too large nor too small . . . ; most were young men . . . ; most were politically experienced . . . ; two carried immense national prestige (Washington and Franklin); and about a dozen others were men of extraordinary intellectual gifts (most notably Madison, Hamilton, and Wilson). It was an accident that certain others did *not* serve as delegates. Adams and Jefferson, whose presence would surely have overloaded the Convention, were abroad. (Jefferson would not have stood for the secrecy rule, and it is hard to believe that without it any sort of agreement could have been reached.) Eight or nine Anti-Federalists who had been appointed refused to serve. . . .

See also Walter Berns, Taking the Constitution Seriously 107–08 (1987) (reporting Herbert Storing's view that only the "providential" tardiness of one delegate and temporary absence of two others permitted approval of the compromise on representation that prevented the convention from breaking up).

63. Ackerman, *supra* note 11 at 169.

64. Lance Banning, Jefferson and Madison 7 (1995).

65. Madison's Notes, *supra* note 5 at 195, 195–96, 228, 232, 236.

66. *Id.* at 209–11. The convention did not formally reject Franklin's proposal but diplomatically allowed it to lapse without a vote.

67. *Id.* at 194, 376, 551.

68. *Id.* at 216.

69. Ackerman, *supra* note 11 at 179.

70. Madison's Notes, *supra* note 5 at 609.

71. *Id.* at 271.

72. *Id.* at 272.

73. *Id.* at 273.

74. For a helpful discussion, see Thomas B. McAffee, The Bill of Rights, Social Contract Theory, and the Rights "Retained" by the People, 16 S. Ill. L.J. 267 (1992).

75. Madison's Notes, *supra* note 5 at 640.

76. *Id.* at 630.

77. *See, e.g.,* Federalist No. 84 (Hamilton), in The Federalist Papers, *supra* note 31.

78. *Cf.* H. Jefferson Powell, The Moral Tradition of American Constitutionalism 63 (1993) (observing that American constitutional thinking sought "to replace the forms of argument of traditional Western European legal systems with a simplified and rationalized code of laws that would require application only, not interpretation"). *See also id.* at 60 (nothing that Enlightenment legalism "rested on 'a confidence, of relatively recent origin, in the capacity of language to confine and control human conduct, to regulate human will and desire by words rather than, always and directly, by the sword . . .'") (quoting Austin Sarat and Thomas R. Kearns).

79. Diggins, *supra* note 32 at 433.

80. Paul Kahn describes the situation of subsequent generations:

No longer were citizens participants in political construction. The inherited constitutional order was no longer a problem to be evaluated by a fresh appeal to political science. Instead, citizens had to understand themselves as the inheritors of an order that made a claim upon them. The political order was not a product of their deliberation and choice; rather, they had to understand themselves as its product.

Kahn, *supra* note 61 at 218. However, Kahn places the shift to a more legalistic conception of reason at a later date. *See* ch. 3, note 1.

81. Marbury v. Madison, 5 U.S. 137, 176 (1803).

82. *Id.* at 176–80.

83. Thomas Jefferson, with his calls for periodic revolution and renewal, was an exception.

84. *See* H. Jefferson Powell, The Original Understanding of the Original Intent, 98 Harv. L. Rev. 885 (1985). *But cf.* Jack N. Rakove, The Original Intention of the Original Understanding, 13 Const. Comm. 159, 171–78 (1996) (observing that Madison and Hamilton *did* sometimes invoke framers' intentions in construing the Constitution). Whether the other, "textualist" as opposed to "intentionalist," variety of originalism is a coherent approach to interpretation presents an interesting question, *see* Paul Campos, Against Constitutional Theory, in Paul Campos, Pierre Schlag, and Steven D. Smith, Against the Law (1996), but one that we need not address here.

85. *See* Morton J. Horwitz, Foreword: The Constitution of Change: Legal Fundamentality without Fundamentalism, 107 Harv. L. Rev. 30, 51 (1993) (arguing that constitutional interpretation in the founding period was "firmly anchored to the premise of originalism," although founders differed in the flexibility that they ascribed to constitutional language).

Chapter Three

1. Lawrence Sager notes the paradox:

> What confidence could the Publius trio have that their audience—"the People of the State of New York"—were capable of understanding and acting upon reasoned arguments on behalf of the Constitution, when these same people were such hopeless candidates for self-government under any but the most well-constructed processes of government? How could Madison undertake to reason so energetically with the unreasonable? More generally, how could anyone with Publius's pessimistic view of political man *en masse* ever hope—except by lucky accident or benevolent dictatorial force—to arrive at a satisfactory scheme of government?

Lawrence G. Sager, The Incorrigible Constitution, 65 NYU L. Rev. 893, 949 (1990).

In a different approach to these issues, Paul Kahn argues that the view of *The Federalist* is that reason must be exercised by the nation in general: "Publius thus relocates science from the convention to the larger body politic." Paul W. Kahn, Legitimacy and History 17 (1992). Of course, there are obvious reasons why *The Federalist* might adopt this view as a rhetorical strategy: In trying to persuade an audience to accept your position, it is not prudent, and perhaps not coherent, to tell them that they should agree with you because you are capable of reason and they are not. The Federalists faced a conundrum that many others have experienced as well: Lacking the power to compel acceptance of your position, you may have little choice but to treat your audience as capable of responding to reasoning, even if in fact you doubt that capacity. (In *The Federalist Papers* Publius tries to turn a difficult situation to his advantage, frequently arguing that opponents of the Constitution must be acting from passion, prejudice, or self-interest.) Kahn observes the same change I have tried to describe—from a more foundational use of reason to a more legalistic reason—but attributes it a later period and especially to Justice Story. "For Story, the science of law separated from the science of politics. Legal science, which the Court was meant to apply, became a science of interpretation of texts." *Id.* at 30.

2. William E. Nelson, Reason and Compromise in the Establishment of the Federal Constitution, 1787–1801, 44 Wm. & Mary Q. 458, 475 (1987).

3. Sager, *supra* note 1 at 951. *But cf.* Jack N. Rakove, The Original Intention of the Original Understanding, 13 Const. Comm. 151, 165 (1996) ("Madison did the best he could to elevate the tone of debate in *The Federalist* and at the Richmond convention, but he did not hold a high opinion of much of the polemical literature and speech-making that ratification occasioned, or of the capacity of most citizens to form independent opinions on as complicated a subject as the Constitution.").

4. Some have doubted the sincerity of the Federalists' professed hostility to a consolidation of national power. For example, Martin Diamond argued that a close reading of the *Federalist Papers* shows that Hamilton and Madison actually expected and wanted such a consolidation, although they carefully disguised this view. Martin Diamond, The Federalist's View of Federalism, in Essays in Federalism 21, 49–51 (1961). A strong form of this suspicion was expressed earlier in this century by William Crosskey, who contended that Madison doctored his notes on the constitutional convention because of "motives [that] were partly petty, personal, and political; and partly, as Madison eventually came to view the matter, patriotic" in order to support the "strange and fantastic theories" of federalism that came to be viewed as orthodox. 1 William Winslow Crosskey, Politics and the Constitution 13 (1953).

5. Richard Epstein, Some Doubts on Constitutional Indeterminacy, 19 Harv. J.L. & Pub. Pol'y 363, 368 (1996).

6. Leonard W. Levy, Constitutional Opinions 113 (1986).

7. For an overview of the constitutional developments leading to expansion of national powers under the commerce clause, see Lawrence Lessig, Translating Federalism: *United States v. Lopez.* 1995 Sup. Ct. Rev. 125, 139–54.

8. Bruce Ackerman observes that it is "clear that the Founding Federalists would have flatly repudiated many of the New Dealers' constitutional innovations." Bruce Ackerman, We the People: Foundations 62 (1991).

9. Alexander Hamilton, Opinion on the Constitutionality of an Act to Establish a Bank (1791), *reprinted in* Paul Brest & Sanford Levinson, Processes of Constitutional Decisionmaking 14, 15 (3d ed. 1992).

10. *Id.* at 17.

11. James Madison, Speech to the House of Representatives (1791), *reprinted in* Brest & Levinson, *supra* note 9 at 10, 11.

12. *Id.* at 12 (emphasis added).

13. 17 U.S. 316 (1819).

14. 22 U.S. 1 (1824).

15. Federalist No. 45 (Madison), in The Federalist Papers 293 (Clinton Rossiter ed. 1961).

16. *See, e.g.,* Wickard v. Filburn, 317 U.S. 111 (1942); Heart of Atlanta Motel v. United States, 379 U.S. 241 (1964).

17. *See, e.g.,* National League of Cities v. Usery, 426 U.S. 833 (1976), *overruled in* Garcia v. San Antonio Metropolitan Transit Authority, 469 U.S. 528 (1985).

18. *See* United States v. Lopez, 115 S. Ct. 1624 (1995).

19. For an analysis persuasively arguing that *Lopez* is unlikely to lead to any significant reduction in the commerce power, see Robert F. Nagel, The Future of Federalism, 46 Case W. Res. L. Rev. 643 (1996). *See also* Lessig, *supra* note 7 at 196–206. For a view predicting more long-term significance for *Lopez,* see Barry Friedman, Legislative Findings and Judicial Signals: A Positive Political Reading of *United States v. Lopez,* 46 Case W. Res. L. Rev. 757 (1996).

20. *See, e.g.,* Federalist No. 78 (Hamilton), in The Federalist Papers, *supra* note 15.

21. *See* Katzenbach v. Morgan, 384 U.S. 641 (1966).

22. *See, e.g.,* South Dakota v. Dole, 483 U.S. 203 (1987) (broadly construing spending power); Missouri v. Holland, 252 U.S. 416 (1920) (broadly construing treaty power).

23. Lessig, *supra* note 7 at 188. *See also* Lynn A. Baker, Conditional Federal Spending after *Lopez,* 95 Colum. L. Rev. 1911, 1914 (1995) (agreeing that "prevailing Spending Clause doctrine appears to vitiate much of the import of *Lopez* and any progeny it may have" and proposing limitations on the spending power).

24. Abner Greene points out that "on a straightforward textualist view, presidential lawmaking would be unconstitutional. But we live with an enormous amount of such lawmaking, and few appear ready to condemn the system as invalid." Abner S. Greene, Checks and Balances in an Era of Presidential Lawmaking, 61 U. Chi. L. Rev. 123, 124 (1994).

25. Martin S. Flaherty, The Most Dangerous Branch, 105 Yale L.J. 1725 (1996). *See id.* at 1727 ("Never has the executive branch been more powerful, nor more dominant over its two counterparts, than since the New Deal.").

26. For a provocative assessment and defense of this situation, see Richard Neely, How Courts Govern America (1981).

27. George W. Carey, In Defense of the Constitution 184–85 (rev. ed. 1995).

28. *See* Gary Lawson, The Rise and Rise of the Administrative State, 107 Harv. L. Rev. 1231 (1994) (surveying the numerous ways in which the modern administrative state deviates from the original constitutional scheme).

29. *See generally* Ackerman, *supra* note 8.

30. *E.g.,* New York v. United States, 505 U.S. 144, 176 (1992); Skinner v. Mid-America Pipeline, 490 U.S. 212, 220 (1989).

31. *Cf.* Carey, *supra* note 27 at 79 (explaining that federalism today is mostly the product of informal understandings and evolutionary growth).

32. Jean Yarbrough notes that "[d]espite calls for a 'new federalism' by both Richard Nixon and Ronald Reagan, it is the early nationalism of Madison which today seems almost irresistible, especially when the message is driven home daily by the thoroughly national media." Jean Yarbrough, Federalism and Rights in the American Founding, in Federalism and Rights (Ellis Katz & G. Alan Tarr eds. 1996).

33. *See, e.g.,* Ronald Dworkin, Freedom's Law (1996); Robin West, Progressive Constitutionalism (1994).

34. *Cf.* Lance Banning, Jefferson and Madison 6 (1995) ("Now, from our perspective, Jefferson and other critics [who objected to the Constitution's lack of a bill of rights] seem so obviously right that readers may be stunned to learn that anyone opposed the first amendments."). *But cf.* Hadley Arkes, Beyond the Constitution 58–80 (1990) (defending framers' decision not to include a bill of rights).

35. *See generally* Daniel A. Farber & Suzanna Sherry, A History of the Constitution 219–44 (1990); Levy, *supra* note 6 at 105–24.

36. *See* Creating the Bill of Rights xii–xiii (Helen E. Veit, Kenneth R. Bowling & Charlene Bangs Bickford eds. 1991).

37. *See* Banning, *supra* note 34 at 3 ("Without James Madison, . . . there would have been no federal Bill of Rights—not, at least, in 1789."); Levy, *supra* note 6 at 124 ("But for Madison's persistence the amendments would have died in Congress"); Thornton Anderson, Creating the Constitution 178 (1993) (asserting that "there might have been no bill of rights at all if Madison had not driven the chariot as well as he did").

Cf. Marci A. Hamilton, The First Amendment's Challenge: Function and the Confusion in the Supreme Court's Contemporary Free Exercise Jurisprudence, 29 Ga. L. Rev. 81, 89 (1994) (conjecturing that but for the resistance to authority reflected in the insistence on conditioning acceptance of the Constitution on the adoption of the Bill of Rights, "the United States Constitution likely would have become just another design for government like the multitudes of others that have passed through history without actually effecting a republican form of democracy").

38. *See* Farber & Sherry, *supra* note 35 at 232.

39. The quotations, reported in Gerard V. Bradley, Church-State Relationships in America 88 (1987), are from, respectively, Pierce Butler and George Mason, Fisher Ames, Robert Morris, Edmund Randolph, and Aedanus Burke.

40. *See* Levy, *supra* note 6 at 119 (describing how the Constitution's opponents "had used the bill of rights issue as a smokescreen for objections to the Constitution that could not be dramatically popularized, and now they sought to scuttle Madison's proposals").

41. Levy, *supra* note 6 at 147.

42. The full discussion as reported in The Congressional Register is reprinted in Creating the Bill of Rights, *supra* note 36 at 187.

43. Lawrence Lessig points out:

Madison believed the Bill of Rights unnecessary, in part because he didn't believe the powers of Congress extended into the domains protected by the Bill of Rights. He didn't believe, for example, that Congress had the power to regulate the press, and therefore he didn't see the need to state a limitation on Congress's power to protect the press.

Lessig, *supra* note 7 at 145. *See also* Hamilton, *supra* note 37 at 84–94.

44. *See* Steven D. Smith, Foreordained Failure: The Quest for a Constitutional Principle of Religious Freedom (1995).

45. *See* Akhil Reed Amar, "Anti-Federalists," *The Federalist Papers* and the Big Argument for Union, 16 Harv. J.L. & Pub. Pol'y 111, 115 (1993).

46. The Sedition Act was pronounced unconstitutional, somewhat belatedly, in New York Times v. Sullivan, 376 U.S. 254 (1964).

47. The Virginia Resolutions are reprinted in Ethelbert Dudley Warfield, The Kentucky Resolutions of 1798: An Historical Study 100–103 (1894).

48. "Madison himself admitted that [the Bill of Rights] mostly offered some additional securities for liberties that Congress was without the power to infringe." Banning, *supra* note 34 at 13.

49. *Cf.* Carey, *supra* note 27 at 124:

[C]learly ours is not a "rights tradition" in the sense the American Civil Liberties Union (ACLU), most academics, and the modern courts would have us believe. And even the adoption of the Bill of Rights soon after ratification does not alter this fact, for how else could Madison, its "father," see fit to declare that these rights could not "endanger the beauty of the Government in any one important feature, even in the eyes of its most sanguine admirers"?

50. *See, e.g.,* Federalist 84 (Hamilton), in The Federalist Papers, *supra* note 15 at 515: "[T]he Constitution is itself, in every rational sense, and to every useful purpose, A BILL OF RIGHTS. . . . [T]he proposed Constitution, if adopted, will be the bill of rights of the Union."

51. *See supra* note 4.

52. For example, arguing that "the entire enterprise of Commerce Clause jurispru-

dence is fundamentally flawed," Richard Epstein urges the Court to "take all the decisions that are regarded as sacrosanct by everyone but Justice Thomas, and overrule them one and all, preferably with a single blow." Richard A. Epstein, Constitutional Faith and the Commerce Clause, 71 Notre Dame L. Rev. 167, 189–90 (1996).

53. Lessig, *supra* note 7 at 129–30.

54. *Id.* at 137–41.

55. *Id.* at 192.

56. *Id.* at 130.

57. *Id.* at 213.

58. Lessig does criticize the modern Supreme Court for failing to understand that fidelity to the original design actually requires the Court to depart from the text in devising new limiting doctrines. *Id.* at 193–215.

59. Richard A. Epstein, Self-Interest and the Constitution, 37 J. Legal Educ. 153, 159 (1987). *See also* Epstein, *supra* note 5 at 373 (arguing that "the vice of so much modern constitutional interpretation" is that the "question it asks for itself is not what the Constitution, fairly read, requires. Rather it is, what methods of constitutional interpretation have to be invented to sustain massive federal power. . . ." *See also* Carey, *supra* note 27 at 185:

> [W]hat is abundantly clear is that modern courts—most especially the Warren Court—have seen fit to read their ideological preferences into the meaning, and hence the requirements, of equal protection, due process, and the Bill of Rights. Long-standing rules of constitutional interpretation were scrapped to advance the goals normally associated with secular liberalism.

60. For example, Justice Black's dissents in free speech cases can be understood as expressing a similar criticism in behalf of a "liberal" cause. *See, e.g.,* Dennis v. United States, 341 U.S. 494 (1951).

61. Robert H. Bork, The Tempting of America 56 (1990).

62. *Id.* at 7.

63. "[D]econstructionism insists that no utterance, no 'text' in the parlance of deconstructionism, in any context has a determinate meaning: any text can be shown to imply its opposite or to bear completely unexpected meanings." Alan R. Madry, Analytic Deconstructionism? The Intellectual Voyeurism of Anthony D'Amato, 63 Fordham L. Rev. 1033, 1034, (1995).

64. Whether American legal academics who claim the label actually understand or practice Derridean deconstruction is questionable, but I am in no position to pronounce on the issue. *See* Pierre Schlag, "Le Hors de Texte, C'est Moi": The Politics of Form and the Domestication of Deconstruction, 11 Cardoza L. Rev. 1631 (1990).

65. *See, e.g.,* Dworkin, *supra* note 33 at 8.

66. *See* Anthony D'Amato, Aspects of Deconstruction: The "Easy Case" of the Under-Aged President, 84 Nw. U.L. Rev. 250, 251 (1989). *See also* Mark Tushnet, Red, White, and Blue: A Critical Analysis of Constitutional Law 60–62 (1988).

67. Anthony D'Amato, Pragmatic Indeterminacy, 85 Nw. U.L. Rev. 148, 150 n.11 (1990).

68. Deconstruction and "creative misreading" are associated with the work of Jacques Derrida; and as Donald Brosnan points out, the Derridean approach to texts is based on "borderline esoterica . . . , maverick insistence on relying on puns and far-flung etymologies and semi-homonyms." Such creative misreadings "must depend on the suspension of logocentric habits and values." Donald Brosnan, Serious But Not Critical, 60 S. Cal. L. Rev. 259, 365 (1987).

69. Richard S. Kay, Adherence to the Original Intentions in Constitutional Adjudication: Three Objections and Responses, 82 Nw. U.L. Rev. 226, 236, 242 (1988).

70. *See* Joseph Vining, From Newton's Sleep 240–41 (1995):

> [In deconstruction] the object in view—or the consequence—of that most meticulous reading is the demonstration of contradictions and therefore incoherence. Again, only elimination of the person—the elimination that is the presupposition of literalism—makes this possible. Without an assumption that words or patterns of words have meanings of their own, it cannot confidently be said that one thing contradicts another. . . . But to say a text itself is incoherent, and to stop there, is to demonstrate the common reification of language that follows the axiomatic elimination of the person. There is no listening really.

71. *See generally* Paul Campos, That Obscure Object of Desire: Hermeneutics and the Autonomous Legal Text, 77 Minn. L. Rev. 1065 (1993).

72. Mark Tushnet observes that "the framers, as liberals, had no reason to think that judges would be any less attached to possessive individualism than were the representatives whom the judges were to restrain." Tushnet, *supra* note 66 at 10.

73. Commenting on a draft of this book, Maimon Schwarzschild questions whether the motivation of the academicians is really so different from that of the politicians. It is a fair question.

74. Federalist No. 10 (Madison), in The Federalist Papers, *supra* note 15 at 78.

75. Madison's Notes, *supra* note 5, ch. 2, at 229.

76. *Id.* at 216.

77. Commenting on a draft of the book, Maimon Schwarzschild makes a point that serves to qualify this conclusion, although not I think to negate it. Schwarzschild points out that some people—*e.g.*, those resisting governmental expansion—will sometimes find it in their interest to read and rely on the text in more purely originalist ways—*i.e.*, because the "framers' intent" happens to coincide with their own interests. So the framers' legalistic strategy at least provided such people with an argument. Still, it seems that this rhetorical or political resource has proven insufficient to prevent the accumulations of national power described earlier in this chapter.

78. For an argument that the Constitution resulted from a politics of reason and compromise quite different from the kinds of politics we are familiar with today, see Nelson, *supra* note 2. *Cf.* James W. Stoner, Jr., Common Law and Liberal Theory 214 (1992) (remarking that "any student of the Convention debates or of *The Federalist Papers* can see [the framers'] care in reasoning and their elevation of purpose").

79. Jay Bybee observes:

> What emerges from the debates [about the Fourteenth Amendment] is not a coalescing of views and intentions, but an uncertain confederation of votes. While many members of Congress cited various provisions of the Constitution, cases, Elliott's *Debates,* and commentators such as Story and Kent, the members were not clear as to what the Constitution meant, and they agreed on little. The views of the Framers of the Fourteenth Amendment are astonishingly imprecise. As legal draftsmen, the Framers of the Fourteenth Amendment were much less accomplished than the Founders; they were surprisingly nonplussed by the mechanics of the amendment they were drafting.

Jay S. Bybee, Taking Liberties with the First Amendment: Congress, Section 5, and the Religious Freedom Restoration Act, 48 Vand. L. Rev. 1539, 1588 (1995) (footnotes omitted).

80. For a description of Madison's unusual combination of public-spirited motivation and sound judgment, see Banning, *supra* note 34 at 12–16. Banning's careful study argues that supposed inconsistencies in Madison's thinking on constitutional matters actually reflect his ability to learn from discussion and political developments. Lance Banning, The Sacred Fire of Liberty: James Madison and the Founding of the Federal Republic (1995). Madison, according to Banning, was also "the most sophisticated constitutional thinker of his time," *id.* at 112; and it is indeed hard to think of any obvious competitors.

81. Madison's Notes, *supra* note 5, ch. 2, at 44.

82. Regarding the enumerated powers strategy, *compare* Madison's Federalist essays nos. 14, 39, and 41 in The Federalist Papers, *supra* note 15 at 102, 245, 263 (expressing confidence in the strategy) *with* Federalist No. 37, *id.* at 228–29 (questioning whether national power could be defined and limited in words). On Madison's reaction to the second bank, see Brest & Levinson, *supra* note 9 at 18.

83. 1 Alexis de Tocqueville, Democracy in America 406–15 (Phillips Bradley ed. 1946).

84. *Id.* at 415.

85. *See* Banning, *supra* note 34 at 10.

86. Federalist No. 10, *supra* note 74 at 79.

87. *Id.* at 80–84.

88. *Id.* at 83. *See* the similar analysis in Federalist No. 51, *id.* at 320, 323–25.

89. George Carey remarks that "Madison at no point in Federalist 10 speaks of constitutional institutions as barriers to factitious majorities. . . ." Carey, *supra* note 27 at 39.

90. Federalist No. 46 (Madison), in The Federalist Papers, *supra* note 15 at 295.

91. This "radically imperfect but better than the alternatives" position is the essence of Federalists Nos. 37 and 38.

Part II

1. *See* ch. 1, n. 94.

Chapter Four

1. *Cf.* Morton J. Horwitz, Foreword: The Constitution of Change: Legal Fundamentality without Fundamentalism, 107 Harv. L. Rev. 30, 116 (1993) (arguing that "[t]he central problem of modern constitutionalism is how to reconcile the idea of fundamental law with the modernist insight that meanings are fluid and historically changing").

2. *See generally* John R. Vile, Rewriting the Constitution: An Examination of Proposals from Reconstruction to the Present (1991).

3. *See* William E. Nelson, The Fourteenth Amendment 114–17 (1988).

4. For an argument that on both descriptive and normative grounds constitutional interpretation is best understood as a common law process, see David A. Strauss, Common Law Constitutional Interpretation, 63 U. Chi. L. Rev. 877 (1996). The common law element in the Constitution and in constitutional interpretation is emphasized in James W. Stoner, Jr., Common Law and Liberal Theory 197–222 (1992), and H. Jefferson Powell, The Moral Tradition of American Constitutionalism (1993). Paul Kahn describes theorizing beginning in the post–Civil War period that self-consciously emphasized the common law dimension of constitutional law. Paul W. Kahn, Legitimacy and History 67–84 (1992). Perhaps more than anyone else, Henry Monaghan has called attention to common law themes in the discussion of current constitutional develop-

ments. *See* Henry Paul Monaghan, Stare Decisis and Constitutional Adjudication, 88 Colum. L. Rev. 723 (1988); Henry P. Monaghan, Foreword: Constitutional Common Law, 89 Harv. L. Rev. 1 (1975).

5. Stoner, *supra* note 4 at 216–22.

6. Robert Lipkin develops an analogous distinction between "deliberative" and "dedicated" cultures. Both kinds of cultures involve reasoning, so that it would be a distortion to say that deliberative cultures are based on "reason" while dedicated cultures are based on "authority." Still, deliberative rationality is in principle more open and more critical than the more tradition-oriented reason of dedicated cultures; in a deliberative culture everything is in principle open to challenge and in need of rational justification. *See* Robert Justin Lipkin, Liberalism and the Possibility of Multicultural Constitutionalism: The Distinction between Deliberative and Dedicated Cultures, U. Rich. L. Rev. 1263, 1284–87 (1995). To borrow Lipkin's terms, our constitutional culture and discourse exhibit both "deliberative" and "dedicated" elements, but it is the more open and critical aspiration that distinguishes our constitutional project and that is the subject of this investigation. *Cf.* Robin West, Progressive Constitutionalism 4 (1994) (distinguishing "democratic deliberation" from "the analogic methods of legal reasoning" and favoring the former as a means of realizing progressive ideals).

7. 478 U.S. 186 (1986).

8. For a discussion of *Bowers* from a "moral reasoning" or "principled" perspective, see Daniel O. Conkle, The Second Death of Substantive Due Process, 62 Ind. L.J. 215 (1987).

9. *See, e.g.,* Alexander M. Bickel, The Morality of Consent (1975); Anthony Kronman, Alexander Bickel's Philosophy of Prudence, 94 Yale L.J. 1567 (1985).

10. Bruce A. Ackerman, Private Property and the Constitution 1–10 (1977). Ackerman took a similar position, though with different vocabulary, in *Reconstructing American Law* (1983).

11. *See* Larry Alexander, Incomplete Theorizing: A Review Essay of Cass R. Sunstein's *Legal Reasoning and Political Conflict*, 72 Notre Dame L. Rev. 531 (1997).

12. Ronald Dworkin, Freedom's Law 3, 37 (1996). *Cf.* Robert C. Post, Constitutional Domains 25 (1995) (suggesting that when the words of the Constitution are not plain, judges must be able to articulate a theory of constitutional interpretation in order to explain and justify their decisions).

13. *Cf.* Strauss, *supra* note 4 at 891 (arguing for a common law "rational traditionalism").

14. Ernest Gellner, Reason and Culture 157 (1992).

15. Craig Evan Klafter, Reason over Precedents: Origins of American Legal Thought (1993).

16. *See* ch. 1, ns. 1–6, 32–35, and accompanying text.

17. In a letter, Michael Perry suggests that reason cannot operate except as grounded in a tradition and that "[w]e now know that the opposition between 'reason' and 'tradition' is utterly false. . . ." Perry may be right; certainly his view is consistent with much in the writings of, say, Alasdair MacIntyre. My purpose here, however, is neither to agree nor disagree with this view, but instead to note that the opposition between reason and tradition *is* a prominent theme in founding era views of reason, *see* ch. 1, and that this theme continues to resonate with a good deal of modern constitutional thinking.

18. Some readers of earlier versions of this book were disappointed that the book did not culminate in any prescription for bringing reason into constitutional law. Although it is not my purpose to formulate any such prescription, readers might note at

this point that governing constitutional law through a common law method of reasoning, if there is one, is a possibility that the criticisms developed in ensuing chapters do not directly address, and that logically remains as one potential alternative to the course that the aspiration to constitutional reason has followed.

19. *Cf.* Laurence H. Tribe, The Idea of the Constitution: A Metaphor-morphosis, 37 J. Legal Educ. 170, 170 (1987) (describing how modern thinking understands "the Constitution less as an object than as a subject of legal social consciousness and discourse"). *See also* Post, *supra* note 12 at 36 (noting that in much modern discourse the "Constitution explicitly loses its character as a specific document or a discrete text").

20. Robert F. Nagel, Rationalism in Constitutional Law, 4 Const. Comm. 9, 13 (1987).

21. For an abbreviated summary of the change, see Mary Ann Glendon, Rights Talk 4–5 (1991):

> At least until the 1950s, the principal focus of constitutional law was not on personal liberty as such, but on the division of authority between the states and the federal government, and the allocations of powers among the branches of the central government. In keeping with Hamilton's observation in *Federalist* No. 84 that "the Constitution is itself, in every rational sense, and to every useful purpose, A BILL OF RIGHTS," the theory was that individual freedom was protected mainly through these structural features of our political regime. The Supreme Court saw far fewer cases involving free speech, association, religion, and the rights of criminal defendants than it does now, not only because such issues were less frequently litigated, but because, until relatively recent times, many important provisions of the Bill of Rights were thought to apply only to the federal government. Gradually, however, the Supreme Court developed its 'incorporation' doctrine, through which more and more of the rights guaranteed by the first eight amendments to the Federal Constitution were declared to have been made binding on the states (incorporated) by the Fourteenth Amendment. This process accelerated in the 1960s when the Warren Court vigorously began to exercise the power of judicial review as a means of protecting individual rights from interference by state as well as federal governments. Today the bulk of the Court's constitutional work involves claims that individual rights have been violated. (citations omitted)

22. *See* David M. Rabban, The First Amendment in its Forgotten Years, 90 Yale L.J. 514 (1981).

23. The establishment clause remained essentially dormant until Everson v. Board of Education, 330 U.S. 1 (1947), after which the Court began to elaborate and enforce it with ever-increasing enthusiasm.

24. Buck v. Bell, 274 U.S. 200, 208 (1927).

25. Lon L. Fuller, The Case of the Speluncean Explorers, 62 Harv. L. Rev. 616, 634 (1949).

26. Bruce A. Ackerman, Constitutional Politics/Constitutional Law, 99 Yale L.J. 453, 522 (1989).

27. Ronald Dworkin, Freedom's Law, *supra* note 12 at 165 (referring to free speech clause).

28. Ronald Dworkin, Taking Rights Seriously 134–36 (1977).

29. Michael J. Perry, The Constitution in the Courts 70–71 (1994).

30. *Id.* at 74.

31. *Id.* at 28–53.

32. *Id.* at 80–81.

33. *See id.* at 74:

The challenge of specifying an indeterminate constitutional directive, then, is the challenge of deciding how best to achieve, how best to "instantiate," in a particular context, the political-moral value—the aspect of human good—embedded in the directive; it is the challenge of deciding how government can achieve the relevant political-moral value in the way that best serves all the various and sometimes competing interests of the political community at stake in the context.

34. Ackerman, *supra* note 26 at 453, 459–60.

35. Michael J. Perry, The Legitimacy of Particular Conceptions of Constitutional Interpretation, 77 Va. L. Rev. 669, 690 (1991) (emphasis added).

36. Dworkin, Freedom's Law, *supra* note 12 at 128.

37. *Id.* at 74.

38. *Id.* at 8, 72.

39. *See id.* at 148–49: "The key clauses of the Constitution's Bill of Rights, after all, are very abstract: they say, for example, that 'due process' is not to be denied, and that all people are to receive 'equal protection of the laws,' but they do not specify what process is due or what counts as equal protection."

40. *Id.* at 78, 73.

41. *Id.* at 31.

42. *Id.* at 343.

43. *Id.* at 37.

44. Ronald Dworkin, Law's Empire 407 (1986).

45. Dworkin, Freedom's Law, *supra* note 12 at 104, 110.

46. *See id.* at 73:

On its most natural reading, then, the Bill of Rights sets out a network of principles, some extremely concrete, others more abstract, and some of near limitless abstraction. Taken together, these principles define a political ideal. . . . It therefore seems unlikely that anyone who believes that free and equal citizens would be guaranteed a particular individual right will not also think that our Constitution already contains that right, unless constitutional history has decisively rejected it.

Cf. Christopher L. Eisgruber, Madison's Wager: Religious Liberty in the Constitutional Order, 89 Nw. U.L. Rev. 347, 354 (1995) ("What is important is to identify the rights the Constitution protects, not to allocate those rights among clauses.").

47. West, *supra* note 6 at 276.

48. *Id.* at 184.

49. *Id.* at 18, 261.

50. *Id.* at 210.

51. *Id.* at 196.

52. Forrest McDonald, Foreword to M. E. Bradford, Original Intentions xii (1993).

53. It is even possible that at the time of enactment these clauses were not vague, and that due to linguistic change and the passage of time we have simply forgotten the more definite meaning they once had. Earl Maltz has argued that when enacted the clauses in the Fourteenth Amendment had a fairly precise and well-understood legal meaning. *See generally* Earl M. Maltz, Civil Rights, the Constitution, and Congress 1863–1869 (1990).

54. Nelson, *supra* note 3 at 129. *See also id.* at 55–56, 122.

55. *Cf.* Mark Tushnet, Red, White, and Blue: A Critical Analysis of Constitutional Law 31 (1988):

> [L]ike Ely and Laycock, Dworkin might be called upon to . . . produce evidence of an originalist sort that the framers knew that they were enacting provisions that embodied a moral content richer than their own moral conceptions. And, simply put, there is no evidence at all that they did. The distinction relies on modern theories of law that were quite foreign, indeed probably would have been incomprehensible, to the framers of the Bill of Rights and the fourteenth amendment. (citations omitted)

56. For further exploration of some of these doubts, see Steven D. Smith, Idolatry in Constitutional Interpretation, in Against the Law 180–86 (Paul F. Campos, Pierre Schlag, & Steven D. Smith, 1996).

57. Of course, it may be that not all amendments *were* made in the spirit of the original conception. Though not all scholars agree, from the notorious uncertainties and ambiguities of the Fourteenth Amendment William Nelson finds himself forced to conclude that "the framing generation understood constitutional politics as a rhetorical venture designed to persuade people to do good, rather than a bureaucratic venture intended to establish precise legal rules and enforcement mechanisms." Nelson, *supra* note 3 at 9.

58. Ackerman, *supra* note 26 at 98, 115, 121, 141, 161.

59. Lawrence Lessig, Translating Federalism: United States v. Lopez, 1995 Sup. Ct. Rev. 125, 146.

60. *Id.* at 193. *See also id.* at 213 ("[W]e must get over this obsession about what is 'made up.' We have no choice, if fidelity is our aim, but to make up limits that better translate founding commitments.").

61. *Id.* at 131.

62. *Id.* at 206–15.

63. *See* Federalist No. 45 (Madison), in The Federalist Papers 288, 289 (Clinton Rossiter ed. 1961).

64. Bork criticizes Laurence Tribe, for example, observing that "[w]hen the original materials stand in the way, he generalizes the principle intended to such an extent that it loses all touch with the ratifiers' understanding of what they were doing." Robert H. Bork, The Tempting of America 201 (1990).

65. *Id.* at 75–82.

66. Gerard V. Bradley, The Bill of Rights and Originalism, 1992 U. Ill. L. Rev. 417, 420 (footnotes omitted).

67. *Consider* Laurence H. Tribe & Michael C. Dorf, On Reading the Constitution 17 (1991):

> The moment you adopt a perspective as open as Dworkin's, the line between what you think the Constitution *says* and what you wish it *would* say becomes so tenuous that it is extraordinarily difficult, try as you might, to maintain that line at all. How can one maintain the line—given the ambiguity of the Constitution's text, the plasticity of its terms, the indeterminacy of its history, and the possibility of making noises in the Constitution's language that *sound* like an argument for just about anything?

68. *See, e.g.,* Dworkin, Freedom's Law, *supra* note 12 at 37. *But cf. id.* at 82 (urging interpreters to "abandon the pointless search for mechanical or semantic constraints and seek genuine constraints in the only place they can actually be found: in good argument").

69. Ralph Ketcham observes that the framers' belief in a universal natural law discernible through reason constituted a "philosophy and cosmology that more basically than anything else separates eighteenth-century thinking from that of our own day" with its dominant "evolutionary, pragmatic, positivist, relativist, or deconstructionist modes of thought." Ralph Ketcham, Framed for Posterity: The Enduring Philosophy of the Constitution 12 (1993).

Chapter Five

1. Ronald Dworkin, Freedom's Law 343 (1996).
2. For a classic inquiry into these developments, see Owen Chadwick, The Secularization of the European Mind in the Nineteenth Century (1975). For an account of the rise of atheism in the United States during that period, see James Turner, Without God, Without Creed: The Origins of Unbelief in America (1985).
3. William Barrett, Death of the Soul 57 (1986). Consistent with this view, John Searle describes the "scientific world view," whose basic tenets are, first, that everything that exists is composed of and reducible to atomic particles in motion and, second, that higher life forms are the product of unguided Darwinian evolution. John R. Searle, The Rediscovery of the Mind 84–91 (1992). Searle stresses that this worldview "is not an option."

> It is not simply up for grabs along with a lot of competing world views. Our problem is not that somehow we have failed to come up with a convincing proof of the existence of God or that the hypothesis of an after life remains in serious doubt, it is rather that in our deepest reflections we cannot take such opinions seriously.

Id. at 90.
4. Bertrand Russell, "A Free Man's Worship," in Why I Am Not a Christian 104, 107 (1957).
5. *See* Louis Dupré, Passage to Modernity 3 (1993):

> The classical notion of *kosmos* (used by Plato and Aristotle), as well as the Roman *natura,* had preserved the idea of the real as an harmonious, all-inclusive whole. . . . At the end of the Middle Ages, however, nominalist theology effectively removed God from creation. Ineffable in being and inscrutable in his designs, God withdrew from the original synthesis altogether. . . . This removal of transcendence fundamentally affected the conveyance of meaning. Whereas previously meaning had been established in the very act of creation by a wise God, it now fell upon the human mind to interpret a cosmos, the structure of which had ceased to be given as intelligible.

6. Dupré acknowledges that "[o]nly recently have we become fully aware of the momentous impact of the abandonment of that theoretical ideal, defined more than two millennia ago." *Id.*
7. Norman Hampson concludes that "[p]erhaps the most striking of the positive qualities and beliefs of Enlightenment Man was his conviction that a beneficent Providence regulated the course of nature and the promptings of his own heart." Norman Hampson, The Enlightenment: An Evaluation of its Assumptions, Attitudes, and Values 155 (1968). But Hampson adds that scientific and philosophical thought was already beginning to point to a darker view: "Chance, or the blind determinism of matter in regular but aimless motion, appeared to regulate the operation of the universe and the destiny of man." *Id.* at 186. Hampson's study amply demonstrates that thinking on these

questions during the period we now describe as "the Enlightenment" was far from monolithic.

8. *See* ch. 1, ns. 52–53 and accompanying text.

9. *See, e.g.,* Franklin I. Gamwell, The Meaning of Religious Freedom 208–09 (1995) (describing Habermas's views of modernity).

10. *Cf.* Dupre, *supra* note 5 at 143 ("Once the human self becomes detached from its cosmic and transcendent moorings, the good can hardly be more than what Hobbes calls it: 'the object of any man's appetite or desire' . . . [Hobbes's] mechanistic view deprived that system from the kind of teleology indispensable to any genuine morality.").

11. For a helpful but more optimistic discussion of essentially the same question by a constitutional scholar, see Michael J. Perry, Is the Idea of Human Rights Ineliminably Religious?, in Legal Rights: Historical and Philosophical Perspectives 205 (Austin Sarat & Thomas R. Kearns eds. 1996).

12. W. T. Stace, "Man Against Darkness," in Man Against Darkness and Other Essays 6 (1967).

13. *Id.* at 5–6.

14. *Id.* at 6–7.

15. *Id.* at 6–7, 1–6, 4, 9.

16. "Vanity of vanities, saith the Preacher, vanity of vanities; all is vanity." Eccles. 1:2.

17. Stace, *supra* note 12 at 7.

18. *Id.* at 12–13. Stace later came to have second thoughts about this dismissive conclusion. *See* Stace, "The Philosophy of Mysticism," in Stace, *supra* note 12 at 18.

19. Stace, "Man Against Darkness," *supra* note 12 at 9.

20. *Id.* at 13.

21. *Id.* at 10.

22. *Id.* at 11, 14, 18. The ideal was to become "genuinely civilized human beings." For Stace, this meant "liv[ing] in quiet content, accepting resignedly what cannot be helped, not expecting the impossible, and being thankful for small mercies. . . ." *Id.* at 16–17.

23. Arthur A. Leff, Unspeakable Ethics, Unnatural Law, 1979 Duke L.J. 1229, 1239.

24. *Id.* at 1229–30, 1233, 1231. Leff's by now famous concluding reflections described our predicament:

All I can say is this: it looks as if we are all we have. Given what we know about ourselves and each other, this is an extraordinarily unappetizing prospect; looking around the world, it appears that if all men are brothers, the ruling model is Cain and Abel. Neither reason, nor love, nor even terror, seems to have worked to make us "good," and worse than that, there is no reason why anything should. Only if ethics were something unspeakable by us, could law be unnatural, and therefore unchallengeable. As things now stand, everything is up for grabs.

Nevertheless:

Napalming babies is bad.
Starving the poor is wicked.
Buying and selling each other is depraved.
Those who stood up to and died resisting Hitler, Stalin, Amin, and
    Pol Pot—and General Custer too—have earned salvation.

> Those who acquiesced deserve to be damned.
> There is in the world such a thing as evil.
> [All together now:] Sez who?
> God help us.

Id. at 1249.

25. *Id.* at 1233.

25. Alasdair MacIntyre, After Virtue 52 (rev. ed. 1984).

27. *Id.* at 12.

28. *Id.* at 55.

29. *Id.* at 60.

30. Philippa Foot, Does Moral Subjectivism Rest on a Mistake?, 15 Oxford J. Leg. Stud. 1, 1 (1995).

31. Charles Taylor reports: "Ask any undergraduate class of beginners in philosophy, and the majority will claim to adhere to some form of subjectivism. This may not correspond to deeply felt convictions. It does seem to reflect, however, what these students think the intellectually respectable option to be." Charles Taylor, Philosophical Arguments 34 (1995).

32. *See* Richard Werner, Ethical Relativism, 93 Ethics 653, 661 (1983) (observing that "ordinary moral argumentation and language tends to presuppose the objectivity of ethics").

33. George Wright points out to me that Elizabeth Anscombe's essay "Modern Moral Philosophy," first published in 1958, cogently explored many of these same problems. *See* G. E. M. Anscombe, Modern Moral Philosophy, *reprinted* in 3 The Collected Philosophical Papers of G. E. M. Anscombe: Ethics, Religion and Politics 26 (1981).

34. *See, e.g.,* Friedrich Nietzsche, Twilight of the Idols, in The Portable Nietzsche 463, 501 (Walter Kaufmann tr. 1968) (first published 1889):

> My demand upon the philosopher is known, that he take his stand *beyond* good and evil and leave the illusion of moral judgment *beneath* himself. This demand follows from an insight which I was the first to formulate: that *there are altogether no moral facts.* Moral judgments agree with religious ones in believing in realities which are no realities. Morality is merely an interpretation of certain phenomena—more precisely, a misinterpretation. Moral judgments, like religious ones, belong to a stage of ignorance at which the very concept of the real and the distinction between what is real and imaginary, are still lacking; thus "truth," at this stage, designates all sorts of things which we today call "imaginings." Moral judgments are therefore never to be taken literally: so understood, they always contain mere absurdity.

35. Leff, *supra* note 23 at 1249.

36. *Id.* at 1232.

37. Probably the most prominent constitutional scholars who have concerned themselves with the need to develop a moral realist basis for constitutional reasoning are Michael Moore and Michael Perry. For a brief review of the renewed interest in moral realism among constitutional scholars, see Steven D. Smith, Moral Realism, Pluralistic Community, and the Judicial Imposition of Principle: A Comment on Perry, 88 Nw. U.L. Rev. 183 (1993). For a particularly probing treatment of the issue, see Graham Walker, Moral Foundations of Constitutional Thought (1990). *See also* Sotirios A. Barber, The Constitution of Judicial Power (1993); Daniel J. Morrissey, Moral Truth and the Law: A New Look at an Old Link, 47 SMU L. Rev. 61 (1993); Kathleen A. Brady,

Putting Faith Back Into Constitutional Scholarship: A Defense of Originalism, 36 Cath. Lawyer 137, 171–72, 176–77. And *see generally* Phillip E. Johnson, Reason in the Balance (1995).

38. *See* Walker, *supra* note 37 at 13–17 (arguing that most constitutional theorists evade the difficult problems of moral reasoning).

39. Although in a defense of "natural rights" Randy Barnett devotes only a footnote to explaining, or at least asserting, that the fundamental difference in worldviews separating us from the eighteenth-century proponents of rights is unimportant, Barnett's peremptory treatment is unusual not so much for its brevity as for its noticing the issue at all. Randy E. Barnett, Getting Normative: The Role of Natural Rights in Constitutional Adjudication, 12 Const. Comm. 93, 106 n.37 (1995). In a similar vein, Robin West observes with concern that natural rights' approaches "simply do not resonate with our modern ways of thinking about political morality," and she urges that "we need to suspend our postmodernist doubts" and learn to think again in this way. Robin West, Progressive Constitutionalism 41, 43 (1994). West does not inquire into overall philosophical, metaphysical, and religious changes in the basic intellectual framework that have made natural rights thinking seem nonsensical or impossible; recovering older ways of thinking, it seems, is simply a matter of suspending doubts and trying harder.

40. Martha C. Nussbaum, Skepticism about Practical Reason in Literature and the Law, 107 Harv. L. Rev. 714, 740 (1994).

41. Ernest Gellner, Reason and Culture 157 (1992).

42. Leff, *supra* note 23 at 1229 ("I also want to believe—and so do you—in no such thing [as natural law], but rather that we are wholly free. . . . What we want, Heaven help us, is simultaneously to be perfectly ruled and perfectly free, that is, at the same time to discover the right and the good and to create it.").

43. For example, *Bradwell v. Illinois*, 83 U.S. 130 (1873), in which the Supreme Court upheld Illinois' denial of a license to practice law solely because the applicant was a married woman, is widely regarded as one of the more benighted episodes in constitutional history; and casebooks and commentators frequently quote language from Justice Bradley's opinion arguing that Illinois' differential treatment of women was consistent with the plan of Nature. ("The paramount destiny and mission of woman are to fulfil the noble and benign offices of wife and mother. This is the law of the Creator. And the rules of civil society must be adapted to the general constitution of things . . . .").

44. *Cf.* Steven L. Winter, Foreword: On Building Houses, 69 Tex. L. Rev. 1595, 1600–01 (1991) (citations omitted):

> There will, of course, always be those who . . . warn against the chaos that will ensue if we abandon "The House of Reason." But it is this very anxiety for some solid foundation that introduces the problem of nihilism. The alternative, however, is neither disorder nor resignation in the face of blind contingency. It is rather, a recognition that "truth" is itself a human product. . . .

45. *See generally* Nelson Goodman, Ways of Worldmaking (1978).

46. Paul Kahn has argued that in much modern constitutional thinking reason has effectively been replaced by will, with the ongoing debates centering on whether the authoritative locus of will is in the community or the individual. Paul W. Kahn, Legitimacy and History 134–70 (1992). *Cf.* Dupré, *supra* note 5 at 133 (observing that collapse of classical notions of cosmos led political thought to "a shift from the law of reason to that of power").

47. Griswold v. Connecticut, 381 U.S. 479, 493 (1965); Snyder v. Massachusetts, 291 U.S. 97, 105 (1934).

48. Adamson v. California, 332 U.S. 46, 67 (1947).

49. Poe v. Ullman, 367 U.S. 497, 544 (1961) (Harlan, J., dissenting); Rochin v. California, 342 U.S. 165, 170–71 (1952).

50. Barber, *supra* note 37 at xi. Barber does not join in this consensus. *See also* Walker, *supra* note 37 at 17 (arguing that most constitutional theorists "deny any moral reality beyond the contrivances of convention").

51. Sanford Levinson, Constitutional Faith 175 (1988).

52. For a more extended criticism, see John Hart Ely, Democracy and Distrust 60–69 (1980).

53. A possible answer might suggest that constitutional principles are based not on general moral conventions, but rather on the conventions of a legal or academic elite. But this position provokes serious objection: It seems not only undemocratic but also internally inconsistent. There is at least a certain internal logic, that is, in a position like that of Plato's *Republic*—which calls for philosophers to rule because they more than others have the ability to discern moral reality. But for philosophers, or the well-educated, to claim a governing function while at the same time *denying* that there is any moral reality accessible to philosophy or education makes little sense. Not surprisingly, therefore, constitutional scholars have not been eager to advocate this position as a normative matter, though some do advance the position descriptively as a way of criticizing modern constitutional orthodoxies. *See* H. Jefferson Powell, The Moral Tradition of American Constitutionalism 10 (1993) (arguing that "[r]ather than explicating the coherence of shared American moral commitments, contemporary [constitutional] theorists offer little more than a veiled apologia for rule by a liberal oligarchy"). *See generally* Robert H. Bork, The Tempting of America (1990).

54. *See* Mark Tushnet, Red, White, and Blue: A Critical Analysis of Constitutional Law 134 (1988). *See also id.* at 140 (remarking that "perhaps the enduring values of our society are what some would describe as racist, sexist, and generally inegalitarian and intolerant"). *Cf.* Brady, *supra* note 37 at 171 (arguing that "even principles which reflect prevailing community values are tyrannical to the dissenter, who becomes the victim of mass collectivism").

55. *See, e.g.,* John Finnis, Natural Law and Natural Rights (1980); Michael Moore, A Natural Law Theory of Interpretation, 58 S. Cal. L. Rev. 277 (1985); Michael J. Perry, Morality, Politics, and Law (1988). *See generally* Natural Law, Liberalism, and Morality (Robert P. George ed. 1996).

56. *See, e.g.,* Griswold v. Connecticut, 381 U.S. 479, 522 (1965) (Black, J., dissenting) (attacking majority position by accusing it of being based on natural law). Randy Barnett points out that "critics of Judge Thomas immediately reacted by characterizing his interest in natural law as kooky and outside the mainstream," and rather than defending the natural law approach Thomas instead disavowed it; he "maintained that natural law had no role to play in constitutional adjudication." Barnett, *supra* note 39 at 95.

57. Lloyd L. Weinreb, The Moral Point of View, in Natural Law, Liberalism, and Morality 195, 195 (Robert P. George ed. 1996).

58. *See* Ely, *supra* note 52 at 48–54; Jeremy Waldron, The Irrelevance of Moral Objectivity, in Natural Law Theory: Contemporary Essays 158, 171–76 (Robert George ed. 1992).

59. Michael Moore, perhaps the most influential moral realist in the American legal academy today, maintains that moral realists will reason about moral issues in the

same coherentist way that conventionalists reason. Whether this position robs moral realism of its practical significance presents a difficult question. For a helpful discussion of Moore's attempt to combine a realist ontology with a coherentist epistemology, see Walker, *supra* note 37 at 128–33.

60. Russell Hittinger, A Critique of the New Natural Law Theory (1987).

61. Steven D. Smith, Nonsense and Natural Law, in Against the Law (Paul F. Campos, Pierre Schlag, and Steven D. Smith, 1996). *See also* Steven D. Smith, Natural Law and Contemporary Moral Thought: Are "Goods" Good Enough?, Am. J. Juris. (forthcoming).

62. Readers interested in alternative ways of bringing reason into constitutional law might note at this point that a natural law constitutionalism, like common law constitutionalism, *see* ch. 4, ns. 4, 9 and accompanying text, represents a possible alternative to the course that constitutional thinking has taken—and one that, if our current approach turns out to be unsatisfactory, might deserve further consideration.

63. *See generally* Patrick Devlin, The Enforcement of Morals (1965).

64. *Id.* at 15.

65. Ronald Dworkin, Taking Rights Seriously 255 (1977). Dworkin's essay had been published in the Yale Law Journal in 1966.

66. *Id.* at 249.

67. *Id.* at 249, 251.

68. *Id.* at 249–50.

69. *See, e.g.,* Joseph Raz, The Relevance of Coherence, 72 B.U. L. Rev. 273, 275 (1992) (describing search for beliefs "not tainted by superstition, prejudice, rashness, jumping to conclusions, or other epistemic defects"). *Cf.* Hilary Putnam, Are Moral and Legal Values Made or Discovered?, 1 Legal Theory 5, 15, 19 (1995) (arguing that "we can distinguish between an intelligent discussion in ethics and one which is prejudiced, closed-minded, etc.," while also rejecting the notion that such a discussion requires "transcendent truth").

70. John Rawls, A Theory of Justice 48 (1971). *Cf.* Larry Alexander & Ken Kress, Against Legal Principles, in Law and Interpretation 279, 306 (Andrei Marmor ed. 1995) ("In the moral realm, reflective equilibrium is championed as the correct epistemological method for discovering (constructing?) correct moral principles.").

71. Taylor, *supra* note 31 at 36.

72. Judith Jarvis Thomson, A Defense of Abortion, Phil. & Pub. Affairs 47–66 (Fall 1971), *reprinted in* The Ethics of Abortion 29 (Robert M. Baird & Stuart E. Rosenbaum eds. 1989).

73. *Id.* at 30.

74. *Id.* at 31.

75. Indeed, we might use something like this "coherence" method even if we are *not* conventionalists, as Michael Moore points out. *See supra* note 59. More generally, even a moral realist may and ought to acknowledge that she cannot step outside her skin and somehow apprehend moral reality directly (whatever that might mean); and so she has no choice but to reason on the basis of her beliefs *about* moral reality. Even so, for a moral realist the point of this exercise will be different; she will be trying to discern the content of an independent reality, not merely to achieve coherence or "reflective equilibrium" in her beliefs as a matter of good intellectual housekeeping.

76. "Subjectivism" and "conventionalism" are somewhat different positions. Subjectivism typically locates morality in the beliefs and attitudes of each individual, while conventionalism finds morality in the beliefs and attitudes of the general community. In a sense, conventionalism is subjectivism writ large, or projected onto the society as a

whole. Despite this difference, both are antirealist positions, and for our purposes the differences between them will usually be unimportant.

77. Nussbaum, *supra* note 40 at 740.

78. *See, e.g.,* Alexander M. Bickel, The Least Danger Branch 24–25 (1962); Ronald Dworkin, A Matter of Principle 24–25 (1985); Michael J. Perry, The Constitution in the Courts 106–10 (1994).

79. *Cf.* Barrett, *supra* note 3 at 78–79:

> For a concept to have meaning, we must be able to represent it, directly or indirectly, through some concrete intuition or intuitions. More simply and crudely: we have to be able to make some kind of mental picture of the concept. Otherwise our thinking becomes empty, and the words we use merely empty verbalisms.

80. Dworkin, A Matter of Principle, *supra* note 78 at 172.

81. *See, e.g.,* Michael Moore, Moral Reality, 1982 Wis. L. Rev. 1061, 1075–79.

82. *See* John H. Garvey, What Are Freedoms For? (1996).

83. *See, e.g.,* John H. Garvey, The Pope's Submarine, 30 San Diego L. Rev. 849 (1993).

84. *See, e.g.,* Dworkin, Freedom's Law, *supra* note 1 at 316:

> The phrase "natural law" refers to an objective moral reality which endows people with fundamental moral rights that are not created by custom or convention or legislation, but rather exist as an independent body of moral principle. As [Clarence] Thomas pointed out, most of the eighteenth-century statesmen who drafted and argued for the Constitution believed in natural law. So, I think, do most Americans now: most of us think that apartheid, or torture, or other forms of brutal repression, for example, are morally wrong, according to objective principles, even when condoned by the laws in force where they occur. (footnote omitted)

85. *See infra* note 92.

86. *See, e.g.,* Philip Soper, Some Natural Confusions about Natural Law, 90 Mich. L. Rev. 2392, 2416 (1992).

87. Michael S. Moore, Metaphysics, Epistemology and Legal Theory, 60 S. Cal. L. Rev. 459 (1987); Barber, *supra* note 37 at 181; Waldron, *supra* note 58 at 162–63. For a thoughtful assessment of the ways in which Dworkin does and does not appear to be a moral realist, see Walker, *supra* note 37 at 42–45.

88. 25 Phil. and Pub. Affairs 87, 127 (1996).

89. *Id.* at 90.

90. *Id.* at 99, 105.

91. *Id.* at 128.

92. Consider in this respect Jules Coleman's assessment: "Frankly, I think [Dworkin is] quite confused about objectivity and its role in . . . legal discourse. . . ." Jules Coleman, Truth and Objectivity in Law, 1 Legal Theory 33, 54 (1995).

An anonymous reviewer objects that extracting a few seemingly inconsistent passages from Dworkin's essay does not amount to a refutation of his argument. I agree, but the objection misunderstands the point of the foregoing discussion. My purpose is not to refute any *argument* made by Dworkin—his argument, for example, that slavery would be wrong whether anyone thought so or not—or even to assert that his position is inconsistent, but instead merely to explain why it is difficult to credit or even make sense of Dworkin's claim that his position is a "realist" one. An analogy may be helpful: Suppose I earnestly claim to believe in ESP; but I go on to ridicule mental telepathy, prescience, and other phenomena that devotees of ESP typically accept; and I also fail to identify any sort of extrasensory perception that I *do* believe in. You might be convinced of my sincerity and yet wonder what I could possibly mean (or whether I mean anything intelligible at all) when I claim to believe in ESP. Likewise for Dworkin's claim to "realism."

93. *See* Robert F. Nagel, Constitutional Cultures 106–07 (1989).

94. *See id.* at 107; T. Alexander Aleinikoff, Constitutional Law in the Age of Balancing, 96 Yale L.J. 943 (1987).

95. *See id.* at 972–83.

96. *See id.* at 984–86. *See also* George W. Carey, In Defense of the Constitution 179 (rev. ed. 1995):

> The Court as an institution is simply not suited for this task [of formulating policy]. Unlike the Congress, it has no reliable means to gauge the relative intensity of the interested parties, what the reactions will be to any given pronouncement or, *inter alia*, what obstacles are likely to arise in its execution. And once having embarked on a path, it can pull back or reverse itself only at great cost to its own prestige and the principle of the rule of law. Moreover, leaving aside the legitimacy of these activities, its members are ill equipped for such tasks because legal training scarcely provides the breadth of knowledge in fields such as philosophy, history, the sciences, and social sciences necessary for this mission.

97. How to determine whether a particular objective is a legitimate "reason" or merely a "prejudice" is an exceedingly difficult question that, fortunately, we need not pursue here. For a thoughtful (if ultimately unsuccessful) discussion, see Ely, *supra* note 52 at 153–70.

98. Romer v. Evans, 116 S. Ct. 1620, 1629 (1996).

99. *Id.* at 1628. *See also id.* at 1627 (asserting that "its sheer breadth is so discontinuous with the reasons offered for it that the amendment seems inexplicable by anything but animus toward the class that it affects").

100. 473 U.S. 432, 450 (1985).

101. 413 U.S. 528, 534 (1973).

102. For example, in correspondence George Wright tells me that although many commercial speech cases fit the pattern described here—the courts in reality are attempting to ferret out illegitimate motives of paternalism—in some cases the courts appear actually to be ranking different but legitimate interests. I defer to Professor Wright's expertise.

103. *See* Aleinikoff, *supra* note 94 at 984–86, 1004.

104. Ely, *supra* note 52 at 145.

105. *Id.*

106. *Id.* at 146.

107. Cass R. Sunstein, Naked Preferences and the Constitution, 84 Colum. L. Rev. 1689 (1984).

108. *Id.* at 1694.

109. *See, e.g., id.* at 1699:

> Heightened scrutiny involves two principal elements. The first is a requirement that the government show a close connection between the asserted public value and the means that the legislature has chosen to promote it. If a sufficiently close connection cannot be shown, there is reason for skepticism that the asserted value in fact accounted for the legislation. The second element is a search for less re-

strictive alternatives—ways in which the government could have promoted the public value without harming the group in question. The availability of such alternatives also suggests that the public value justification is a facade. (footnotes omitted)

110. *Id.* at 1689.

111. *See, e.g.,* Frederick Schauer, Cuban Cigars, Cuban Books, and the Problem of Incidental Restrictions on Communications, 26 Wm. & Mary L. Rev. 779 (1985).

112. *See* Steven D. Smith, Free Exercise Doctrine and the Discourse of Disrespect, 65 U. Colo. L. Rev. 519, 545–70 (1994).

Chapter Six

1. *See generally* Lynne Henderson. The Dialogue of Heart and Head, 10 Cardozo L. Rev. 123 (1988).

2. On the difficulty of classifying Dworkin and many other legal scholars as moral "realists," "antirealists," or "conventionalists," see ch. 5, ns. 79–92 and accompanying text.

3. *Cf.* Mary Ann Glendon, Tradition and Creativity in Culture and Law, 27 First Things 13, 13 (Nov. 1992) (describing "in our time, the tradition of antitraditionalism").

4. Within a conventionalist framework it is not so easy to say what constitutes inconsistency, but this is an objection we need not pursue here.

5. Aristotle, Metaphysics IV.4.

6. *See* ch. 5, n. 81 and accompanying text.

7. To be sure, even a moral realist might not accept a general consistency requirement. For example, she might hold a sort of Yin-Yang view of moral reality. Or to borrow an analogy from modern physics, which has found itself forced to describe certain atomic phenomena as in some sense like particles and in some other sense like waves, a moral realist might believe that moral reality is inherently complex or in tension with itself, so that what seem to be inconsistent descriptions might both be true. *Cf.* Blaise Pascal, Pensees 224 (A. J. Krailsheimer tr. 1966):

> *Two contrary reasons.* We must begin with that, otherwise we cannot understand anything and everything is heretical. And even at the end of each truth we must add that we are bearing the opposite truth in mind.

See also id. at 208: "A hundred contradictions might be true."

8. Suzanna Sherry, who vigorously contends for the necessity of consistency to reasoned discourse, *see* Suzanna Sherry, The Sleep of Reason, 84 Georgetown L.J. 453, 475 (1996), appears alternately to perceive and not to perceive that this requirement presupposes a commitment to some form of objectivism or realism. Early in her essay Sherry asserts that the possibility of reason "must therefore depend on a commonly shared perception of reality." *Id.* at 456. This *sounds* at least vaguely objectivist. But Sherry never explains what sort of reality moral discourse depends on, and her objectivist insight gradually slips away. Midway through the essay she insists that "[t]here is a difference between objective truth and justified beliefs, and suggesting that only beliefs informed by reason are justified does not take any stand on the existence or accessibility of objective truth." *Id.* at 473. Shortly thereafter she demands consistency in discourse, but despite her commitment to reason, Sherry offers no reasons for making consistency mandatory.

9. *See* Michael Moore, Moral Reality Revisited, 90 Mich. L. Rev. 2424, 2462 (1992)

(arguing that conventionalism provides no basis for requiring consistency). *See also* Arthur Allen Leff, Unspeakable Ethics, Unnatural Law, 1979 Duke L.J. 1229, 1238:

> Let us say that person A decides that one ought to do X under particular circumstances. Person B believes that under those circumstances one ought to do Y. Person A's conclusion is based upon deep and mature thought and comes out of an intellectual structure such that doing X will work no discernible contradiction with anything else he might think one ought to do. Not so Person B. He thinks one ought to do Y, but he has not thought about it, and if he did think about it he would recognize that doing Y is totally, flagrantly inconsistent with a host of other things he thinks one ought to do. Should one not in such a situation give more weight to A's position than to B's? Only if *someone* has the power to declare careful, consistent ethical propositions "better" than the sloppier, more impulsive kinds. Who has that power and how did he get it?

10. Walt Whitman, Song of Myself, verse 51. In the same spirit, recall Emerson's oft-quoted statement—"A foolish consistency is the hobgoblin of little minds." Ralph Waldo Emerson, Self-Reliance, in Selected Writings of Ralph Waldo Emerson 263 (William H. Gilman ed. 1965).

11. Robert M. Baird, Dworkin, Abortion, Religious Liberty, and the Spirit of Enlightenment, 37 J. Church & State 753, 766 (1995) (emphasis added).

12. *See supra* note 5 and accompanying text.

13. Even in academic culture, however, these preferences and aversions surely vary. I have argued elsewhere, for example, that as matter of temperament legal theorists who claim the label of "pragmatism" exhibit less need for complete coherence, and more tolerance for inconsistency, than those (such as Dworkin) who attack legal pragmatism typically display. *See* Steven D. Smith, The Pursuit of Pragmatism, 100 Yale L.J. 409, 438–39 (1990).

14. Michael S. Moore, Metaphysics, Epistemology and Legal Theory, 60 S. Cal. L. Rev. 453, 458–59 (1987) (arguing that Dworkin's is a "subtle and much more appealing conventionalism than Devlin's").

15. Moore, *supra* note 9 at 2453, 2462, 2467.

16. Ronald Dworkin, Taking Rights Seriously 249–51 (1977).

17. I use "prejudice" here in what I think is a common understanding of the term—that is, a belief that one has received but not really examined or thought about. Dworkin himself offers what seems a rather peculiar definition; he says prejudices are "considerations our conventions exclude." Dworkin, *supra* note 16 at 249. But Dworkin's definition seems either to render the criterion irrelevant—if a consideration is contrary to convention in the first place then there should never be any question of its determining conventional morality anyway—or else to collapse the criterion of "prejudice" into some other criterion such as "consistency."

18. Bruce A. Ackerman, Beyond *Carolene Products*, 98 Harv. L. Rev. 713, 737 (1985).

19. *Id.* at 739.

20. *See* Karl N. Llewellyn, The Common Law Tradition 521–35 (1960).

21. The discussion here will not attempt to summarize Dworkin's entire book; it covers only Dworkin's treatment of one issue—although his resolution of that issue provides the foundation for the rest of his analysis of abortion. For a more comprehensive review and assessment, see Frances M. Kamm, Abortion and the Value of Life: A Discussion of *Life's Dominion*, 95 Colum. L. Rev. 160 (1995). For a thoughtful discussion of Dworkin's claim that life is sacred, see Michael J. Perry, Is the Idea of Human

Rights Ineliminably Religious?, in Legal Rights: Historical and Philosophical Perspectives 205, 232–39 (Austin Sarat and Thomas R. Kearns eds. 1996).

22. Ronald Dworkin, Life's Dominion 9 (Vintage ed. 1994).

23. *Id.* at 13–14, 39–40.

24. *Id.* at 13.

25. Preface to the Vintage Edition, xi (emphasis in original).

26. *Id.* at 13 (emphasis added).

27. *See* Ronald Dworkin, Freedom's Law 46 (1996): "[I]t is entirely consistent to think, for example, that a fetus is just as much a human being as an adult, or that it has a soul from the moment of conception, and yet that the Constitution, on the best interpretation, does not grant a fetus rights competitive with the rights it grants other people."

28. Of course, the moral beliefs and conventions that provide the material for Dworkin's analysis might themselves implicitly presuppose some kind of moral reality. *See* ch. 5, n. 81 and accompanying text. But Dworkin's own argument, though it might be said indirectly to trade on that presupposition, would not itself endorse the presupposition.

29. "I do hope to convince such people, if they are willing to listen, that they have misunderstood the basis of their own convictions." *Id.* at x.

30. *See* Baird, *supra* note 11 at 762: "The problem is that an individual cannot be shown not to hold a belief by demonstrating that the individual holds another belief incompatible with the first. It is simply the case that individuals sometimes really do believe contradictory propositions."

31. For a similar argument, see Kamm, *supra* note 21 at 168–69.

32. *See* Dworkin, *supra* note 22 at 14, 32, 47.

33. Mary Ann Glendon, Rights Talk 45 (1991).

34. Cass Sunstein remarks that "almost every right is defeasible at some point. . . . In American law, no right is absolute." Cass R. Sunstein, Rights and Their Critics, 70 Notre Dame L. Rev. 727, 736 (1995). *See also* Kamm, *supra* note 21 at 168–69, 185–225.

> 35. The equal protection clause requires states to extend the protection of their laws against murder and assault equally to all persons, and if fetuses were constitutional persons any state legislation that discriminated against them in that respect, by permitting abortion, would be suspect, under equal protection principles, and the Supreme Court would have an obligation to review such legislation to determine whether the state's justification for the discrimination was "compelling." In some cases it would be: when a state permitted abortion to protect the health of a mother, for example, or perhaps in cases of rape or incest.

Dworkin, *supra* note 27 at 47–48.

36. For a different argument leading to the same conclusion—*i.e.,* that the supposedly inconsistent beliefs Dworkin discusses are *not* by-and-large inconsistent—see Gerard V. Bradley, *Life's Dominion:* A Review Essay, 69 Notre Dame L. Rev. 329, 382–84 (1993).

37. Dworkin, *supra* note 22 at 39–50.

38. For a critical assessment of Dworkin's analysis of Catholic doctrine, see Bradley, *supra* note 36 at 364–69.

39. *Cf.* Mark Tushnet, Red, White, and Blue: A Critical Analysis of Constitutional Law 51 (1988):

In a legal system with a relatively extensive body of precedent and well-developed techniques of legal reasoning, it will always be possible to show how today's decision is consistent with the relevant past ones, but, conversely, it will also always be possible to show how today's decision is inconsistent with the precedents. This symmetry, of course, drains "consistency" of any normative content.

40. *See, e.g.,* Gorgias 462c–463c; Sophist 291c, 303c.

41. *See* T. H. Irwin, Plato: The Intellectual Background, in The Cambridge Companion to Plato 51, 54 (Richard Kraut ed. 1992).

42. "Socrates' efforts to define the virtues assume that objectively correct answers can be found, and that they must correspond to some objective realities independent of our beliefs and inquiries." *Id.* at 69.

43. *See, e.g.,* Laws 889e–890a:

ATHENIAN: [T]his party asserts that gods have no real and natural, but only an artificial being, in virtue of legal conventions, as they call them, and thus there are different gods for different places, conformably to the convention made by each group among themselves. . . . Then they actually declare that . . . as for right, there is absolutely no such thing as a real and natural right, that mankind are eternally disputing about rights and altering them, and that every change thus made, once made, is from that moment valid, though it owes its being to artifice and legislation, not to anything you could call nature. All these views, my friends, come from men who impress the young as wise, prose writers and poets who profess that indefeasible right means whatever a man can carry with the high hand. . . .
CLINIAS: What an awful creed you describe, sir! . . .

44. Republic 493a–b (729).
45. Gorgias 462c–463c.
46. Sophist 291c (1060).
47. *Id.* 303c (1074).
48. Laches 196b (139).
49. Republic 498e–499a (734).
50. Gorgias 489e (272).
51. Gorgias 503c, 515e.
52. Republic 508a–509b.
53. Gorgias 455–457.
54. Republic 338d, 340d, 341c.
55. *Id.* at 343c.
56. *Id.* at 345b.
57. Gorgias 473e.
58. *Id.* at 482e, 489b. Of course the citizens of Athens, unable to either refute or silence Socrates, go beyond this sort of verbal violence; they ultimately resolve their differences with Socrates by having him executed.
59. Dworkin, *supra* note 22 at x.
60. His attack on pro-lifers is hardly Dworkin's only resort to this tactic. *See, e.g.,* Dworkin, Freedom's Law, *supra* note 27 at 37 (judges who deny relying on their own moral convictions in judging are guilty of "mendacity"), at 74 (legalistic view of the Constitution is "the political huckster's dream"), at 81 (legalistic view amounts to "hypocrisy"), at 243 (Catherine MacKinnon thrives on "calling names . . . personal sensationalism, hyperbole, and bad arguments"). Dworkin has been especially liberal in his ad hominem attacks against Robert Bork. Bork, he says, is "a constitutional radical" and a "crude moral skeptic." *Id.* at 265, 273. Bork "has made a career of grossly unfair

charges against those who disagree with his views." *Id.* at 288. Bork is "shrill and mendacious"; he "deploys . . . wild charges" that are "irresponsibly false," and he "debases the quality of the debate." *Id.* at 288–90. Bork's jurisprudence is "rigid, parochial, and depressing." *Id.* at 305. Of course, Dworkin is not the only scholar who resorts to name-calling or pejorative characterization, and he is sometimes the target of that tactic. *See id.* at 239 ("Professor MacKinnon says that my review of her book is incompetent, inconsistent, ignorant, appalling, shocking, rock-throwing junk, and that there is next to no difference between me and 'kept writers in pornography magazines.'"). And some readers will surely regard the present discussion as a pejorative characterization of Dworkin.

61. John Rawls, Political Liberalism 243 n. 32 (1993).

62. *Id.*

63. *Cf.* Paul Campos, A Heterodox Catechisms, in Paul F. Campos, Pierre Schlag, & Steven D. Smith, Against the Law 10 (1996) (describing "the tautological or even shamanistic invocation of the signifier 'reasonable'").

64. In this respect, Rawls's conclusory assertions arguably mirror the judicial decision they serve to affirm—that is, *Roe v. Wade.* Noting that "[i]t seems to be generally agreed that, as a matter of simple craft, Justice Blackmun's opinion for the Court was dreadful," Mark Tushnet suggests that "[w]e might think of Justice Blackmun's opinion in *Roe* as an innovation . . .—the totally unreasoned judicial opinion." Tushnet, *supra* note 39 at 53–54.

65. Robert Lipkin has tellingly criticized Rawls's notions of "public reason," showing that in the end Rawls merely asserts positions that enjoy a liberal consensus without attempting to offer further justifications for those who do not already share that consensus. Robert Justin Lipkin, In Defense of Outlaws: Liberalism and the Role of Reasonableness, Public Reason, and Tolerance in Multicultural Constitutionalism, 45 DePaul L. Rev. 263, 279–303 (1996). Thus, Rawls's position "is an explication of liberalism for liberals." *Id.* at 291. "He never really demonstrates why threatening nonliberal views are unreasonable. . . ."; consequently, "it could be argued that Rawls is simply intolerant of nonliberal attitudes." *Id.* at 288.

66. One might seek to excuse Rawls's meager effort by observing that it comprises only a single, albeit lengthy, footnote; his chapter is not primarily devoted to discussing abortion, but rather uses the issue only as an illustration of "public reason." But this excuse is dubious, because it seems that Rawls believes he *has* explained why approximately the current legal compromise on abortion is in fact required by "public reason." It was Rawls, after all, who saw fit to deal with the issue of abortion in an extended footnote. To put the point differently, although it is true that the teaching of "public reason" on the issue of abortion is, in Rawls's discussion, brief and conclusory, this brief and conclusory pronouncement appears to convey pretty much all that Rawlsian "public reason" has to say on the subject.

67. For a similar complaint about Rawls's conclusory treatment, see Richard H. Posner, Overcoming Law 188–90 (1995). Compare Paul Campos's observation about Rawls's pervasive invocation of "reasonableness":

> "[R]eason" functions as the master concept that transcends the enumeration of particular reasons: *invoking* "reason" becomes equivalent to *giving* reasons. The obvious circularity of this argument illustrates how a discourse that presents itself as a model of rational explication is, rationally speaking, indistinguishable from the . . . emotive language games upon which the . . . moral intuitionist must more openly rely.

Paul F. Campos, *supra* note 63 at 197.

68. Robert F. Nagel, Constitutional Cultures at 147 (1989).

69. Posner, *supra* note 67 at 192 (footnotes omitted).

70. Jean Yarbrough observes that "[i]n area after area of American life, claims that might once have been framed in terms of sound and fair public policy are clothed in the more strident, uncompromising idiom of enforceable legal rights. . . ." Jean Yarbrough, Federalism and Rights in the American Founding, in Federalism and Rights 57, 57 (Ellie Katz & G. Alan Tarr eds. 1996). *See generally* Mary Ann Glendon, Rights Talk (1991).

71. *Compare* Robin West, Progressive Constitutionalism 35 (1992) *with* Richard A. Epstein, Takings 314–29 (1985).

72. For a range of views and constitutional arguments on this issue, see Symposium: The Role of Religion in Public Debate in a Liberal Society, 30 San Diego L. Rev. 643 (1993). Kent Greenawalt has perhaps done more to explore the subject than anyone else. *See* Kent Greenawalt, Private Consciences and Public Reasons (1995); Kent Greenawalt, Religious Convictions and Political Choice (1988).

73. Robin West argues that the state has violated the Thirteenth and/or Fourteenth Amendments by "fail[ing] to protect these women against the resulting state of servitude" involved in housewife status, although she is unclear about what sort of remedy the Constitution requires. West, *supra* note 71 at 36. The vagueness of West's position on this issue makes it difficult to think of advocates who directly oppose it, although it is hard to imagine that any remedies West might propose for housewife status would not run afoul of the constitutional theories of, say, Richard Epstein.

74. *Compare* West, *supra* note 71 at 261 (arguing that the Fourteenth Amendment requires anti-pornography ordinances) *with* American Booksellers Ass'n v. Hudnut, 771 F.2d 323 (7th Cir. 1985), aff'd, 475 U.S. 1001 (1986) (striking down such an ordinance under the First Amendment).

75. *Compare* West, *supra* note 71 at 263 (arguing that the Constitution requires affirmative action) *with* Adarand Constructors v. Pena, 115 S. Ct. 2097 (1995) (striking down an affirmative action program and suggesting the unconstutionality of such programs).

76. Tushnet, *supra* note 39 at 52.

77. Sanford Levinson, Constitutional Faith 191–92 (1988). Levinson adds that when said in the language of the Constitution "some things will sound strange and 'off the wall,'" but even this qualification may be temporary: "Today's frivolity may be tomorrow's law." *Id.* at 192 (quoting D. M. Rissinger).

78. Laurence H. Tribe & Michael C. Dorf, On Reading the Constitution 17 (1991).

79. Paul W. Kahn, Legitimacy and History 195 (1992).

80. West, *supra* note 71 at 15, 261, 16.

81. Laurence H. Tribe, Taking Text and Structure Seriously: Reflections on Free-Form Method in Constitutional Interpretation, 108 Harv. L. Rev. 1221, 1235 (1995).

82. *See* Jordan Steiker, Sanford Levinson, and J. M. Balkin, Taking Text and Structure *Really* Seriously, 74 Tex. L. Rev. 237 (1995). The authors conclude their essay with a question:

> Must we in the legal academy teach every opinion of a Justice of the Supreme Court seriously? Or can we properly say that some (but which?) are parodies of legal argument? As Shakespeare reminded us, even "[a] dog's obeyed in office." This only underscores, though, that some parodies are the occasion for tears rather than laughter.

Id. at 257 (citation omitted).

83. Robert F. Nagel, Name-Calling and the Clear Error Rule, 88 Nw. U. L. Rev.

193, 199 (1993). *See also* Steven D. Smith, Free Exercise Doctrine and the Discourse of Disrespect, 65 U. Colo. L. Rev. 519, 552–57, 575–76 (1994).

84. H. Jefferson Powell, The Moral Tradition of American Constitutionalism 11 (1993).

85. *See, e.g.,* ch. 7, ns. 2–11 and accompanying text.

Chapter Seven

1. *Cf.* Pierre Schlag, The Enchantment of Reason (forthcoming) manuscript at 54 (noting how in legal discourse "the partisans of reason" so often "resort to dogmatic assertions, to rhetorical bluster, to political posturing, to ethical bullying, to shallow circularities and to ad hominem arguments").

2. George W. Carey, In Defense of the Constitution 181, 185 (rev. ed. 1995).

3. Michael Stokes Paulsen, Captain James T. Kirk and the Enterprise of Constitutional Interpretation: Some Modest Proposals from the Twenty-Third Century, 59 Albany L. Rev. 671, 674, 677, 677 n.7 (1995). *See also* Kenneth Lasson, Scholarship Amok: Excesses in the Pursuit of Truth and Tenure, 103 Harv. L. Rev. 926, 942 (1990) (depicting legal scholarship as "bleak and turgid").

4. Morton J. Horwitz, Foreword: The Constitution of Change: Legal Fundamentality without Fundamentalism, 107 Harv. L. Rev. 30, 40 (1993).

5. Duncan Kennedy, American Constitutionalism as Civil Religion: Notes of an Atheist, 19 Nova L. Rev. 909, 919 (1995).

6. Sanford Levinson, Constitutional Faith 172 (1988).

7. Paul W. Kahn, Legitimacy and History 210 (1992).

8. T. Alexander Aleinikoff, Constitutional Law in the Age of Balancing, 96 Yale L.J. 943, 992, 983 (1987).

9. H. Jefferson Powell, The Moral Tradition of American Constitutionalism 263, 7, 262, 47 (1993).

10. Daniel A. Farber, Missing the "Play of Intelligence," 36 Wm. & Mary L. Rev. 147, 147, 154, 157 (1994).

11. Leslie Gielow Jacobs, Even More Honest Than Ever Before: Abandoning Pretense and Recreating Legitimacy in Constitutional Interpretation, 1995 U. Ill. L. Rev. 382, 372, 364.

12. As we have seen, Ronald Dworkin holds that for moral reasoning in general, a rationalization does not "count" as a reason. *See* Ronald Dworkin, Taking Rights Seriously 249–50 (1977). Whether Dworkin would impose this restriction on constitutional reasoning seems more dubious. *See, e.g., supra* note 22 and accompanying text.

13. Although in this book I am concerned with constitutional reasoning, I do not mean to suggest that the phenomenon of rationalization is limited to constitutional law. Much of the discussion in this chapter seems applicable to law, and legal scholarship, generally; and some of the discussion draws on sources not primarily concerned with constitutional law.

14. *See* ch. 6, ns. 68, 69 and accompanying text.

15. *See, e.g.,* Jean Appleman, Persuasion in Brief Writing 2–3 (1968):

> Reacting as mortals, [judges] are no more persuaded by cold, lifeless syllogisms than are other mortals. Rather, they must first become interested in the case and then be made to see its rightness or wrongness—that justice and equity are on the side of the advocate. . . . And if the attorney can so present the facts, sincerely, but without exaggeration or hysteria, that the courts will react to them as he did, they will find a way of shaping the law to meet the desired results.

16. Joseph C. Hutcheson, Jr., The Judgment Intuititve: The Function of the "Hunch" in Judicial Decision, 14 Cornell L. Rev. 274, 279 (1929).

17. *See, e.g.,* Ruggero J. Aldisert, Opinion Writing 31–34 (1990).

18. *See, e.g.,* Richard A. Wasserstrom, The Judicial Decision 25–30 (1961); Paul Brest, Processes of Constitutional Decisionmaking 3–5 (1975).

19. For example, Ronald Dworkin argues that judges are often loathe to admit the inevitable role of moral reasoning in their opinions; consequently, they "try to explain their decisions in other—embarrassingly unsatisfactory—ways." Ronald Dworkin, Freedom's Law 4 (1996).

20. Of course, legal scholars do not always end up *approving* constitutional decisions; often they *criticize* these decisions. It nonetheless seems fair to characterize constitutional scholarship broadly as a rationalizing enterprise because this scholarship typically justifies constitutional decisions in two senses. First, the bulk of constitutional scholarship has sought to support and justify the landmark constitutional decisions such as Griswold v. Connecticut, 381 U.S. 479 (1965) Roe v. Wade, 410 U.S. 113 (1973), New York Times v. Sullivan, 376 U.S. 254 (1964), Brandenburg v. Ohio, 395 U.S. 444 (1969), and especially Brown v. Board of Education, 347 U.S. 483 (1954). *See infra* notes 22, 27–30, 40 and accompanying text. Indeed, scholarly criticisms of lesser decisions often consist precisely of arguing that these decisions do not adhere to or fulfill the promise of these landmark cases. Second, even in criticizing particular decisions legal scholars typically reaffirm and provide accounts (inevitably, if the accounts are to serve as standards for criticizing particular decisions, *supportive* accounts) of the overall enterprise of constitutional law and judicial review. To say that a legal decision is *incorrect*, in other words, entails that there is a standard or method of reasoning for determining what a *correct* decision would be.

21. Richard A. Posner, Overcoming Law 214 (1995).

22. Ronald Dworkin, A Matter of Principle 326–27 (1985). *Cf.* Dworkin, Freedom's Law, *supra* note 19 at 102 ("I take the principle of procreative autonomy to be an elaboration of Brennan's suggestion [in *Griswold*].") It seems Dworkin has done a good deal of tidying up after Justice Brennan. *See also id.* at 199–209 (offering improved rationale for Brennan's opinion in New York Times v. Sullivan).

23. *Cf.* Larry Alexander and Ken Kress, Against Legal Principles, in Law and Interpretation 279, 291 (Andrei Marmor ed. 1995):

> In article after article, treatise after treatise, legal scholars survey a doctrinal field and conclude that the legal materials in that field are best justified as expressions of this or that set of legal principles. Their arguments are not that such principles are moral principles, for they may not be morally ideal, and they owe their very existence to specific human decisions. Nor do their arguments depend upon these principles having been explicitly adopted by courts or legislatures, for frequently no court or legislature has done so. Rather, their arguments for these principles consist of showing that the principles are morally attractive even if not ideal, and that following these principles would have resulted in most of the legal decisions in the field, even if not their actual rationales.

24. In light of these later decisions, Jefferson Powell notes, *Brown* "appeared to stand for a conclusion that its reasoning did not even purport to reach." Powell, *supra* note 9 at 167.

25. *See, e.g.,* Wenona Y. Whitfield, Brown v. Board of Education: A Substitute Opinion, 20 S. Ill. U. L.J. 15, 15 (1995) ("I adamantly reject the notion that the basis of the plaintiffs' rights should be placed on social science data.").

26. Mark V. Tushnet, Reflections on the Role of Purpose in the Jurisprudence of the Religion Clauses, 27 Wm. & Mary L. Rev. 997, 999 n.4 (1986).

27. *See* Steven D. Smith, Brown v. Board of Education: A Revised Opinion, 20 S. Ill. U. L.J. 41 (1995). *See generally* Symposium, Brown v. Board of Education, 20 S. Ill. U. L.J. 1 (1995).

28. Mark Tushnet, Red, White, and Blue: A Critical Analysis of Constitutional Law 53–54 (1988).

29. Bruce Ackerman, We the People: Foundations (1991).

30. *Id.* at 99.

31. Posner, *supra* note 21 at 215.

32. Laurence H. Tribe, Taking Text and Structure Seriously: Reflections on Free-Form Method in Constitutional Interpretation, 108 Harv. L. Rev. 1221, 1290 (1995).

33. Robert Wiebe, The Opening of American Society 25 (1984).

34. *Cf.* Lance Banning, The Sacred Fire of Liberty: James Madison and the Founding of the Federal Republic 171 (1995) (describing *The Federalist* as a "systematic rationalization" of the convention's work).

35. *See, e.g.,* Tribe, *supra* note 32; Terrance Sandalow, Abstract Democracy: A Review of Ackerman's *We the People,* 9 Const. Comm. 309 (1992); Steven L. Winter, Indeterminacy and Incommensurability in Constitutional Law, 78 Cal. L. Rev. 1441, 1527–34 (1990) (arguing that Ackerman misreads and distorts *Brown*).

36. *Cf.* Tushnet, *supra* note 28 at 133 ("Earl Warren had humane instincts, not a systematic philosophy.").

37. Oliver Wendell Holmes, Jr., The Common Law 1 (1991) (first published 1881).

38. John 3:8.

39. *See* Wasserstrom, *supra* note 18.

40. With respect to *Roe,* for example, Judge Posner comments:

> *Roe v. Wade* has been the Wandering Jew of constitutional law. It started life in the due process clause, but that made it a substantive due process case and invited a rain of arrows. Laurence Tribe first moved it to the establishment clause of the First Amendment, then recanted. Dworkin now picks up the torch, but relies upon the free exercise and establishment clauses in combination. Feminists . . . have tried to squeeze *Roe v. Wade* into the equal protection clause. Others have tried to move it inside the Ninth Amendment . . . ; still others (including Tribe) inside the Thirteenth Amendment, which forbids involuntary servitude. I await the day when someone shovels it into the takings clause, or the republican form of government clause (out of which an adventurous judge could excogitate the entire Bill of Rights and the Fourteenth Amendment), or the privileges and immunities clause of the Fourteenth Amendment. It is not, as Dworkin suggests, a matter of the more the merrier; it is a desperate search for an adequate textual home, and it has failed.

Posner, *supra* note 21 at 180–81.

41. For example, the plurality opinion in Planned Parenthood v. Casey, 505 U.S. 833 (1992), expressed doubt about whether *Roe* had been properly decided but nonetheless reaffirmed the decision, emphasizing the value of adhering to precedent. James Boyd White singles out precisely this aspect of the opinion for praise. James Boyd White, Acts of Hope 153–83 (1994). *See also* Dworkin, Freedom's Law, *supra* note 19 at 72–73 (peremptorily dismissing one plausible but disappointingly unpretentious reading of the Fourteenth Amendment due process clause because "history" has rejected it).

42. This is not to deny, of course, that law professors can sometimes exercise in-

fluence over judges in more direct but less "rational" ways—for instance, by supplying judges with law clerks trained to think (or perhaps recommended *because* they think) in much the same way the professor does. Moreover, people of prominence and prestige in general may have the power to influence judges simply on the basis of their ability to dispense public praise and blame, and some law professors—a very few, probably—are people of prominence and prestige. Academic speculation sometimes suggests, for instance, that Justice Kennedy's votes in cases like *Casey* and *Evans v. Romer* reflect the fact that Kennedy has come under the sway of Professor Laurence Tribe in one or both of these ways; though impossible to verify, such speculation is not implausible. But this sort of influence is quite different than the direct exertion of "reasoned" argument in which a scholar might write an article that is so convincing on its merits that a judge would read it and be persuaded. *Cf.* Robert F. Nagel, Liberals and Balancing, 63 U. Colo. L. Rev. 319, 323–24 (1992) (suggesting that "less intellectually distinguished" judicial nominees, such as Kennedy and Souter, who have only "an undeveloped, mushy legal philosophy," will be more susceptible to influence by academic litigators because "they will have fewer resources of their own to cause them to consider theoretical or institutional or long-run considerations").

43. Douglas Laycock, A Survey of Religious Liberty in the United States, 47 Ohio St. L.J. 409, 450 (1986).

44. *Cf.* Sanford Levinson, Constitutional Faith 159 (1988) (describing the "omnipresent indeterminancy" of constitutional law).

45. *See* ch. 3, ns. 35–50 and accompanying text.

46. The quotation from Madison is reported in Gerard V. Bradley, Church-State Relations in America 88 (1987).

47. *See* Walter Berns, Taking the Constitution Seriously 126–27 (1987) ("What is also beyond dispute, although very little attention has been paid to it, is that during what is still the greater part of our history (1789–1925), the Bill of Rights played almost no role in the securing of rights.").

48. For an argument that both the establishment and free exercise clauses were intended solely to prevent federal interference with the states' jurisdiction over religion, see Steven D. Smith, Foreordained Failure 17–50 (1995).

49. United States v. Carolene Products, 304 U.S. 144, 152 n.4 (1938).

50. *See* Louis Lusky, Footnote Redux: A *Carolene Products* Reminiscence, 82 Colum. L. Rev. 1093, 1099 (1982).

51. *Id.*

52. Lewis F. Powell, Jr., *Carolene Products* Revisited, 82 Colum. L. Rev. 1087, 1087 (1982).

53. Probably the most elaborate outgrowth of the footnote is John Ely, Democracy and Distrust (1980).

54. Plato, Ion. Though in the dialogue Ion accepts this account of his art, whether Plato intended the account to be taken at face value seems dubious.

55. The following observations are based on G. W. F. Hegel, Reason in History (Robert S. Hartman tr. 1953) (first published 1837).

56. *Id.* at 26.

57. *Id.*

58. *Id.* at 31.

59. *Id.* at 44.

60. *Id.* at 39–41.

61. *Id.* at 40. Because of their special status and role, these heroes cannot be bound by the ordinary rules and conventions of morality. "But so mighty a figure must

trample down many an innocent flower, crush to pieces many things in its path."
Id. at 43.

62. The dedication in Ely's classic *Democracy and Distrust* reads:

For Earl Warren.

You don't need many heroes
if you choose carefully.

63. *See supra* note 61.

64. Ernest Gellner, Reason and Culture 157 (1992).

65. Hegel, *supra* note 55 at 47.

66. *See* Gellner, *supra* note 64 at 77–78.

67. *Id.* at 71–79.

68. Robin West, Progressive Constitutionalism 267–68 (1994).

69. Lawrence G. Sager, Justice in Plain Clothes: Reflections on the Thinness of Constitutional Law, 88 Nw. U. L. Rev. 410, 410 (1993).

70. This description is taken from the ironic title of Henry Monaghan, Our Perfect Constitution, 56 NYU L. Rev. 353 (1981).

71. Quoted in Michael Kammen, A Machine that Would Go of Itself 44 (1986).

Epilogue

1. Michael Oakeshott, The Tower of Babel, in Rationalism in Politics and Other Essays 465 (Timothy Fuller ed. 1991) (essay first published in 1948) [hereinafter "Tower I"]; Michael Oakeshott, The Tower of Babel, in On History and Other Essays 165 (1983) [hereinafter "Tower II"].

2. Oakeshott, Tower II, *supra* note 1 at 165–66.

3. *Id.* at 166. Oakeshott also described the story as one about the "project of finding a short cut to heaven" or about the "pursuit of perfection as the crow flies." Oakeshott, Tower I, *supra* note 1 at 465–66. For such a social project, he believed, "the penalty is a chaos of conflicting ideals, the disruption of a common life, and the reward is the renown which attaches to monumental folly." *Id.* at 466.

4. Gen. 11: 1–9.

5. Josephus, The Jewish Antiquities, Bk. I, 109–18, in IV Josephus 53–57 (H. St. J. Thackeray trans. 1930) (footnotes and verse numbers omitted).

6. Augustine, City of God 14.13.

7. Ernest Gellner, Reason and Culture 156 (1992).

8. *Cf.* Norman Hampson, The Enlightenment 146 (1968) ("The Enlightenment was an attitude of mind rather than a course in science and philosophy.").

9. *Id.* at 158.

10. *See* Introduction, note 1.

11. Ronald Dworkin, Law's Empire 407 (1986).

12. *See* Chapter 4, note 44 and accompanying text.

13. Planned Parenthood v. Casey, 505 U.S. 833 (1992). For an encomium by a leading legal scholar, see James Boyd White, Acts of Hope 153–83 (1994).

14. The Joint Opinion acknowledged this. "Men and women of good conscience can disagree, and we suppose some always shall disagree, about the profound moral and spiritual implications of terminating a pregnancy, even in its earliest stage." 505 U.S. at 850.

15. *See, e.g.,* Mary Ann Glendon, A Nation Under Lawyers 112 (1994) (describing Justice Kennedy's lackluster background and surprise nomination).

16. *Id.* at 867.

17. *Id.* at 860–69.

18. *Id.* at 868.

19. Robert F. Nagel, Judicial Power and American Character 138 (1994). *See also id.* at 61–62 (plurality opinion reflects an "outpouring of self-important romance" reminiscent of a "late-night fit of drunken sentimentality").

20. Glendon, *supra* note 15 at 113.

21. A qualification is in order here: Though one can tentatively assess the persona of the author of a writing, one cannot confidently judge the actual character of the human being behind the persona. Someone who seems arrogant may *be* arrogant; on the other hand, it is a common observation that people who lack self-assurance sometimes put on an excessive display of confidence in an effort to conceal their own deficiencies, or perhaps to impress those who dispense praise and blame. In the end, who can judge?

22. Steven G. Calabresi & Gary Lawson, Foreword: Two Visions of the Nature of Man, 16 Harv. J. Law & Pub. Pol'y 1, 1 (1993).

23. Reinhold Neibuhr, "The Tower of Babel," in Beyond Tragedy: Essays on the Christian Interpretation of History 25 (1937) [hereinafter "Babel"]; Reinhold Niebuhr, The Irony of American History 159 (1952) [hereinafter "Irony"] ("The builders of the Tower of Babel are scattered by a confusion of tongues because they sought to build a tower which would reach into the heavens. The possible destruction of a technical civilization, of which the 'skyscraper' is a neat symbol, may become a modern analogue to the Tower of Babel.").

24. Neibuhr, Babel, *supra* note 23 at 28.

25. *Id.* at 46.

26. Niebuhr, Irony, *supra* note 23 at 48.

27. Niebuhr, Babel, *supra* note 23 at 29–30.

28. "Yet we know, or should know, by this time, that our material riches imply a spiritual, cultural, and moral poverty that is perhaps far greater than we see." Thomas Merton, Christian Culture Needs Oriental Wisdom, in A Thomas Merton Reader 295 (rev. ed. Thomas P. McDonnell, ed. 1974). *See also* Oakeshott, Tower I, *supra* note 1 at 481 (asserting that "[l]ike lonely men who, to gain reassurance, exaggerate the talents of their few friends, we exaggerate the significance of our moral ideals to fill in the hollowness of our moral life").

29. Niebuhr, Babel, *supra* note 23 at 39.

30. Sanford Levinson, Constitutional Faith 172 (1988). Levinson claims no certainty in this respect; he concludes his book on a questioning note:

> It would be essentially misleading to attribute to constitutional faith the longevity that we associate with the great religious faiths that have provided the metaphors for this book, particularly Judaism and Christianity. We might think instead of the great Egyptian, Greek, and Roman religions that today stock museums with their treasures but are otherwise dead as informing visions of how we the living might structure our own lives. Whether constitutional faith maintains itself depends on our ability to continue taking it seriously. I have tried to show that this is no easy task. I also hope that I have demonstrated, at least in part, that the question is worth asking and that answers can emerge, if at all, only out of conversation.

Id. at 193–94.

31. Niebuhr, Irony, *supra* note 23 at 46. *See also id.* at 70:

[I]n both the Calvinist and the Jeffersonian concept of our national destiny the emphasis lay at the beginning upon providence rather than human power. Jefferson had proposed for the seal of the United States a picture of "the children of Israel, led by a cloud by day and a pillar of fire by night."

32. *See, e.g.,* Republic 493:

For the divine, as the proverb says, all rules fail. And you may be sure that, if anything is saved and turns out well in the present condition of society and government, in saying that the providence of God preserves it you will not be speaking ill.

33. Niebuhr, Irony, *supra* note 23 at 70.
34. *See* Gellner, *supra* note 7 at 159.
35. Niebuhr, Irony, *supra* note 23 at 4.
36. *Id.* at 49.
37. For a discussion of the Turner thesis and variations, see Carl N. Degler, Out of Our Past: The Forces that Shaped Modern America 121–34 (rev. ed. 1970). For an argument that the country's character and institutions derive from its unique material circumstances, see David M. Potter, People of Plenty (1954).
38. *See, e.g.,* Glenn Harlan Reynolds, Chaos and the Court, 91 Colum. L. Rev. 110 (1991) (reflecting on application of chaos theory to judicial behavior).
39. *See, e.g.,* Robert W. Gordon, Unfreezing Legal Reality: Critical Approaches to Law, 15 Fla. St. U. L. Rev. 195, 200 (1987) (asserting that history is a product of "complexity, variety, irrationality, unpredictability, disorder, cruelty, coercion, violence, suffering, solidarity, and self-sacrifice" but that conventional legal discourse "regularly filter[s] out" these factors).
40. *Cf.* Niebuhr, Irony, *supra* note 23 at 88:

Perhaps the real difficulty in both the communist and the liberal dreams of a "rationally ordered" historic process is that modern man lacks the humility to accept the fact that the whole drama of history is enacted in a frame of meaning too large for human comprehension or management. It is a drama in which fragmentary meanings can be discerned within a penumbra of mystery; and in which specific duties and responsibilities can be undertaken within a vast web of relations which are beyond our powers.

41. *Id.* at 49.
42. Niccolo Machiavelli, The Prince 91, in The Prince and The Discourses (Modern Library ed. 1950).
43. Gellner, *supra* note 7 at 159.
44. Niebuhr, Irony, *supra* note 23 at 174.

▣ Index